Thinking the Limits of the Body

SUNY Series in Aesthetics and the Philosophy of Art
Mary C. Rawlinson, editor

Thinking the Limits of the Body

edited by
Jeffrey Jerome Cohen and Gail Weiss

State University of New York Press

Material from chapter 3 originally appeared in Linda Kauffman, *Bad Girls and Sick Boys: Fantasies in Contemporary Art and Culture,* © 1998 Regents of the University of California

Published by
State University of New York Press, Albany

For information, address State University of New York Press,
90 State Street, Suite 700, Albany, NY 12207

Production by Dana Foote
Marketing by Patrick Durocher

Library of Congress Cataloging-in-Publication Data

Thinking the limits of the body / edited by Jeffrey Jerome Cohen and Gail Weiss.
    p. cm. — (SUNY series in aesthetics and the philosophy of art)
    Includes bibliographical references and index.
    ISBN 0-7914-5599-8 (alk. paper) — ISBN 0-7914-5600-5 (pbk. : alk. paper)
    1. Body, Human—Social aspects. 2. Body, Human (Philosophy) I. Cohen, Jeffrey Jerome. II. Weiss, Gail, 1959– III. Series.

HM636 .T55 2003
306.4—dc21   2002036684

10 9 8 7 6 5 4 3 2 1

CONTENTS

PART IV
DIS-ABLING ALLIANCES

PART V
LIMINALITIES

ACKNOWLEDGMENTS

This volume would not have been possible without the generous funding provided by the Consortium of Washington Universities. The themes examined here originated in an interdisciplinary faculty research seminar on the body that has been meeting since 1994. We would like to thank all of the past and present members of the seminar for creating the collegial, stimulating environment that led to this volume. We are grateful to Mary Rawlinson, editor of the SUNY series in Aesthetics and the Philosophy of Art, for her support and to Jane Bunker, Dana Foote, and the SUNY Press staff for seeing *Thinking the Limits of the Body* to completion. Our thanks also go to the English Department at The George Washington University for their financial assistance and to Valerie Hazel for producing the index. Finally, we want to state our appreciation to the Human Sciences graduate program at The George Washington University. This interdisciplinary program in language, culture, and society has fostered an intellectual community of graduate students and faculty that is all too rare in the academy today.

Introduction
Bodies at the Limit

Jeffrey Jerome Cohen and Gail Weiss

Poked, probed, sliced, prosthetically enhanced and surgically diminished, transplanted, and artifically stimulated, the body in contemporary culture is the volatile subject of both textual and material fascination. The explosion of technologies and methodologies that claim to give us better access to "the truth" of the body have made the body more visible and yet more elusive. Intricate mappings of human genes have reduced the body to a series of secret codes to which our geneticists alone hold the keys. Performance artists use their bodies to challenge our understanding of corporeal signification. As a signifying power that does not refer back to a simple origin, the body revealed in the work of Orlan, Annie Sprinkle, Bob Flanagan, Cindy Sherman, and other "flesh artists" belies the stability of conventional formulations of subjectivity. Critical race theorists, queer theorists, and disability theorists have shown us that the body is as problematic when it is marked (e.g., by its race, sex, class, ethnicity, age, abilities, etc.) as when it is un(re)marked and viewed as natural or universal. Clearly, the body is well on its way to becoming the interdisciplinary subject of study par excellence. But what are its limits as concept and category?

"The body." The term suggests a bounded and autonomous entity, universal but at the same time singular, atemporal, and therefore unmarked by history. To think the limits of the body is to interrogate this abstract, strangely dematerialized vision, appealing as it may be in its Cartesian simplicity. If we take the notion of limit seriously, we must ask to what extent our continual invocation of "the body" limits our very attempts to think beyond its pregiven ontology, its supposed unity. Just as Martin Heidegger maintains in *Being and Time* that every attempt to question Being already presupposes a certain understanding of Being, when we inquire into what "the body" means, we must recognize that both the question and any possible answers to it always unfold against historically contingent, yet nonetheless powerfully enduring frames of interpretation.[1] Moreover, if, as Heidegger argues in "What Is Metaphysics?," "every metaphysical question always encompasses the whole range of metaphysical problems," then to ask about the status of "the body" is also to examine all those other aspects of existence to which the body is intrinsically related (Heidegger 1993: 93). These include language, perception, agency, culture, textuality, desire, and intersubjectivity. Any investigation of the body in relationship to these intertwined phenomena is further complicated by Heidegger's second point, namely, that "every metaphysical question can be asked only in such a way that the questioner as such is present together with the question, that is, is placed in question" (Heidegger 1993: 93). Here, Heidegger suggests that we cannot interrogate the body without also interrogating our own implication in the phenomena we are examining, a reflexivity that affects the very process of questioning itself.[2]

With these complications in mind, how can we simultaneously acknowledge the weight of the traditions that have shaped the very questions we are now asking about the body and, at the same time, critically position ourselves to read this body at its limits? Clearly we cannot put these interpretative frames behind us or simply move beyond them. Is there, however, a middle space between the body as a set of historically predetermined constructs and possible futures where the body (and therefore we ourselves) can be otherwise? Gloria Anzaldua calls such a space *la frontera*/the borderlands, a "place of contradictions," a landscape of "shifting and multiple identity and integrity" (Anzaldua 1999: 19). She recognizes that to dwell within the borderlands "is like trying to swim in a new element, an 'alien' element" insofar as it requires that we refuse both to abandon history and to embrace uncritically the future (Anzaldua 1999: 19). Rather than conceptualize epistemological and geographical frontiers as that beyond which nothing further exists, however, Anzaldua emphasizes that these limits are their own centers, enriched by the clash of multiple cultures, multiple languages, multiple ways of thinking the world.

Following Anzaldua, thinking the limits of the body demands that we be attuned to the conflicts and tensions that enliven the body's own borderlands, and not seek to diminish or negate them in the interests of a specious clarity, a monologic history. Thinking about historicality from within the hermeneutical tradition, Hans-Georg Gadamer reminds us that the labor of interpretation always involves a movement backward and forward in time. This process, he argues, necessitates a "fusion of horizons" wherein past and present comprise an ongoing dialectic, ensuring that neither the past nor the present can be viewed as fixed. "In fact," Gadamer tells us,

> the horizon of the present is being continually formed, in that we have continually to test all our prejudices. An important part of this testing is the encounter with the past and the understanding of the tradition from which we come. Hence, the horizon of the present cannot be formed without the past. There is no more an isolated horizon of the present than there are historical horizons. Understanding, rather, is always the fusion of these horizons which we imagine to exist by themselves. (Gadamer 1982: 273)

As with Anzaldua, this fusion preserves rather than eliminates difference. It requires an awareness of the body's own otherness, its inassimilability to what Kaja Silverman calls the "dominant fiction," in this case cultural narratives which determine in advance the contours of corporeality.

Simply put, limits need not foreclose. We are interested in what limits produce (a Deleuzian middle—a combinatory space of multiplicity), what they make possible (unexpected futures, altered horizons, new pasts), what they incorporate (their own disavowals, their abjected others), as well as how the limits are themselves constructed in and through particular cultural matrices which they cannot escape but always exceed.[3] Limits, in other words, are grounded in desire, indeed, in multiple desires. Deleuze and Guattari describe desire as infinitely connective, as ceaseless movement toward new heterogeneities. As Elizabeth Grosz observes, in Deleuze and Guattari's account, desire "is what produces, what makes things, forges connections, creates relations, produces machinic alignments . . . desire is an actualization, a series of practices, action, production, bringing together, making machines, making reality (Grosz 1994: 195). In opposition to an understanding of desire as lack (e.g., a craving for something one does not yet have), Deleuze and Guattari view it as active, as impossible to contain within *any* social structuration: "Desire's turbulent restlessness defies coding into signs, significations, meanings; it remains visceral, affective, which is not to say that it is in any way reducible to physiology" (Grosz 1995: 196). Always embodied, it can never be limited to or by discrete bodies. On this model, desire exhibits its own agency; the body, marked by multiple desires, becomes as we shall see, the site of multiple agencies.

Desiring bodies always inhabit a borderlands between liberatory expansion and tight social circumscription. They are always articulated within and responsive to specific, delimiting cultural frameworks such as "the straight mind" described by Monique Wittig, the habitus discussed by Pierre Bourdieu, or the disciplinary regimes examined by Michel Foucault. These hegemonic matrices produce and classify bodies binaristically and hierarchically, engendering such foundational divisions as normal/abnormal, licit/illicit and permitted/forbidden (Foucault 1990: 83). According to Judith Butler:

> This exclusionary matrix by which subjects are formed thus requires the simultaneous production of a domain of abject beings, those who are not yet "subjects," but who form the constitutive outside to the domain of the subject. The abject designates here precisely those "unlivable" and "uninhabitable" zones of social life which are nevertheless densely populated by those who do not enjoy the status of the subject, but whose living under the sign of the "unlivable" is required to circumscribe the domain of the subject. This zone of uninhabitability will constitute that site of dreaded identification against which—and by virtue of which—the domain of the subject will circumscribe its own claim to autonomy and to life. In this sense, then, the subject is constituted through the force of exclusion and abjection, one which produces a constitutive outside to the subject, an abjected outside, which is, after all, "inside" the subject as its own founding repudiation. (Butler 1993: 3)

Disavowals and abjections produce tangible limits for the embodied subject, demarcating the body from what it is not. Yet, as Butler eloquently points out, these attempts to establish "clean and proper" borders between bodies always ultimately fail. This failure occurs not only because those who have been designated as abject can refuse the margins assigned to them and infiltrate the centers from which they have been excluded, but also because all subjects, all bodies, are fundamentally impure (their morphogenesis having occurred through a series of repudiations that simultaneously sustains and destabilizes them).

Butler's account challenges any attempt to establish an impermeability between inside and outside, forcing a reconceptualization of the very notion of limit. Rather than continuing to view limit merely as something that operates externally, dividing one body from another, we must also recognize that limits are chiasmatic, sites of reversibility in which, like the Moebius strip, inside becomes outside and vice versa (Grosz 1994). The body is, in other words, a crossroads, a space of limit *as* possibility.

The very act of drawing a limit is, moreover, neither ethically nor politically neutral. Without question, limits foreclose possibilities even as they open them up. The "zones of uninhabitability" discussed by Butler take on a special force when they are materialized as slums, ghettos, resettlements, refugee camps, or mass graves. Corporeality is limned by violence. We must therefore be sensitive to the lived consequences of limits, which are never merely abstract. While we will never get away from the abjections that make identity possible, it is also crucial that we continue to challenge self-imposed and other-imposed limits that are arbitrary, unjust, and oppressive. As Elaine Scarry has argued in her work on torture, our bodies not only have the capacity to make the world, but also to unmake it (Scarry 1985: 50). And indeed, it is through acts of oppression that the world-destroying effects of limiting bodies are most poignantly realized.

Corporeal Connections

The imbrications of body and world, self and other, limit and possibility have animated recent work across the disciplines. The following chapters sketch a cartography of what we take to be the very best efforts to think the body at its limits, a collaborative project that seeks transdisciplinary points of resonance and divergence. Because the body encompasses communities (social and political bodies), territories (geographical) bodies, and historical texts and ideas (a body of literature, a body of work), we are especially interested in how disciplinary metaphors materialize specific bodies, and where these bodies break down and/ or refuse prescribed paths. Postmodern theorizations of the body often neglect its corporeality in favor of its cultural construction. *Thinking the Limits of the Body* demonstrates the inseparability of textuality, materiality, and history in any discussion of the body. More specifically, the limits of the body are most evident precisely at the points where dominant cultural discourses, elemental resistances, and different temporalities collide.

These collisions have produced a plethora of responses that range from a questioning of the body's humanity, a celebration of the body's pleasures, and the often violent effacement of the body itself. "The Future" predominates in many of these explorations of corporeal limits. Indeed, the future has become the fantasy field in which contemporary problems of embodiment are articulated. Theorists of artificial intelligence have offered us visions of a disposable body, a creature of Consciousness unhampered by flesh. Dreams of a cyborgian future occlude the possibility that we have always been "posthuman." The chapters in this collection, by contrast, insist that the past and the present provide equally fecund domains for an exploration of the body at its limits. The danger of investing all of one's hopes or fears in the future (as utopia or dystopia) is that, on the one hand, we may fail to recognize the ways in which our conceptions of the future are themselves a function of the present and the past, and, on the other hand, we may also fail to recognize the transformative potential that is already latent in both.

In "Histories of the Present and Future: Feminism, Power, Bodies," Elizabeth Grosz argues for a reconceptualization of the past in its relation to the future. Traditional, historical understandings of the past view it as exhibiting particular patterns and structures that are in turn replicated in the present and, ultimately, in the future. On such a view, the past is directly related to the present and the present in turn provides the framework for what will come. Grosz claims that this model fails to do justice to the dynamic, openended nature of both past and future. Instead of viewing the relation between past and future as grounded in repetition, Grosz argues for the creation of "histories of the future" through a continual rewriting of the past. Drawing from the work of Bergson, Deleuze, Derrida, and Irigaray, she maintains that both past and future are realms of openness, contingency, vectors of possibility which feminism must mine from one moment to the next. By mapping (and remapping) this largely uncharted territory, feminist theorists can provide new formulations of power, knowledge, and the corporeality of sexual difference.

Gail Weiss's "The Body as a Narrative Horizon" explores the role that the body plays in situating human narratives. Philosophers Paul Ricoeur, Alasdair McIntyre, Mark Johnson, and others have claimed that we structure our lives narratively: discrete episodes take on specific configurations (constellations of meaning) to produce coherent experiences as well as a distinctive sense of self. Critically examining these accounts, Weiss asks: "What role does the body play in these narratives? How might the notion that we live our lives narratively need to be reconfigured to do justice to the body's (often invisible) contribution to these narratives?" This chapter seeks to demonstrate that the body is a narrative horizon for all texts, and in particular, for all of the stories that we tell about (and which are indistinguishable from) ourselves. As such, the body grounds our quest for meaning, and, in so doing, establishes our accountability for the quest itself, an accountability that includes our failure to complete the quest.

Together, Grosz's and Weiss's chapters foreground the temporal and corporeal horizons that have functioned as an "absent presence" in contemporary
identity politics. In *Dermal Boundaries,* Linda Kauffman and William A. Cohen
turn our attention to the body's own less visible horizon, namely, the skin. Linda
S. Kauffman has long been interested in woman artists like Carolee Schneemann
and Annie Sprinkle who perform their bodies as an antiaesthetical art. "Cutups
in Beauty School" analyzes the work of Orlan, whose ongoing project transforms
cultural understandings of beauty and pathology. Through public plastic surgeries, her face has been reconstructed to cite famous icons of femininity. This
medical transformation of her flesh exposes how arbitrary, unnatural, and un-
attainable cultural ideals of feminine beauty are. By making exorbitantly visible
what ordinarily unfolds in the secrecy of the operating room, Orlan's bloody
surgical theater (connected to the outside world via satellite, fax, email) reflects
how deeply the body has been transformed through its alliances with technology.
As the first "woman-to-woman transsexual," she reveals that gender and identity
are processes that are impossible to complete; opening her body, she finds it
empty of interiority, possessed of nothing but its infinitely plastic surface.

William A. Cohen's chapter, "Deep Skin," shows us how Victorian readings of the flesh of the colonized other undercuts artificial divisions between the
corporeal and the noncorporeal. More specifically, Cohen offers a critical analysis
of Anthony Trollope's "The Banks of the Jordan," in order to highlight the skin's
"peculiar status as both physical embodiment and psychical envelope, both a
surface projected from inside and a mask immediately comprehensible from
without, the [skin's] crucial, if sometimes conflicting, psychological, spiritual, and
social functions." Cohen argues that the narrator's fears about physical and
spiritual contamination through close contact with the native's skin serves as a
metonymic displacement of a pressing domestic concern in England in the late
1850s, namely, fear of exposure to the germs and disease circulating throughout
the polluted, unembanked rivers of England including, most prominently, the
Thames. Not surprisingly, the solution recommended for the latter problem,
containing the rivers and ridding them of their noxious elements, finds resonance
as a formula for addressing the bodily habits, cultural practices, and spiritual
beliefs of the colonized other. Fixing the rivers turned out to be a more successful
project than establishing "proper" boundaries between colonizer and colonized,
however; as Cohen powerfully reveals, the effort to keep bodies and souls pure is
forever undercut by the skin's own resistances.

As William A. Cohen makes explicit in his excavation of a colonialist
history, dermal boundaries invariably become racial edges. Laura Doyle's chapter, "Ontological Crisis and Double Narration in African American Fiction:
Reconstructing *Our Nig,*" turns our attention to the enslaved other and describes
how severe racial oppression can lead to self-fragmentation. Though in many
ways debilitating, this splintering of the self can be, as Doyle shows, a paradoxical
form of self-preservation. Her essay offers us a "disjunctive ontology," a descrip-

tion of lived experience as a series of disjointed fragments that do not add up to a single whole. Through the perspectives of Harriet Wilson's main character and narrator, Frado, Doyle portrays a recognition of self in and through the other that generates a split subject. This split subject, which Doyle identifies with Merleau-Ponty's notion of the chiasm, allows for reversible relations between (unequal) subjects that simultaneously bind and divide them. Through her reading of this 1859 novel, we see how the project of constructing a self is both diminished and enabled by the dominating power of race.

The complex relationship between conquest, colonization, modernity, and cannibalism is explored in Sara Castro-Klarén's "Parallaxes: Cannibalism and Self-Embodiment, or, The Calvinist Reading of Tupi A-Theology." Challenging Jean de Léry's famous 1578 ethnographic treatise on Tupinamba culture, the scientific authority of which has seldom been questioned, Castro-Klarén shows how Lery's detailed accounts of ritualistic cannibalism among the Tupinamba were the product of colonialist fantasies of the "New World other." Human consumption of human flesh, and theophagy—the human consumption of Divine flesh—were doctrinal issues that the Church struggled to resolve. Léry's fascination with anthropophagy, she argues, originates in European anxieties about the status of the Eucharist *as* body in the wake of the Protestant reformation. Through a rereading of the myths of the contemporary Awareté tribe in Brazil, Castro-Klarén provides an alternative history of the body's limits that places the very practice of ethnography into question.

The insistence on making difference visible in the flesh, a process which inevitably normativizes the hierarchies that emerge in and through that differentiation, is the central focus of "Making Freaks: Visual Rhetorics and the Spectacle of Julia Pastrana." Rosemarie Garland-Thomson depicts the "visual cannibalism" that marks what might be called the logic of the stare. The complex emotions and desires evoked in spectators of nineteenth-century freak shows, she argues, simultaneously challenged and reinforced the traditional binaries of self/other, normal/abnormal, male/female, human/nonhuman, and civilized/primitive. Staring at the "monstrous other," Garland-Thomson suggests, ultimately assuages the spectator's own cultural insecurities even as it destines the spectacular other to a liminal existence, exiled by the visible signs of his or her imagined social transgression.

Like Garland-Thomson, Robert McRuer is a leading voice in the emerging discipline of disability studies. His chapter, "Critical Investments," takes as its focus the uncanny confluence of two media events featuring Christopher Reeve, a Superbowl commercial for an investment company in which the actor's disability is imagined as spectacularly "cured" and a television movie directed by Reeve in which a man with AIDS returns home to die. McRuer examines how disability and the queer limn the heterosexual, able body, challenging its self-presumption of normalcy. He finds in AIDS activism and scholarship nonbinary models for the explication of identity, models which bring queer theory not only to the study of sex and gender but to a nuanced reading of race, nationality, and other categories. The deconstructive impetus of AIDS-focused queer theory shares much with disability theory, likewise concerned with detailing the historical contingency of minority identities and the ideological work such identities are made to perform. Against systems of power that would "immunize" dominating identities from their differences, both queer theory and disability studies offer ways of thinking the body outside of the constricting parameters of ablebodied heterosexuality.

The final section of our volume, *Liminalities,* extends the investigation of corporeal boundaries by emphasizing the porousness between bodies and world. If we cease to grant each body an absolute integrity, one that has too often been achieved by viewing the body as a self-sufficient entity, we become more sensitive to the complexities of intersubjective and intercorporeal relations. Whereas McRuer allies queer theory and disability studies to bring about a more just future, Jeffrey Jerome Cohen's chapter conjoins queer theory and medieval studies to create a richer past. "The Inhuman Circuit" excavates a posthuman body in the Middle Ages. Reading Deleuze and Guattari alongside chivalric romance, Cohen argues that contemporary queer theory has jettisoned the notion of an atemporal, inherently natural sexuality without abandoning the humanism on which such a claim is founded. In medieval culture, the horse, its rider, the bridle, saddle, and armor together form a Deleuzian "circuit," a network of meaning that includes the inanimate and the inhuman. No single object or body has meaning within this assemblage without reference to the other forces, intensities, affects, and directions to which it is conjoined. "The Inhuman Circuit" stresses the limits of the human as a useful conceptual category and maps out the transformative bodily possibilities that were always already present in the past.

If, as Luce Irigaray claims, the question of sexual difference is the most pressing of our time, Debra B. Bergoffen's "Mourning the Autonomous Body" asks why it is that so few find Irigaray's sense of urgency compelling. Appealing to Freud's *Mourning and Melancholia,* Bergoffen argues that our indifference to the question of sexual difference is itself a form of resistance to relinquishing the autonomy of the unsexed body. Although autonomy has traditionally been extolled as a basis for a politics of freedom, Bergoffen maintains that an overvaluation of autonomy betrays the meanings of erotic bodies and distorts the experience of sexual desire. In this betrayal and distortion the autonomous body becomes the ground of the politics of patriarchy upholding mastery, domination, and violence. Just as Nietzsche insisted on the murder of God, Bergoffen holds that we must murder the autonomous body, properly mourn our loss, and learn to love ambiguous bodies and their inscriptions of sexual difference.

Together, these chapters problematize the very notion of bodily limits at precisely those junctures where they seem most visible and insurmountable. Through the convergence of queer theory, postcolonial studies, disability studies, feminist theory, medieval studies, literary theory, phenomenology, and history,

Thinking the Limits of the Body argues against disciplinary isolation and for interdisciplinary approaches to corporeality. We have grouped the ten chapters that comprise this volume under five section headings, each of which captures a different facet of the body at its limits; however, as our discussion above suggests, the themes that link the various chapters to one another prohibit precise delineations, spilling over their fixed groupings. Exceeding their own textual limits, these chapters in their interconnections can—we hope—provide an important link between past discourses on the body and future interdisciplinary work. The body at its limits, this collection insists, need not be a site of collapse, negativity, and failure, but rather can become a locus of proliferation, mystery, and possibility.

Notes

1. See Martin Heidegger, introduction to *Being and Time* (1996).

2. The reflexivity Heidegger is calling our attention to is one that is always mediated by an intersubjective linguistic and cultural tradition; the self always comes back to itself via that which is other, namely its world.

3. According to Gilles Deleuze and Félix Guattari, "The middle is by no means an average; on the contrary, it is where things pick up speed. *Between* things does not designate a localizable relation going from one thing to the other and back again, but a perpendicular direction, a transversal movement that sweeps one *and* the other away, a stream without beginning or end that undermines its banks and picks up speed in the middle" (Deleuze and Guattari 1987: 25).

References

Anzaldua, Gloria (1999). *Borderlands/La Frontera: The New Mestiza.* 2d ed. San Francisco: Aunt Lute.

Boundas, Constantin V., and Dorothea Olkowski (1994). *Gilles Deleuze and the Theater of Philosophy.* New York: Routledge.

Bourdieu, Pierre (1990). *The Logic of Practice,* trans. Richard Nice. Stanford: Stanford University Press.

Butler, Judith (1993). *Bodies that Matter: On the Discursive Limits of "Sex."* New York: Routledge.

Deleuze, Gilles, and Félix Guattari (1987). *A Thousand Plateaus: Capitalism and Schizophrenia,* trans. Brian Massumi. Minneapolis: University of Minneapolis.

Douglas, Mary (1988). *Purity and Danger: An Analysis of the Concepts of Pollution and Taboo.* London: Routledge.

Foucault, Michel (1978). *The History of Sexuality Volume 1: An Introduction,* trans. Robert Hurley. New York: Vintage.

——— (1978). *Discipline and Punish: The Birth of the Prison,* trans. Alan Sheridan. New York: Vintage.

Gadamer, Hans-Georg (1982). *Truth and Method.* New York: Crossroad.

Grosz, Elizabeth (1994). *Volatile Bodies: Toward a Corporeal Feminism.* Bloomington: Indiana University Press.

Heidegger, Martin (1996). *Being and Time,* trans. Joan Stambaugh. Albany: State University of New York Press.

——— (1993). "What is Metaphysics?" *Martin Heidegger: Basic Writings,* trans. and ed. David Farrell Krell. New York: HarperCollins.

Irigaray, Luce (1993). *An Ethics of Sexual Difference* trans. Carolyn Burke and Gillian C. Gill. Ithaca: Cornell University Press.

Scarry, Elaine (1985). *The Body in Pain: The Making and Unmaking of the World.* New York: Oxford University Press.

Silverman, Kaja (1992). *Male Subjectivity at the Margins.* New York: Routledge.

Wittig, Monique (1992). *The Straight Mind and Other Essays.* Boston: Beacon.

PART I
HORIZONS

1

Histories of the Present and Future
Feminism, Power, Bodies

Elizabeth Grosz

There is much about feminist theory that is in a state of flux right now; major transformations are occurring regarding how feminist politics and its long- and short-term goals and methods are conceived. The debates about the place of identity in political struggle, attempts to make feminism more inclusive, the ways in which even the body is conceptualized, the impact of feminism on young women and men, have, instead of producing a new more focused and cohesive feminist movement, simply witnessed the growing fragmentation and division within its ranks. I would like to look at some of the effects that some key theoretical/political changes have on the ways in which feminist scholarship and theory have changed or should change.

In particular, I want to look at two paradigm shifts—shifts that have affected the ways we understand knowledge and power—which have occurred over the last decade or so and have transformed, or hopefully will transform, the way feminist scholarship and politics is undertaken and what its basic goals are. The first consists in transformations in our understanding of knowledges, discourses, texts, and histories, which politicizes them not only in terms of their contents—that is, in terms of what they say—but also in terms of the positions from which they are articulated (their modes of address)—what they cannot say—and what their positions are within a network of other texts that constitute both their milieu and the means by which they become both comprehensible and tamed. The second involves transformations in the ways in which women and femininity are understood, that move away dramatically from the prevailing feminist models of earlier generations of women's identity, their absence from prevailing practices and forms of knowledge, their unique features, qualities, and characteristics. Instead of focusing on women's unique identities, their roles as unrecognized agents in histories and practices, it may be time instead to focus on the disparate and disunified processes, or rather agencies (in the plural), forces and impulses that comprise such an identity.

This dual politicization of knowledges, discourses, and writing, on the one hand, and of identity politics, on the other hand, have come together to raise new feminist questions about knowledge, subjectivity, and power. It is no longer clear, in the wake of antihumanist assaults on the general question of identity, whether the strategic value of identity-politics, a politics developed around the affirmation of minority identities, remains as strong as it was two or three decades ago. Subjects cannot be understood as powerless, oppressed, defeated, marginalized, and stripped of action; nor conversely can they be affirmed as self-contained and pregiven agents, agents who control their actions, their effects, their social milieu. Though useful in bolstering a sense of fragility, both concepts of the subject conceived as victim and the subject conceived as agent are equally fictitious. It is perhaps now time to undertake more profound and braver experiments in conceptualization by attempting to think the subject, identity, agency, community—all terms reliant on a notion of some internal force—explicitly in terms of forces, agencies (in the plural), operative vectors, points of intensity, lines of movement, resistance, or complacency. We need to think subjects in terms of their strategic placement within power networks; that is, in terms of what they are able to do, more than in terms of who they are.

Both these tendencies, now beginning to have major impacts on feminist theory, owe an enormous debt to the radical antihumanism and the postulation of the inherent entwinement of power and knowledges developed in the genealogical works of Michel Foucault, Gilles Deleuze, and other postmodern thinkers. I would like to divide this chapter into a discussion of these transformations. I want first to look at how these transformations may affect our understanding of history and historical research. I will then go on to discuss how they affect our understanding of power, and finally I will suggest how this provides us with more complex and subtle ways of understanding bodily differences and thus sexual difference.

I will use the philosophical writings of some late-twentieth-century French philosophers—Michel Foucault, Jacques Derrida, Gilles Deleuze, and Luce Irigaray—to raise the question of what history is, how its readings, its reconstitution, functions politically, and how alternative histories remain to be written. In raising these questions (I don't dare claim to be able to answer them!) I hope to focus on the contemporary political context in which feminist history, the production of an alternative feminist canon, or the problematization of historiography, can take place.

Past, Present, and Future

The status and place of temporality and of the past remains one of the elided ingredients in much current discussion about social change, upheaval, transformation, or even revolution, that is, in speculation about the future. How we understand the past, and our link to it through memory, reconstruction, and scholarship, prefigure and contain corresponding and unspoken conceptions regarding the present and future. Implicit in the very procedures of conventional historical research is the presumption that the past provides us with the means (or at least some of them) for understanding the present, a series of potential lessons to learn, an anticipation of events to come, a mode of repetition that revivifies and enlivens the past by linking its relevance, its sense, to the present (and by implication, the future). Rethinking the relations between past and present, reconstituting historical "memory" as a form of production, may thus exert a powerful influence on reconsidering the ways in which the past is traditionally represented in both history in its various methodologies, as well as in dominant philosophical and feminist conceptions of time. The ways we rethink this relation will, of course, also have direct implications for whatever conceptions of the future, the new, creation, and production we may develop.

Much historical and historiographic research is mired in a certain belief that human beings, or even life in its generality, are essentially functions of repetition. The same kinds of issues reappear over and over again, and if we know how to read history carefully enough, perhaps we can learn from the first or second replaying of historical forces what we need not live through again. In short, history as a discipline is in large part motivated by the belief that we can learn from the past, and by reflecting on it, can improve the present. The past is fundamentally like the present, the present is a mode of continuity of the past, and insofar as this similarity continues, the past will provide a preeminent source for the solution of contemporary problems and the issues the future may throw up. The more and the better we understand the past, the more well armed we are to face a future that is to a large extent a copy or reformulation—the variation on a theme—of historical events. It is for this reason we need to cultivate memory, as the art and scholarship appropriate to memorialize the past. Such a view of history can only understand the present in terms of a concretization of the past, the culmination or fruition of what has been as a form of contained repetition. It thus sees the future in terms of tendencies and features of the past and present. Where the past is a retrospective projection of a present real, on such an understanding, the future can only be understood in terms of the prospective projection or extrapolation of the present. The problem with such a model of time and history is that it inevitably produces a predictable future, a future in which the present can still recognize itself instead of a future open to contingency and the new, the future as fundamental surprise. What is needed in place of such a monumental history is the idea of a history of singularity and particularly, a history that defies repeatability or generalization, and that welcomes the unexpectedness of the future and the new as it makes clear the specificities and particularities, the events, in the full sense of the word, of history.

This, as I understand it, must be one of the paradoxes of historical research in general: histories—stories and reconstructions of the past—are in fact illuminations of a present that would not be possible without this past. The time of the historian is strangely dislocated, somewhere between the past and the present, but not entirely occupying either. For the feminist historian, these paradoxes, the paradoxes of temporality, are particularly exacerbated: a feminist or radical historian (this point is of course not confined to feminists but could apply equally to the postcolonial or antiracist historian) the task is not simply to openly acknowledge that the writing of past is more a story about the present, but also that it is the linking of the past and present to a possible future, of providing a connection between past potential and a future that does *not* resemble the present. The project of the feminist historian must be, in part at least, the forging of relations between the sexes, and of each sex, along lines that dramatically diverge from what is present. The past, a past no longer understood as inert or simply given, may help engender a productive future, a future beyond patriarchy. Time, the very matter and substance of history, entails the continual elaboration of the new, the openness of things (including life, texts, or matter) to what befalls them. This is what time *is* if it is anything at all, the indeterminate—the unfolding and emergence of the new.

The future is the domain of what endures. But what endures, what exists in time and has time as part of its being is not what remains the same over time, what retains an identity between what it was and what it will be. Time involves the divergence between what was, (that is, what exists in virtuality) and that which is actualized or capable of actualization. The past is what endures, not in itself, but what is open to becoming, to something other. This becoming infects not only beings in/as duration, but the world itself:

> The universe *endures*. The more we study the nature of time, the more we shall comprehend that duration means invention, the creation of forms, the continual elaboration of the absolutely new. It is true that in the universe itself two opposite movements are to be distinguished. . . , 'descent' and 'ascent'. The first only unwinds a roll ready prepared. In principle, it might be accomplished almost instantaneously, like releasing a spring. But the ascending movement, which corresponds to an inner work of ripening or creating, *endures* essentially and imposes its rhythm on the first, which is inseparable from it. (Bergson 1944: 14)

Even if our primary orientation is to the past, the past is never adequately conceivable except insofar as it propels a new future, a future beyond the limit of the present. This is why feminist history is so crucial: not simply because it informs our present, but more so, because it enables other virtual futures to be conceived, other perspectives to be developed, than those which currently prevail. In this sense, the astute historian stands on the cusp of the folding of the past into the future, beyond the control or limit of the present.

The Past Lives into an Unknowable Future

I want to raise a series of hypotheses, some of them quite speculative, some of them meant to surprise more than to convince or aspire to truth, some meant to highlight rather than obscure social and political issues, which I hope will help us to raise in relief the question of what feminist history might be and what feminist theory must be in order to support feminist history, feminist writing, feminist knowledges (which for me are *not* about women's history, women's writing, women's knowledge but about writing *otherwise*). To write a history of the past from the point of view of the future: the task, at least one of the most urgent, is to think in the *future anterior,* the tense that Irigaray favors in her textual readings: what will have been, what the past and present will have been in the light of a future that is possible only because of them.

Three working hypotheses, then, about history and its inherent binding of past to present and future:

1. Augmenting Foucault (in *Discipline and Punish*), I would suggest that history is always a history of the present, and that the best history is not only one that is a history of the present, a reconstitution of the conditions of the present, but also a *history of the future.* In studying history, we are not simply gleaning texts, artifacts, and events as they occurred in themselves: we are not unearthing "facts" from the past, like little nuggets of gold, each of which have their own intrinsic value. Rather, what *counts* as history, what is regarded as constituting the past is that which is deemed to be of relevance to concerns of the present. It is the present that writes the past rather than, as positivist historiography has it, the past that gives way to the present. This is not to say that the present is all that is left of the past; quite the contrary, the past contains the resources to much *more* than the present. Rather, it is only the interests of the present that serve to vivify and reinvigorate the past. The past is always propelled, in virtual form, in a state of compression or contraction, to futures beyond the present;

2. Instead of the past being regarded as fixed, inert, given, unalterable, and rock-solid even if not knowable in its entirety, it must be regarded as being inherently open to future rewritings, as never "full" enough, or present enough, to retain itself as a full presence that propels itself intact into the future. This is Derrida's crucial claim about identity and iteration (particularly in *Of Grammatology* and *Limited Inc.*). The identity of any statement, text, or event, is never given in itself. Neither texts nor objects nor subjects have the kind of self-presence that gives them a stable and abiding identity; rather, what time is, and what matter, text, and life are, are becomings, openings to time, change, rewriting, recontextualization. The past is never exhausted in its virtualities, insofar as it is always capable of giving rise to *another* reading, another context, another framework that will animate it in different ways. What Derrida makes clear is that the significance, value, or meaning of a text or an event is only given in the infinitely deferred future. So that when we are "doing" history, not only are we writing the event, we are positively reinscribing it, producing it anew, writing it as an opening up to a life that is not exhausted in its pastness.

The historian, especially the radical or critical historian (such as a feminist or an antiracist historian must be) is crucially poised at the intersection of two virtualities, to use the language of Gilles Deleuze (*Bergsonism, Cinema 2: The Time-Image, Difference and Repetition*). The past is not a diminished or receded former present, a present that has faded into memory or carried in artifacts that intrude in the present. The past is the virtual that coexists with the present. The past, in other words, is always already contained in the present, not as its cause or its pattern but rather, as its latency, its virtuality, its potential for being otherwise. This is why the question of history remains a volatile one, not simply tied to getting the facts of the past sorted out and agreed on. It is about the production of *conceivable futures,* the future here being understood not as that which is similarly contained in the present, but rather, that which diverges from the present, that which produces a new future, one uncontained by and unpredicted from within the present. This indeed is what I understand feminist politics—at least at its best—to be about: the production of futures for women that are uncontained by any of the models provided in the present. Rewriting, reinscribing the past is a way to activate these possible futures and, indeed, is their only political rationale. The inventive historian is poised between a past that is not dead and a present as the place for the inauguration of new and unpredicted futures. We can call these futures modes of becoming, modes of becoming-other; and

3. The past is the virtuality that makes both history and memory possible. Neither history nor memory should be equated with the past itself. As latency or virtuality, the past is larger, more complex, more laden, than any history can present—including feminist history. There can be no complete, or even partial history, no objective reconstruction, no extraction of the truth of history. What I am getting at is that the past always and essentially gives rise to multiple histories, histories undertaken from different perspectives of the present. This multiplicity is not given through the complexity that the present adds to the past, the present layering or enriching, spotlighting the details of the past. Such a picture is rendered more complex through the necessity of recognizing what the fissured and latent past enables, for the past is uncontainable within any one history, or even all cumulative histories.

This claim is based on Irigaray's understanding of sexual difference as the perspective that has yet to take place, yet when it occurs, it will transform the ways in which all knowledges, all practices, all relations can be understood, from perspectives whose positioning has never been occupied, or taken place before. There is another way of undertaking history—even feminist history—or another way of undertaking any activity or discipline, than that which is presently available. The past, in short, cannot be exhausted through its transcription in the present, because it is also the ongoing possibility (or virtuality) that makes *future* histories, the continuous writing of histories, necessary. History is made an inexhaustible enterprise only because of the ongoing movement of time, the precession of futurity, and the multiplicity of positions from which this writing can and will occur.

Taken together, these hypotheses imply that history is always—whether archivally or textually based, whether it appears to offer a haven away from the present or a way into the problems of the present—an intensely political matter, a matter of one's political interests and alignments in the present. This is *not* a limitation of the discipline of history but is the condition of all historical research, even the most traditional: it is always invested, and its investments dictate what counts as being historically relevant information. This is not really a new claim: history, like politics and philosophy, is always an invested framework, always wedded to paradigms that are involved in political schemas. What I want to add to these claims is a feminist slant. In other words, I would like to take on one of the possible, future, anterior positions on the question of histories of the present and future, one articulated in terms of sexual difference. It is here that my work owes an immense debt to the writings of Luce Irigaray, who remains the most insistent and clear-sighted proponent of sexual difference and its ontological and epistemological implications. I will not talk about her texts in detail, but rather will use her insights to develop some of the implications of a sexually different understanding of history. But first, a brief detour through a Foucauldian and Deleuzian understanding of power.

Power and Knowledges

I want to return to the impact of antihumanist theory on feminism, how, inflected through the writings of those I have already mentioned as postmodern philosophers—Foucault, Derrida, Deleuze—it may provide us with new kinds of questions and new modes of utilizing existing intellectual frameworks for new ends. If these disparate thinkers share anything in common that is of direct relevance to feminist concerns, it is a broadly conceived understanding of power and its productivity, one that I believe is implicitly assumed in the writings of Irigaray as well.

Until very recently (until the work of Irigaray and, in particular, Spivak) power has been seen as the enemy of feminism, something to be abhorred, challenged, dismantled, or at best, something to be shared more equally. Power is not the enemy of feminism but its ally. The goal of feminism is no longer the dismantling of power or its equal distribution, for power must be understood more carefully as that which administers, regulates, and enables, that which flees and produces, as well as that which disqualifies and subordinates, limits, and contains. If feminists believe that their goal is to abandon power, then they have already lost in a game from which they cannot withdraw. Feminism must aim at the reordering of power and not its elimination, at the expedient use of power and its infinite capacities for transformation and rewriting, its fundamentally openended character, its capacity to be worked on and opened up to a future set of unpredictable uses and effects. Power is not something that feminism should disdain or rise above, for it is its condition of existence and its medium of effectivity. To understand how this different, indeed positively affirmative relation of power marks the present state, or rather, the cutting edge, of feminist theory, we must ask, then, what power is and how it functions. This too can be summarized in a few terms:

1. Power is a fluid medium within which we are produced and function, within which we operate, have effects, and are effected, act and are acted upon. It is not something we can deny, resist, or dispense with except in the very terms that it provides. It is only within power that power can be transformed, and only through its operations that change can be (and is) effected. It is not as if we can separate ourselves, our passions, our daily concerns, and our intimate relations from power, because it is that through which we have effects and are acted upon, the field of our effectivity. Such an understanding of power implies that many preconceptions we hold, or have inherited, must be abandoned if we are to accept, to intervene into, and be able to utilize power.

2. Power must no longer be conceived as a perfect, systematic, structural, or homogeneous whole. It is heterogeneous, multiple, contradictory, sporadic, uneven, calculating but not predictable, viscous or thick with its capacity to absorb what it finds recuperable about its unpredictable permutations. Moreover, it has what might be called recoil effects, which transform or modify the intentionalities directed toward its subversions. This is what is power's mode of effectivity, as well as its resistance to concerted manipulation.

Power is neither perfect nor ineffable, neither secure nor consciously manipulable by individuals or groups, churches or elites, however well placed or apparently lacking in strategic position or resources. Its functioning cannot be explained by universal laws or general rules, for it is haphazard, expedient, calculating (and thus also prone to miscalculation). Neither hidden nor clandestine, power always functions openly (if we know how to recognize it), through its modes of material constitution, arrangement, organization, distribution, and its administration and regulation of objects, subjects, practices, events, and institutions. It produces sites of particularly intense investment, and correlatively, sites of relative underinvestment, which vary historically, culturally, and geographically.

3. Resistance is precisely a function of its haphazard operations (and not, as Marxism asserts, of power's internal contradictions—as if it were a system of logic: contradiction has never stopped practices from occurring, power from functioning), its modes of expediency and its necessarily excessive self-production (in particular, its fascinating capacity to generate more than it needs, to produce in excess of any functionality or systematicity), an excess that can be turned in on itself. These very excesses (the sites of over- or under-investment in power's uneven spread over culture) are what enable, indeed at times, insist on the conversion of power into its ever-newer forms, into its unpredictable future.

I have made no claims about individuals or groups "having" power, or exerting it over others; I have not discussed the issue of more or less power, because none of this makes sense if power is understood as a set of material forces and effects. However, issues of oppression, subordination, domination, and control are not simply evaporated or defined out of existence (as some feminists, particularly those opposed to poststructuralism and antihumanism, suggest) but must be reconceived beyond the model of woman as passive victim of male power who is robbed of agency and efficacy. This victimology continues to be the dominant rationale and presumption behind the establishment of most forms of feminist politics and most feminist theoretical studies, which tend to presume an understanding of power and powerlessness, of power as systematically regulated enforcement of men's dominant and women's subordinate positions. Such a model is ironically unable to explain the very possibility of feminism itself, women's capacity to move beyond *ressentiment* and anger, righteous indignation or moral outcries, to produce something new, women's capacities to move beyond what attempts to debilitate or contain them, to devise strategies, harnessing what they know about power, about their daily lives, their experiences, their positions.

This is a much more complicated and murkier understanding of power—power as a mode of negotiation, implication, and complicity—that feminism must address if its theoretical projects, including those directed to the past, are to be more than a litany of the woes suffered by women, a position that I believe is inherently antithetical to feminism, for it cannot explain how feminism is itself possible. The task ahead, the challenge facing feminist theory will be that of taking power responsibly, of working with and through it, of producing and activating knowledge not against power, but against the prevailing assumptions that have regulated the production and use of knowledge against women's interests. The task ahead, then, is not to seize power (power has never been lacking) but to refigure knowledges so that they help position women to utilize power strategies, to regulate their lives, to produce differently and to recognize differently the kinds of production undertaken by women in the past.

Sexual Difference

I have thus far discussed how notions of temporality, relations between past, present, and future, are always implicated in power relations; and also, how all knowledges and discourses—in this case, histories—are, in one way or another, bound up with power relations. I would now like to see what implications that has for the question of sexual difference. I would like to explain how I understand this phrase, as its definition seems crucial to the ways in which is it used and abused in feminist circles. Sexual difference, like the very notion of difference itself, can be understood in one of two ways. First, as a difference between two preexisting entities (such as the difference between oranges and apples); and second, as a constitutive difference, a difference that preexists the entities that it produces. This second notion, shared by both Derrida and Deleuze, is also a constitutive ingredient in Irigaray's understanding of sexual difference. Sexual

difference is not the differences between the sexes as we know them today, or as
we know them from the past. This is because, as Irigaray has argued, the
differences between the sexes have never taken place (*This Sex Which Is Not One*).
Here she is not claiming unique experiences that one sex has that the other does
not: rather, she is arguing that there has never been a space in culture for women
as women. Women have only ever been represented as a lack, the opposite, the
same as, or the complement of the one subject, the unique human subject. In
making the claim that sexual difference is yet to take place, she is arguing that
there is no space in culture, in representation, in exchange, in ethics, in politics, in
history, or in writing, for the existence of *two* sexes, only the one sex and its
counterpart. Insofar as women are conceived as the afterthought, the reflection,
the augmentation, the supplement, the partner, of men, they are contained within
a phallocentrism that refuses alternative positions and spaces, that refuses the
right of any autonomous representations, that eradicates sexual difference, that
refuses to accord women the possibility of being otherwise than defined in some
necessary relation to men.

Phallocentrism is explicitly *not* the refusal of an identity for women (on the
contrary, there seems to be a proliferation of identities—wife, mother, nun,
secretary, etc.), but rather, the containment of that identity by other definitions
and other identities. Thus Irigaray does not seek the "real" woman somehow
beyond her patriarchal containment, instead she aims to challenge conceptual
systems that refuse to acknowledge their own limitations and their own specific
interests. This is a challenge less to do with harnessing the lives, experiences, and
energies of "real" women than to do with challenging and undermining the
legitimacy of modes of their representation, models, and systems that represent,
theorize, and analyze the world and that help to produce them. Irigaray's questions are thus not questions about what to do, how to act, how to write in such a
way as to be faithful to the lives and experiences of "real women": her strategies
instead are philosophical and methodological. She asks: how to develop conceptual schemas, frameworks, and systems that reveal what is at stake in dominant
representational systems, and how to develop different ways of theorizing, based
on the recognition of what has been left out of these dominant models. In other
words, how to think, write, or read *not* as a woman, but more complexly and less
clearly, how to think, write, and read otherwise, whether one is a man or a
woman, how to accommodate issues, qualities, concepts that have not had their
time before.

It is this challenge that Irigaray issues to feminist thought—not to simply
take women as the objects of intellectual investigation (though of course this is
not to be very easily accomplished in some contexts), but rather to open up the
position of knowing subject to the occupation of women. To enable women to
inhabit the position of knower so that knowing itself may be done differently,
different questions be asked, different criteria of evaluation be developed,
different intellectual standards and goals to emerge. Irigaray cannot specify in

advance how women, and men, might occupy positions of knowing when sexual difference finally takes place: that would be to preempt the specificities of other women's positions and their specific modes of occupation of positions.

The lessons that history can teach us are only as profound and adventurous as our own intellectual mindsets and political allegiances will allow: history is not a series of stories and texts that only illuminate the past. History is not the recovery of the truth of bodies or lives in the past; it is the engendering of new kinds of bodies and new kinds of lives. History is in part an index of our present preoccupations, but perhaps more interestingly, the past as rich as our futures allow. Insofar as those futures come to approximate the minimal conditions for an understanding, recognition, and celebration of sexual difference, what history, and the struggles of the past, have to teach us is still wide open, open to us rather than to them, to forge.

References

Bergson, Henri (1944). *Creative Evolution,* trans. Arthur Mitchell. New York: Random House.

———— (1988). *Matter and Memory,* trans. N. M. Paul and W. S. Palmer. New York: Zone.

Deleuze, Gilles (1991). *Bergsonism,* trans. H. Tomlinson and B. Habberjam. New York: Zone.

———— (1994). *Difference and Repetition,* trans. Paul Patton. New York: Columbia University Press.

———— (1986). *Cinema 1: The Movement-Image,* trans. H. Tomlinson and B. Habberjam. Minneapolis: University of Minnesota Press.

———— *Cinema 2: The Time-Image,* trans. H. Tomlinson and R. Galeta. Minneapolis: University of Minnesota Press.

Derrida, Jacques (1974). *Of Grammatology,* trans. G. C. Spivak. Baltimore: Johns Hopkins University Press.

———— (1988). *Limited Inc.,* trans. S. Weber. Evanston, Ill.: Northwestern University Press.

Foucault, Michel (1977). *Discipline and Punish: The Birth of the Prison,* trans. Alan Sheridan. London: Allen Lane.

Irigaray, Luce (1984). *This Sex Which Is Not One,* trans. C. Porter. Ithaca: Cornell University Press.

2

The Body as a Narrative Horizon

Gail Weiss

By now, we are all familiar with the postmodernist claim that the body (and this is usually intended to refer to the human body) is a text. To say that the body is a text in turn means that it is not outside of or opposed to discourse, but is itself discursively constructed. This claim, in particular, has had the (intended) effect of destabilizing the body, insofar as it opposes a more traditional conception of the body as a purely material, biological organism that is separate from (and usually viewed as resistant to) cultural influences.

By rejecting this dualistic model, we avoid the intractable problem of determining exactly how two allegedly distinct phenomena—the natural and the cultural—interact to comprise a unified sense of self. At the same time, by dislodging the body from one side of this false dichotomy, the "integrity" of the body as a distinctive metaphysical substance appears to be abolished as well. Thus, once this opposition between the natural and the cultural is undone, as it is undoubtedly undone when one shows that the body does not exist independently of culture but is cultural through and through, we no longer have to account for how nature and culture work together. Yet we now have a new problem, namely, that of determining whether or not the body has any ontological standing at all. For if the body is a text, on what basis, if any, are we to differentiate it from other kinds of texts? In what sense can the body be said to "be" at all?

While I, too, accept the notion that the body can and should be viewed as a text, I am also concerned about the ethical implications of such a position, implications that are rarely acknowledged and, for that very reason, all the more urgent to consider. These implications, I would argue, can and must be understood in narrative terms, since understanding the body as a text means that it has its own narrative structure, and any ethics that arises out of this narrative structure must itself be narratively constructed.[1]

To say that the body has its own narrative structure is itself a problematic claim, however, to the extent that it once again seems to set the body apart from everything else, from all that is not part of the body. Indeed, one of the virtues of the position that the body is a text is precisely that it emphasizes the intrinsic connection between the body and language, and therefore, with all aspects of our experience. But, if the body doesn't play a distinctive role in narrative construction, then on what basis can we claim that bodies have a distinctive moral standing, a moral standing that implies a measure of responsibility (for that narrative) that propositions and stories in and of themselves seem to lack?

Perhaps there are some who would argue that propositions or stories actually do have moral standing in their own right, that they need not be associated with a particular author or even a Foucaultian "author-function" to have ethical force. I'm not unsympathetic to such a claim but I would argue that it can be made only on the basis of an appeal to the "body" of the text itself. To account for the moral imperatives that can and do issue from texts, we must recognize not only that the body is discursively constructed, and thus that the body cannot be separated from discourses about it, but also that texts are themselves embodied, which means that they have their own materiality, which is precisely what defines them (and differentiates them from one another) as texts.

My focus in this chapter will be on how to come to terms with this embodied dimension of texts, for, while much has been written on the body as text, very little attention has been paid to the text as body. Correcting this imbalance will, I believe, provide a much more fruitful means of getting beyond the admitted artificiality of the nature/culture divide as well as the equally problematic "solution" that makes the body just one cultural product among others. Recognizing the materiality, or more precisely, the materialities, of texts (including the body as text), is to acknowledge that all texts are necessarily embodied just as all bodies can be understood textually. What I am especially interested in establishing is *not* that texts can be reduced to their materiality or that materiality can be reduced to textuality, but rather, that the body serves as a narrative horizon for all texts, and, in particular, for all of the stories that we tell about (and which are indistinguishable from) ourselves.

First, let me clarify what I mean by the expression "narrative horizon." The term "horizon" has a particular significance within the phenomenological tradition, one that is associated first and foremost with Edmund Husserl. According to Husserl, horizons are an integral aspect of each and every one of our experiences. When I perceive an object, for instance, that object is situated within a perceptual field that itself serves as a kind of background or horizon against which, and by means of which, the object is perceived. The determinacy (i.e., clarity and distinctness) of the object is directly proportional, for Husserl, to the indeterminateness of this background. This is because, as Maurice Merleau-Ponty notes,

> it is necessary to put the surroundings in abeyance the better to see the object, and to lose in background what one gains in focal figure, because to look at the object is to plunge oneself into it, and because objects form a system in which one cannot show itself without concealing others. (Merleau-Ponty 1962: 67–68)

The claim that a determinate figure requires an indeterminate ground does not originate with Husserl or Merleau-Ponty, moreover, but is indebted to the empirical research of nineteenth-century Gestalt psychologists who maintained that to perceive any object (or group of objects) at all always involves isolating a figure against a ground. What distinguishes Husserl's own contribution from the Gestalt psychologists' recognition of the mutual dependence of the ground upon the figure and the figure upon the ground, are his claims that (1) there is not one but multiple horizons that situate a given figure (indeed, he argues that every intentional object has both internal as well as external horizons); (2) these horizons do not have clear boundaries but are marked by a "zone of indeterminacy"; and (3) this figure/ground structure is exemplified not only within the perceptual domain but is the primary organizational principle for all of our actual and possible experience. "Thus," Husserl observes,

> the particular object of our active consciousness, and correlatively the active, conscious having of it, being directed toward it, and dealing with it—all this is forever surrounded by an atmosphere of mute, concealed, but cofunctioning validities, a *vital horizon* into which the active ego can direct itself voluntarily, reactivating old acquisitions, consciously grasping new apperceptive ideas, transforming them into intuitions. Because of this constantly flowing *horizonal* character, then, every straightforwardly performed validity in natural world-life always presupposes validities extending back, immediately or mediately, into a necessary subsoil of obscure but occasionally available reactivatable validities, all of which together, including the present acts, make up a single indivisible, interrelated complex of life. (Husserl 1970: 149)

What Husserl is suggesting is that there is no such thing as a simple act of perception since anything we are perceiving appears against a dense backdrop of past, present, and future experiences. When we imagine something, for instance, the thing we are imagining has its own horizons, horizons that include our memories of previous imaginings, our past, present, and future perceptions, our attitudes, and the memories, perceptions, and attitudes of others. Thus, these multiple "grounds" for any given figure include temporal horizons, spatial horizons, intersubjective and imaginary horizons, horizons that are not separate from one another but overlap and together provide a context for each and every one of my experiences, a context that situates them in relation to one another and which therefore plays a definitive role in establishing the meaning of those experiences.

The zone of indeterminacy, then, refers to the inexhaustibility of these horizons for they are, by definition, incapable of being rendered determinate (or being converted into "figures" in their own right) without new horizons arising to replace them. Rather than viewing the indeterminacy or inexhaustibility of these horizons as a barrier to the construction of coherent texts or meaningful narratives, however, they are precisely what make it possible for us to create new narratives and to embrace old ones. For, as Merleau-Ponty argues, while this figure/ground perspective characterizes our possible as well as actual experience, and could therefore be viewed as a limitation insofar as it means that we can never obtain an aperspectival or "God's eye" view of that experience, it is nonetheless possible to change the terms of the relationship between figure and ground. For instance, we can turn our attention to some aspect of the ground and transform it into the figure (which in turn means that what had hitherto been the figure will now become part of the ground), an ongoing process that facilitates the development of new perspectives.

At the end of his essay on painting, "Eye and Mind," Merleau-Ponty sums up the "limits" of perspective by reminding us that

> no thought ever detaches itself completely from a sustaining support; that the sole privilege of speaking thought is to have rendered its own support manageable; that the figurations of literature and philosophy are no more settled than those of painting and are no more capable of being accumulated into a stable treasure; that even science learns to recognize a zone of the "fundamental," peopled with dense, open, rent beings of which an exhaustive treatment is out of the question . . . that, in the end, we are never in a position to take stock of everything objectively or to think of progress in itself. (Merleau-Ponty 1993: 149)

To the extent that we find the inexhaustibility of disciplines such as literature and philosophy to be limitations, this disappointment itself, he argues,

> issues from that spurious fantasy which claims for itself a positivity capable of making up for its own emptiness. It is the regret of not being everything, and a rather groundless regret at that. For if we cannot establish a hierarchy of civilizations or speak of progress—neither in painting nor even elsewhere—it is not because some fate impedes us; it is, rather, because the very first painting in some sense went to the farthest reach of the future. If no painting completes painting, if no work is itself ever absolutely completed, still, each creation changes, alters, clarifies, depends, confirms, exalts, recreates or creates by anticipation all the others. If creations are not permanent acquisitions, it is not just that, like all things, they pass away: it is also that they have almost their entire lives before them. (Merleau-Ponty 1993: 149)

For Merleau-Ponty, this process according to which one creation in turn becomes the horizon for others, rather than serving as an obstacle to meaning, itself guarantees that there will always be new meanings insofar as there will always be new figures and new horizons that provide the context for their interpretation. Moreover, Merleau-Ponty's claim that each painting anticipates all the others emphasizes the intersubjective dimension of these horizons and of the narratives that are constructed by means of them.

To acknowledge the overlapping of horizons, then, involves a recognition that my horizons and your horizons mutually inform one another and therefore mutually inform the way in which we configure our experiences. As Alasdair MacIntyre and Mark Johnson argue, the narratives we tell about our lives are always coauthored.

Before turning to their respective work for insight into the role that horizons play in these intersubjective narratives, we need to know more about how the narratives themselves are constructed. According to Paul Ricoeur:

> All narratives combine in various proportions, two dimensions—one chronological and the other non-chronological. The first may be called the episodic dimension. This dimension characterizes the story as made out of events. The second is the configurational dimension, according to which the plot construes significant wholes out of scattered events. (Ricoeur 1991: 106)

Ricoeur views both dimensions, the episodic/chronological dimension and the configurational/achronological dimension to be equally constitutive of our narratives, however he argues that both structuralist literary critics and antinarrativist historians tend to ignore the configurational dimension altogether.

Ricoeur is especially interested in the act of configuration because it does not obey a conventional chronology but nonetheless produces meaning by drawing from past, present, and future events. Following Louis O. Mink, Ricoeur argues that the configurational act is a "grasping together" an act of "eliciting a pattern from a succession" (Ricoeur 1991: 106). In connection with our earlier discussion, I would maintain that the configurational act, as a spontaneous organizational strategy, can itself be understood as a Gestalt, or figure/ground organization that produces what Riceour calls a "constellation of meaning."

Metaphorical statements, on this account, could themselves be understood as configurational acts. They arise, Ricoeur asserts, not *ex nihilo,* but in response to a "semantic impertinence" or a "clash" between semantic fields. More specifically, he claims that

> every metaphor, in bringing together two previously distant semantic fields, strikes against a prior categorization, which it shatters. Yet, the idea of semantic impertinence preserves this: an order, logically antecedent, resists, and is not completely abolished by, the new pertinence. In effect, in order that there be a metaphor, it is necessary that I continue to perceive the previous incompatibility through the new compatibility. Therefore, predicative assimilation contains a new sort of tension, one no longer solely between subject and predicate, but between incompatibility and the new compatibility. (Ricoeur 1991: 125)

In *Fables of Responsibility: Aberrations and Predicaments in Ethics and Politics,* Thomas Keenan makes a similar point about how tropes function and expands upon it through the metaphorical example "Achilles is a lion." In this example, he asserts:

> "Lion" means something new, now, but it only means it to the extent that it preserves its bond to the "primitive meaning." The resourcefulness by which language turns "its own poverty into wealth" in this economy of re-use works on a principle of substitution: words change places, stand in for each other, cross over from one meaning to another. The hegemony of meaning is far from being questioned: on the contrary, rhetoric is designed to exploit the exchangeability of words to expand the horizon of meaning. (Keenan 1997: 143)

Ricoeur's understanding of metaphor as a configurational act that preserves the incompatibility between semantic fields in and through its presentation of a "new compatibility" is, I would argue, a promising point of departure for an understanding of how narratives are constructed and reconstructed. Keenan's emphasis on the "economy of re-use" according to which a word with a fairly "stable" connotation (e.g., lion, a four-legged animal) both retains its old meaning and takes on a new one (through being applied to Achilles to signify his courageousness), shows, moreover, that the process of creating new meanings, and by extension, new narratives, need not involve the creation of new languages. That is, the richness of the reciprocal relationship between figure and ground is such that it can be infinitely reworked and this reworking can reinforce existing meanings even as it creates new ones.[2]

Keeping this reversibility between figure and ground in mind, let us return to our initial inquiry into the body of the text or, more precisely, into the bodily dimension of the process of narrative construction that makes texts readable as such. Ricoeur prepares the way for such an investigation in his claim that

> It is as if metaphor *gives a body, a contour, a face to discourse.* . . . But how? It seems to me, it is in the moment of the emergence of a new meaning from the ruins of a literal predicament that imagination offers its specific mediation. (Ricoeur 1991: 124 my emphasis)

While Ricoeur turns to the imagination as a site of productive reference in order to explicate this point, I would like to turn to the body itself and the ongoing role that it plays as a narrative horizon in discourse (a role that it continues to play even in discourses about the body).

By displacing the focus from the imagination to the body, however, I do not mean to deny the primacy of the imagination in the construction of narratives. "Human beings," Mark Johnson claims, "are imaginative synthesizing animals." Johnson, like Ricoeur, stresses the productivity of our imaginative activity, and, more specifically, he claims that this activity is precisely what enables us to pursue what Alasdair MacIntyre calls a "quest" for narrative unity, a quest that has as its goal the organization and production of an integrated sense of self. As Johnson observes:

> In order for us to have coherent experiences, to make any sense at all of what happens to us, to survive in our environment, and to enhance the quality of our lives, we must organize and reorganize our experience from moment to moment. (Johnson 1993: 152)

MacIntyre argues that this continual organization and reorganization is guided by a particular *telos,* not one that lies outside of this process of narrative construction but, rather, one that emerges in and through it. This telos takes the form of what MacIntyre calls an "intelligible" narrative, a narrative that creates its own unity by giving a meaningful structure to a series of experiences that, in principle, could always have been configured differently. Moreover, our ability to produce intelligible narratives (and therefore intelligible selves), is, for MacIntyre, precisely what grounds our moral responsibility for those narratives. For, MacIntyre notes,

> human beings can be held to account for that of which they are the authors; other beings cannot. To identify an occurrence as an action is in the paradigmatic instances to identify it under a type of description which enables us to see that occurrence as flowing intelligibly from a human agent's intentions, motives, passions and purposes. *It is therefore to understand an action as something for which someone is accountable, about which it is always appropriate to ask the agent for an intelligible account.* (MacIntyre 1981: 195; my emphasis)

Intelligibility, as MacIntyre emphasizes here and elsewhere, arises out of the agent's "intentions, motives, passions and purposes." If, to use one of his examples, I see a man gardening and I want to understand the meaning of this act, I must find out "why" he is engaged in this activity. Is he, MacIntyre asks, gardening to please his wife or because he enjoys the physical labor, both, or neither?

A primary difficulty with MacIntyre's account, aside from the limited possible interpretations he offers of the gardener's motivation for gardening, is his claim that meaningful narratives are constructed by recourse, first and foremost, to the intentions of the agents who are implicated in them. That is, for MacIntyre, a narrative becomes intelligible precisely to the extent that it can be seen as arising out of one or more agents' intentions. When we are incapable of generating an intelligible narrative because our own or others' intentions are opaque to us, MacIntyre argues, communication breaks down.

Although I agree with MacIntyre that our ability to be accountable for our actions is directly tied to our ability to ground these actions in specific narrative constructions, I find his claim that the meaning of these narratives stems from the agent's or agents' intentions to be overly reductive and therefore untenable. This is because he seems to reduce meaning to narrative intelligibility and the intelligibility of narratives to the intelligibility of the intentions that allegedly motivate them. These claims appear to me to be problematic on at least two counts.

First, I would argue that meaning cannot and should not be equated with narrative intelligibility. As both Husserl and Merleau-Ponty have shown, the horizons that situate our experience are themselves meaningful, however their very role as grounds for our experience means that they are often left out of account in the process of narrative construction, even when this latter depends on these horizons from the outset. Secondly, and relatedly, the intelligibility of narratives (and the same point goes for their unintelligibility) always includes more than the "intentions, motives, passions, and purposes" associated with them. There is, I am suggesting, a tacit organization to our narratives that is due not to cognition or emotion but to the body itself as the ultimate ground of all narrative construction. Whereas for MacIntyre, narratives seem either to be intelligible or unintelligible depending on the presence or absence of coherent intentions and/or on the ability or inability of the agent to discern coherent intentions, intentions that are in turn rendered coherent to the extent that they can be situated within a unified narrative, I would maintain that our bodies themselves contribute to the construction of narrative intelligibility and that this occurs even and precisely when the kind of coherence MacIntyre is privileging cannot be found.

Finally, MacIntyre's assumption that an action cannot be meaningful unless it is situated within an intelligible narrative is also problematic because, I would argue, along with Merleau-Ponty, that meaning does not require or presuppose the rationalist notion of intelligibility with which MacIntyre associates it. In our earlier discussion of Ricoeur, we noted that metaphors arise out of a clash between semantic fields and that they do not eliminate this clash but preserve it through the creation of a new meaning that creates a "new compatibility" on the basis of an existing "incompatibility." The very claim that metaphor involves a clash between semantic fields that generates a new compatibility out of an incompatibility poses a challenge to a rationalist conception of intelligibility. To explore this challenge further, we must ask, "How does this clash occur?" "What is the 'semantic impertinence' that brings it about?" For, it is clear that the semantic fields themselves must be configured in a certain way for such a clash to be experienced as such.

What I would like to propose is that the body is itself a semantic impertinence, that the body (whether this be an actual human body or the body of a text or the body of some other artifact, creature, or event) serves as the site for the production of semantic fields and, accordingly, of the inevitable tensions that arise among them. To make such a claim is not to deny the crucial role played by the imagination, for the imagination, as Mark Johnson emphasizes, is not a cognitive faculty but an embodied activity.

Despite his recognition of this crucial embodied dimension of all narrative activity, however, Johnson also offers far too reductive an explanation for narrative construction. Specifically, he contends that "all forms of action (from mundane tasks, to large-scale projects, to life plans) can be understood metaphorically as journeys" (Johnson 1993: 168). This "protonarrative," he holds, is structured by means of two basic imaginative schemas, the "source-path-goal" schema and the "balance" schema. Like MacIntyre then, Johnson privileges coherent narratives. Unlike MacIntyre, he acknowledges the crucial role the body plays in their intelligibility but, at the same time, he tends to understand the body's role in narrative construction in terms of a set of cognitive "image schemas" that emerge out of and, in turn, structure our embodied experiences.

While Johnson recognizes that "our lives are shot through with gaps, disjunctions, reversals, fractures, and fragmentations that constitute what Ricoeur calls the 'discordance' of human existence" and that "in Ricoeur's terms, both narratives and human lives have a 'discordant concordance,' an ineliminable tension that resists our attempts to construct a total unity and harmony" (Johnson 1993: 170), his cognitivist account of this process tends to view the "discrepant" data as meaningless to the extent that they resist incorporation into a coherent narrative.

More than anything, I am arguing that the body itself is this very "discordant concordance," that which frustrates our attempts at narrative unity, while simultaneously making the quest for narrative coherence possible. We can best see how this is so, I think, by turning to literature.

MacIntyre faults Kafka for the unintelligibility of the endings of his stories despite their initial intelligibility. Although Kafka's "failure" is acknowledged by MacIntyre to be deliberate, MacIntyre nonetheless refuses to probe deeper into the source of this failure, contenting himself with the dismissive, parenthetical assertion that "It is no accident that Kafka could not end his novels, for the notion of an ending like that of a beginning has its sense only in terms of intelligible narrative" (MacIntyre 1981: 198).

MacIntyre makes these remarks in the context of Kafka's *The Trial* and *The Castle,* however I would like to respond to them and conclude this chapter by referring to *The Metamorphosis*. Indeed, I think Kafka is exemplary in showing how the body serves as the continual narrative horizon that drives the quest for narrative intelligibility and, at the same time, thwarts it.

The everlasting debate over exactly *what* kind of bug Gregor Samsa becomes, an obsession Kafka anticipated and refrained from indulging by refusing to allow an image of this "monstrous vermin" to appear on the cover of his novella, reflects a desire to achieve narrative coherence by "normalizing," albeit in a manner that accepts its abnormality, Samsa's bodily metamorphosis. The irony is that even if Kafka had given in to this desire for clarity by specifying exactly what kind of creature Gregor had become, neither the metamorphosis itself nor the narrative in which it is configured would be clearer. Indeed, Samsa's changing body (which continues to change in shape, size, and abilities even after

his alleged metamorphosis) constitutes the crucial, narrative horizon that continually resists, more than anything else, Samsa's, his family's, and the reader's
attempts to persist in the illusion of narrative intelligibility.

To the extent that we read the ambiguities of Samsa's bodily changes as a
metaphor for those "semantic impertinences" that are our own bodies, we can
understand Kafka to be suggesting that the body continually transgresses all
attempts to make it or the narratives grounded upon it fully intelligible. And yet,
the body can never be dispensed with altogether, for the body is, indeed, the
omnipresent horizon for all the narratives we tell (about it). As such, it grounds
our quest for narrative coherence and, in so doing, establishes our moral accountability for the quest itself, an accountability that includes our failure to complete
the quest.

Finally, I think this failure can best be understood in Merleau-Pontian
terms, not as a lack of intelligibility but as a challenge to the very notion of the
intelligible, a challenge that we must not try to "solve" but whose very insol-
ubility gives richness, meaning, and depth to our experience. To use Ricoeur's
language, to take up this challenge is not to avoid but actively to produce the
clash between semantic fields that gives birth to new meanings and makes
possible the creation of new narratives.

Notes

1. While it is beyond the scope of this chapter to address the ethical
implications of the narrative structure of corporeal experience, what I hope to do
here is to provide a grounding for just such a discussion.

2. Gertrude Stein's 1914 collection of poems, *Tender Buttons,* offers an
excellent example of the malleability of language. By displacing ordinary words
from their ordinary contexts she is able to generate new meanings that, at the
same time, never lose their traditional referents. This makes the reading of the
poems a playful exercise for those who can revel in the elasticity of expression and
a frustrating experience for those who seek univocal and stable meanings. Moreover, as Lisa Ruddick and others have argued, Stein's experimental strategy does
not preclude the ability to raise serious issues within her work, including an
ongoing challenge to reductive interpretations of everyday domestic experience
within patriarchy.

References

Husserl, Edmund (1970), *The Crisis of European Sciences and Transcendental
Phenomenology,* trans. David Carr. Evanston, Ill.: Northwestern University
Press.

Johnson, Mark (1987). *The Body in the Mind: The Bodily Basis of Meaning, Imagination, and Reason.* Chicago: University of Chicago Press.

———— (1993). *Moral Imagination: Implications of Cognitive Science for Ethics.* Chicago: University of Chicago Press.

Kafka, Franz (1972). *The Metamorphosis,* trans. Stanley Corngold. New York: Bantam.

Keenan, Thomas (1997). *Fables of Responsibility: Aberrations and Predicaments in Ethics and Politics.* Stanford: Stanford University Press.

MacIntyre, Alasdair (1981). *After Virtue: A Study in Moral Theory.* Notre Dame: University of Notre Dame Press.

Merleau-Ponty, Maurice (1962). *Phenomenology of Perception,* trans. Colin Smith. London: Routledge and Kegan Paul.

———— (1993). "Eye and Mind," *The Merleau-Ponty Aesthetics Reader,* ed. Galen A. Johnson. Translation editor Michael Smith. Evanston, Ill.: Northwestern University Press.

Ricoeur, Paul (1991). *A Ricoeur Reader: Reflection and Imagination,* ed. Mario J. Valdés. Toronto: University of Toronto Press.

Ruddick, Lisa (1990). *Reading Gertrude Stein: Body, Text, Gnosis.* Ithaca: Cornell University Press.

Stein, Gertrude (1914). *Tender Buttons.* Los Angeles: Sun and Moon Press.

PART II
DERMAL BOUNDARIES

3

Cutups in Beauty School

Linda S. Kauffman

Emma's head was turned towards her right shoulder, the corner of her
mouth, which was open, seemed like a black hole at the lower part of
her face . . . her eyes were beginning to disappear in a viscous pallor, as
if covered by a spiderweb. . . . They had to raise the head a little, and a
rush of black liquid poured from her mouth, as if she were vomiting.

—Gustave Flaubert, *Madame Bovary*

Madame Bovary was not banned merely because of the sex scenes— it was the
nihilism of passages like this, which by repudiating the teachings of the Church
posed an "outrage to public morals." Flaubert confessed that he could never look
at a beautiful woman without visualizing her corpse. Since his father was a
doctor in Rouen, the hospital was his childhood playground; its scenes and smells
were a gritty antidote to what he called "the cancer of Romanticism," which he
cauterized by writing *Madame Bovary,* "a book about nothing . . . held together
by the strength of its style."[1]

The cancer of Romanticism, nevertheless, lives on. In the fall of 1993, *Time
Magazine* devoted a special issue to "The New Face of America: How Immi-
grants are Shaping the World's First Multicultural Society". The cover girl is 15
percent Anglo-Saxon, 17.5 percent Middle Eastern, 17.5 percent African, 7.5
percent Asian, 35 percent South European, and 7.5 percent Hispanic. While
seeming to promise racial tolerance and assimilation, the cover girl is merely
a composite created by cybergeneticists who combined six races to create a
"morph" (short for metamorphosis) of their ideal beauty. No wonder minorities
are skeptical of the buzzword "assimilation": the composite eliminates all racial
and ethnic markers, although the cybergeneticists seem blithely unaware that
this oversight could conceivably be perceived as racist. *Time's* editor writes: "As
the onlookers watched the image of our new Eve begin to appear on our computer screen, several staff members promptly fell in love. Said one, 'it really breaks
my heart that she doesn't exist.'"[2] The men do not seem to grasp that no
breathing woman could match their ideal. They have fallen in love with their
own invention, like the frustrated infertility researcher in David Cronenberg's
*Dead Ringer*s who protests petulantly, "We have the technology! It's the woman's
body that's all wrong!"

Was there ever a time when woman's body was not "all wrong"? Ever
since the Judgment of Paris, anonymous young women have paraded before

Figure 3.1 "The New Face of America." Cover of *Time* magazine (fall 1993), Special Issue, © Time Pix.

male judges, who inevitably find all but one wanting. Centuries of mythology, art, culture, and commerce capitalize on that lack, exploit that (invented) inadequacy. Whatever else divides twenty-something women from feminists over forty, at least they agree that beauty is a racket.[3]

No wonder so many women artists are "Gorilla Girls" and *Angry Women* (Vale and Juno 1991), actively creating a new antiaesthetic by interrogating those who have the power to define beauty and to proclaim that the woman's body "needs work." I call them "cut-ups" because they are often bawdy comics, satirizing the culture's investments in femininity. Beneath the comedy, however, lies a serious shared objective: to examine the vicissitudes of psychic life, particularly the drives that lead men to turn the female body into a fetish, icon, or cut-out. However much they lust after their ideal beauty, *Time's* cybergeneticists would never actually want to *see* the gruesome plastic surgery that would be necessary to make a woman's face match the computer morph. Where the virtual and the visceral fuse, one finds Orlan.

"Orlan" is the fictional name of a French art history professor and performance artist who, through plastic surgery, has transformed her face into a composite of the icons of feminine beauty. She tracks the interrelationships between sexuality and pathology, between the female body and the body politic, deconstructing femininity. Through a series of plastic surgeries, she has acquired the chin of Botticelli's Venus, the nose of Diana, the forehead of the Mona Lisa, the mouth of Boucher's Europa, the eyes of Gérôme's Psyche. She chose these women not for their looks but because she was intrigued with the weave of *stories* surrounding them: the rumor that the Mona Lisa was a self-portrait of Leonardo in drag; the mythological tales of the adventuress, Diana.[4] Like *Time's* cybergeneticists, Orlan relies on digital computers to visualize her ideal morph, but by putting their theories into practice, she exposes all the implications they overlooked: the arbitrariness of the standards, the impossibility of meeting them, the unchallenged assumption that every woman *wants* beauty.

Orlan has variously been described as "a beautiful woman who is deliberately becoming ugly";[5] "a slightly plump woman of average height" (Fox 1993); or "46 and still rather ugly—even after six operations . . . her pug-like face would need something more than the skill of a surgeon's knife to reach the Grecian ideal of perfection" (Rosen 1993). Attitudes like these explain why it took Orlan two years to find a surgeon who understood that her aim was *not* to make herself more beautiful. In New York City, she finally found a feminist surgeon (and amateur sculptor) whom she calls a "surgical aesthetician."[6] Hilton Kramer remarked dismissively that if Orlan *really* wanted to do something transgressive, why not put both eyes on one side of her head, like a Picasso? In fact, Orlan comes as close as she can: cheek implants were implanted above her brow, giving her the owlish look of a Star Trekker.

"What," Simone de Beauvoir asked, "is Woman?" The answer: a person of the female sex. Only in certain relations of power and exchange does she become

Figure 3.2 Orlan with implants above eyebrows, 1993. Courtesy Orlan and Sandra Gering Gallery, New York.

a servant, a womb, or a sexual partner (de Beauvoir 65–66). "Woman," Orlan shows, is a projection of male fantasies compiled through the centuries in myth, art, religion. Orlan exposes the process of projection, production, distribution, and exchange. She peels away the sedimentary layers that have made this artificial process seem "natural." As Barbara Rose observes,

> Orlan's performances might be read as rituals of female submission. . . . But actually she aims to exorcise society's program to deprive women of aggressive instincts of any kind. . . . If the parts of seven different ideal women are needed to fulfill Adam's desire for an Eve made in his image, Orlan consciously chooses to undergo the necessary mutilation to reveal that the objective is unattainable and the process horrifying. (B. Rose 1993: 125)

I'll return again to the issue of aggression at the end. For the present, Orlan points out that there are not many images that cannot be looked at; one has only to turn on the evening news to see murder, rape, massacres in living color. As J. G. Ballard notes, "The hidden logic at work within the mass media—above all, the inadvertent packaging of violence and cruelty like attractive commercial products—has already spread throughout the world" (Ballard 1990: 93). There-fore, it's all the more remarkable how difficult it is to watch Orlan under the knife. Her skin is essentially cut away from her face, laid across her nose, whereupon implants "lift" the skin and pull it taut. Blood is everywhere. Orlan is awake, submitting only to local anaesthetic. "I try to suffer as Christ did," she says, reminding us that the etymological meaning of "passion" is "suffering."

Generic Antecedents and Implications

While heralding the world of the posthuman, that world is thus paradoxically peopled with ghosts: primitive rituals of sacrifice and purification, medieval rituals of fleshly mortification, mystical Indian rites, baroque transports of ec-stasy. She calls one operation "The Reincarnation of St. Orlan," and poses as a Baroque White Virgin, in imitation of Bernini's "The Ecstasy of St. Theresa." For over twenty years, Orlan has worked specifically with Baroque iconography. Her namesake is Caravaggio's *St. Orlan and the Elders;* she carved a prototype out of marble, then sent it out to be enlarged to full scale. But to subvert the madonna/whore dichotomy of the Old Masters, she leaves one breast exposed (Hirschorn 1994).

Peter Greenaway's *The Baby of Macon* is an intriguing analogue to Orlan's work; they share an abiding fascination with the history of painting in general, the Baroque in particular. The *Baby of Macon*'s deepest theme is pictorial repre-sentation of Madonna and Child. The plot revolves around an infant who may or may not be Christ. A beautiful young woman claims to be his mother, after she murders his true mother, an old hag, who is "unseemly" in the regime of representation. The surrogate Madonna is subsequently condemned as a whore and raped to death. The infant is first adored, then sacrificed and dismembered by his worshipers.[7] As allegorical as a medieval morality play, the film raises disturbing questions about articles of faith and the suspension of disbelief, as does Orlan. Orlan's *femme morcélé* parallels Greenaway's *bébé morcélé;* both trace the links between sacrifice and eroticism, death and sensuality, following Bataille's theories on transgression and taboo. In the chapter on "Christianity," Bataille laments that Christianity reduces religion to its benign aspect. He argues that the modern view of the orgy must be rejected, for "Bacchic violence is the measure of incipient eroticism whose domain is originally that of religion" (Bataille 1986: 117).[8] Surrounded in the operating room by nearly naked black men doing a striptease, Orlan arranges all the props for an orgy; the orgies in Greenaway's film are so numerous and violent that watching is almost unbearable. *The Baby of Macon*'s juxtaposition of innocence and violence tests several film taboos, oscillat-ing repeatedly between reality-film, morality play-within-a-play. Greenaway desacralizes Christianity in general, the Catholic Church in particular, as does Orlan. As Greenaway explains:

> The Baroque age was the first time various art forms were combined to
> create a certain form of propaganda which . . . was put to use for the
> church . . . here in the end of the 20th century we're now again in an
> enormous Baroque period, this time with a small b. . . . In our lives, we
> have seen the Baroque used as propaganda for the two great C's, capitalism
> and communism. (Shulman 1994: H18)

Both Orlan and Greenaway illustrate that in order for the institution of Christianity to be erected, Christ himself had to be ejected. Without the crucifixion,
there would have been no church. The "eject," as Kristeva points out in her
discussion of Bataille, is always *abject*. Like the artists in the *Abject Art* show,
Greenaway and Orlan are obsessed with the way subjects are sutured into the
cinematic or visual space. They examine how subjects simultaneously subject
themselves and others to institutionalized violence and power.

    In Orlan's work, the juxtaposition of posthuman technology and ancient
religion serves several additional functions. First, it provides an apocalyptic
frame of reference, for while *apocalypse* generally connotes catastrophe, it also
signifies revelation of what was, is, and will be. Orlan is Janus: one side faces the
past, which memorializes the obsolete body, carefully preserving its viscera as
reliquaries. The other side faces the cyborg future, when the inorganic far
outweighs the organic elements of the body. Artificial hearts, breasts, hair implants, reproductive technologies, and organ transplants have already trans-
ported us into the world of tomorrow; Orlan serves as intermediary between
present and future. Her installation at the Pompidou Center's *Hors Limites* show
in 1994 was called "Entre" ("In Between Two"): she stands between past and
future, human and posthuman. (When she learned about Jeffrey Deitch's *Post
Human* show, she let him know that she should have been included. She is right.)
She did participate in the "Virtual Futures" Conference at the University of
Warwick in England in the summer of 1995, which had the declared aim

> to bury the 20th century and begin work on the 21st. We are children of the
> 21st century and live already in the future unknown, uncovering every day
> vast new landscapes for exploration. We will not know the results of the
> tumultuous global changes we are undergoing and creating for a hundred
> years or more, if we can survive them, but we are less interested in
> knowledge than in experiencing these changes.[9]

Orlan's own aims are not quite so utopian, for she does not approach the millennium with either fervor or fear; instead she dissects both ideological poles with
surgical precision. Like Ballard, she embodies a new psychopathology of everyday life.

    Orlan's actions cut through three discrete genres: (1) Western classical
painting, from Leonardo da Vinci forward; (2) the genre of the psychoanalytic

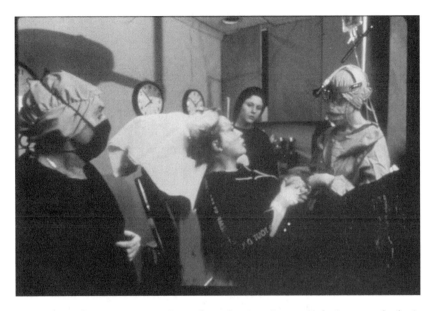

Figure 3.3 Orlan, *Omnipresence*. Scene from the operating room during seventh plastic surgical operation, November 21, 1993. Courtesy Orlan and Sandra Gering Gallery, New York.

case study, with specific attention to Lacan and Freud (who wrote a famous essay on Leonardo);[10] and (3) the genre of epistolarity, which has undergone several recent transformations as a result of technology. Jean Cocteau was the first to link ancient epistolary conventions to a new communications technology—the telephone—in *La Voix Humaine,* a woman's dramatic monologue on the telephone with the lover who abandoned her. Nicholson Baker's 1991 novel *Vox* substitutes anonymous phone sex for the letter, but his title pays homage to Cocteau. Email novels have already begun to appear: Avodah Offitt's 1994 *Virtual Love* consists of online correspondence between two psychiatrists.

Orlan invents a new model for epistolarity and simultaneously performs it. While the surgeons operate, Orlan opens a window to the world via satellite, visiophone, picture Tel, fax, and modem. Well-wishers around the globe "correspond" with her; everybody is plugged in and hooked up. While she is on the operating table, she receives messages from Tokyo, Moscow, Paris, Latvia. Epistolarity is now international, instantaneous, and interactive. She makes the verbal and the visual intersect, for Orlan's "correspondents" can see as well as hear her, just as she sees, hears, and responds to their questions and comments. This takes epistolary communication far beyond the powers even of email. The "correspondence" is *visual, aesthetic and clinical*—all at the same time. It is *multiple, spontaneous, and staged*—all at the same time.

Orlan is our age's Cocteau, the missing feminist link between the Surrealists' exploration of the unconscious, the Situationists' of spectacle, and Baudrillard's simulacra. Like Virtual Reality and God, Orlan is everywhere and nowhere. She stages the problematic of belief, its causes and consequences. Lying prone and vulnerable, she shares with the world an overwhelming desire to communicate (Adams 1996: 154). Orlan's New York show at the Sandra Gering Gallery in 1993 combined the concept of "Omnipresence" and virtual interactivity: while the surgeons operated, supporters around the globe not only watched the operation but transmitted messages back to her instantaneously. One fax transmittal: "Paris is with you, Orlan"—the *city* of Paris—*not* the mythological beauty contest judge.[11]

"I was able," she says, "without feeling any pain, to answer people who were feeling their own pain as they were watching me." Those words are an uncanny description of the psychoanalyst's function—*to answer people who [are] feeling their own pain.* "To answer," however, means "to respond"; it does not imply that either the analyst or Orlan *provides* the answers. Orlan invests "the talking cure" with new significance. Just as her face is a composite of many icons, she combines the functions of intercessor, cyborg, mother, and analyst (on whom one projects one's loves and hatred). Orlan uses the new technologies in medicine and telecommunications to create a psychological self-portrait, one that reflects how profoundly the human senses have been reorganized by those technologies. Rather than "playing" the passive patient, Orlan plays the pedagogue: during surgery, she reads from Lacan's "The Mirror Stage" and Kristeva's *Powers of Horror.* Small wonder that Orlan would one day like to do a whole exhibition on Abjection— she is Exhibit A. What is it about the body, she asks, that evokes such revulsion—particularly the female body? Why is every stage of women's art, history, and subjectivity repressed, disavowed—right up to the present moment—with herself? As a panel participant with Orlan, I have witnessed firsthand the hostility she arouses. She recalls a New York dinner party for art dealers, curators, and collectors with whom she hoped to discuss her work. Instead, they were suspicious of her, particularly the women. Suddenly, she noticed that all the women had the same nose! Her very presence simultaneously affronted and exposed their psychic and economic investments, quite literally.

If the Mirror Stage is the structuring moment when an ideal of unity, harmony, wholeness (with self and other) is imprinted on the mind's eye, Orlan cracks the mirror, exposing the optical trick that makes it up. She never lets the spectator forget that the ideal is illusory. "I no longer recognize myself in the mirror," says Orlan. Re-cognition: the act of knowing involves doubling, repetition, re-creation. The agency of the ego is founded in a fictional direction; subjectivity is not only fractured but based on misrecognition. Narcissism, Lacan argues, is ontological, which illuminates Orlan's numerous comments about her own image: "I've worked with my own image for twenty years," she tells me.

"Being a narcissist isn't easy when the question is not of loving your own image, but of re-creating the self through deliberate acts of alienation."

Although many feminists have taken issue with Freud for equating femininity with narcissism, Orlan *performs* that equation—with a Medusan vengeance. She documents each step of the process, photographing her bruised and bandaged face every day for forty-one days. She emphasizes the *plasticity* of her body as an aesthetic—and technological—medium. Since psychoanalysis involves "working through" old materials (dreams, fantasies, traumas), it seems fitting that Orlan recycles every material thing. (One of the defining traits of the fetish is its untranscended materiality; its status as a material object.) As the French representative to the Sydney Biennial in December 1992, she included in the exhibition vials containing samples of her liquified flesh and blood drained off during the "body-sculpting" part of the operations. These "relics" were marketed to raise funds for the remaining operations.

As gruesome as all this sounds, Orlan actually transforms the operating room into a carnival of campy humor. She and the medical team don costumes designed by Paco Rabanne or other couturiers; a pair of black men do a striptease. Orlan brandishes a skull's head, pitchfork, or crucifix, delighting in absurd juxtapositions, like the Surrealists' *Exquisite Corpse* projects, collaborative artworks in which one artist designs the head, another the torso, a third the feet for a single painting. It almost seems as if she wants to transform the famous Surrealist image of an umbrella and a sewing machine on an autopsy table into a tableaux vivant. Orlan shares Peter Greenaway's and Jeffrey Deitch's view that "the body is obsolete." Orlan herself is the "exquisite corpse"; the body merely a costume. She sheds one "costume" after another, staging femininity literally as masquerade. She is a "relic" in both senses of the word—a religious relic and a relic of an age that will soon seem long ago and far away.

Just as her own body is a "cadavre exquis," she grafts Brecht's theory of the "alienation effect" with Artaud's "theater of cruelty." Her studio on Rue de Raspail (the celebrated scientist) is next to the asylum where Artaud died, and one of her staged facelifts was performed in homage to Artaud. Artaud defined "Cruelty" as the painful reorganization of the theater and the urgent demand for a new type of corporeal speech: "We need above all a theater that wakes us up: nerves and heart." His manifesto exhorts actors to create a spontaneous corporeal force between actor and the "shocked" neuro-muscular responses of the spectator.[12]

The Viennese Actionists took up the historical legacy of Artaud, exposing the process-oriented, ritualistic, performative characteristics that characterized "body art" of the l960s and 1970s (Export 1992). From Marcel Duchamp, Orlan took the idea of using cast-off materials, found objects as art, an idea Orlan takes to an extreme by using her own body as a "ready-made." Orlan calls her own work "carnal body art for the 1990s." Yves Klein also had a dramatic impact on her work.[13] The art movement Fluxus (whose members include Valie Export,

Yoko Ono, Henry Flynt, Joseph Beuys, and Jean Dupuy) are also Orlan's precursors, especially with their emphasis on "chance operations," indeterminacy, and the unconscious.

Many of these artists were represented in the *Hors Limites* show in Paris at the Pompidou Center in 1994–95, an ambitious comprehensive retrospective from 1952 forward which, appropriately, begins with Guy Debord. Orlan's early art suggests the kind of agitation synonymous with Debord and the Situationists, so named because they became notorious for staging absurd "situations" that mocked both state power and the art establishment. Orlan shares their aim of transforming life through art. The Situationists argued for a collective view of play; play must invade life (Export 1992: 28–29). In the wake of Debord's *Society of Spectacle,* Orlan improvised a series of absurd *feminist* spectacles—like lying down in the streets of Paris and using her own body as a ruler to measure Rue Lamartine, Rue Victor Hugo, as well as streets named for famous men in other cities. She uses her petite body to "take their measure." Other measuring actions related her body to a medieval convent and to the Guggenheim Museum. Like the Situationists, Orlan wants to launch a cultural revolution against consumer society. In 1977, *Le Baiser de l'Artiste* featured a life-size photo of her torso transformed into a slot machine, which she labeled "automatic kiss-vending object." By inserting five francs, customers could watch the coin descend from her breasts to her crotch, whereupon she leapt from her pedestal to kiss the customer, a burlesque of the processes that idealize and objectify woman, while commodifying the art *and* the artist.

As in the *Post Human* exhibition, Orlan points to a new concept of the self, ruled not by metaphors of depth but of surface. It is in this sense that she develops a new metaphorology. She demonstrates that subjectivity doesn't control the image; instead the image shapes subjectivity, whether the image comes from Renaissance art or contemporary advertising. (In *The Physical Self,* Greenaway uses the Benetton image of a newborn to make the same point.) When her metamorphosis is complete, Orlan—a synthetic name for a synthetic identity-in-process—will let an ad agency assign her a new name to go with her new "look."

Orlan and Greenaway are trying to drive the same point home: subjectivity itself has undergone a profound transformation as a result of televisual technologies. A recent essay entitled "Television" asks whether television fundamentally *determines* our experience:

> *Is the television a—or the—dominant but unacknowledged epistemological model of subjectivity?* Do we understand ourselves as presentational constructions, moved by prefabricated, precoded information, precipitated—in a strangely evacuated but somehow 'electric' space? (Byfield and Tobier 1992)

Orlan traveled to India to obtain enormous flashy billboards of the type used to advertise Indian films, because they have the kitschy look of 1950s Hollywood posters. Her pilgrimage testifies to the lengths to which she will go to show how our self-images are cobbled from advertisements and films. She is expert in the hyperreal, the saturation of reality by simulacra.

Nevertheless, sensationalistic media coverage in both Europe and the United States consistently portrays her as a freak. When Orlan was interviewed by CBS's Connie Chung in 1993, Chung could not disguise her revulsion, which was particularly hypocritical, since *she* went under the knife years ago to make her eyes look more "Western." Orlan merely takes to an extreme what Chung and many other celebrities take halfway. She merely exposes the processes that doctors and patients go to such lengths to disavow. Orlan has nothing against plastic surgery per se. Her critique is directed against the regime of beauty it so rigidly enforces, to which celebrities (and New York art dealers) so slavishly conform.

When Orlan calls herself the first "woman-to-woman transsexual," she destroys the neat divisions between male/female, culture/nature, outside/inside. That litany of dismantled dichotomies is by now familiar, but Orlan uses the phrase with surgical precision, for where the transsexual undergoes sex reassignment in order to be "complete," Orlan is never complete (Adams 1996: 158–59). The whole point is to avoid perfection, fixity, positiveness. Parveen Adams calls Orlan "an image *trapped* in a woman's body," but it is Orlan who sets the trap, Orlan who upsets the tranquil categories of gender and genre. Adams is, however, right to conclude that the image is empty. It is not a face but a gap (Adams 1996: 158)—not unlike "the black hole at the lower part of her face" that opens in Emma Bovary's corpse, spewing out black liquid.

Along with artists like "supermasochist" Bob Flanagan, Orlan points to a newly emerging aesthetic, generated from or driven by the insides of the body. With Greenaway and Deitch, they are not just creating *performances* for the twenty-first century, but *bodies*. If Flanagan is Sacher Masoch, Orlan is de Sade. Both are stoic comedians, exhibitionists, displaying the corporeal self as an "Atrocity Museum." They interpret medicine's texts: codes, alphabets, letters, sequences, and blueprints are the signatures of all things they are here to read.

No wonder the medical establishment weighed in on the "issue" of Orlan. In 1991, the *Revue Scientifique et Culturelle de Santé Mentale* devoted a special issue to the question of whether she is sane or mad, and whether her work is art or not. (The strictly regimented dichotomy of options is revealing: sane/insane, art/not-art.) Essays by psychologists, critics, and artists explored the relationship of her work to psychopathology and aesthetics and concluded that her surgery projects are indeed art (*VST: Revue Scientifique et Culturelle de Santé Mentale* 23/24, 1991).[14] Not everyone agreed: Hollander finds in her work symptoms of Body Dysmorphic Disorder (BDD):

> Orlan has literally become "detached" from her original body, the new creation being something distant, foreign, unnatural. The further disloca-

tions produced by the constant photographing, videotaping and filming of several "before" and "after" images can only lead to an extreme case of identity confusion, a state that would fall within the psychiatric diagnosis of Depersonalization Disorder, another mental disorder related to BDD (cited in Augsburg 1995: 43).

Hollander sounds exactly like one of J. G. Ballard's parodies of clinical psychiatric manuals in *The Atrocity Exhibition.* The culture of experts has the technical lingo, but it comprehends nothing, it tells us nothing. It is judgmental and prescriptive, not descriptive. Orlan could not have helped but be amused by the *Revue;* she rolled her eyes as she told me how fixated the interviewers were on her relationships with her mother and father. First she parodies the genre of the psychiatric case study, then the experts proceeded to turn her into one.

Having traced Orlan's generic antecedents, let me mention some of the important implications of her work for theorists of genre. The first implication: however much the genre is deformed, traces of its roots remain visible, even when radically altered by technology. In *The Handmaid's Tale,* for instance, a tape cassette stands in for a letter, but all the generic characteristics of epistolarity remain intact, as clearly visible as in Cocteau's *La Voix Humaine.* Exhibit A is certainly *Madame Bovary,* prosecuted for its "outrage to public morals." Only later did it become clear that by the end of the first chapter, point of view in the novel had changed forever; the collective "we" who observe Charles Bovary's first day of school disappear, and *indirect discours libre* makes it impossible to determine how "we" are to interpret from that point forward. Flaubert is perhaps the first to make "looking awry" part of narrative structure itself.

The same applies to Orlan's innovations: no one theory adequately explains her work, *even though she reads theory during her performances!* Just as the epistle (according to Derrida) "is not a genre, but all genres, literature itself," Orlan illustrates Derrida's theory of genre: the trait that enables one to determine genre does not appear in genre itself. It is important to remember that when Orlan's operations are complete, she will not look like the Mona Lisa, the Botticelli Venus, or the other paintings—instead, she will be a composite of them all. In this sense, she perfectly embodies Derrida's definition of genre: "A sort of participation without belonging—a taking part in without being part of, without having membership in a set" (Derrida 1980).

Genre also has important implications for theories of spectatorship. *Obscenity's* etymology may derive from *ob-scene,* and suggests "that which takes place offstage, off to the side" (Williams 1993: 47), but the very fact that Orlan uses multiple visual technologies *onstage* indicates that we are witnessing a paradigm shift in the making where spectatorship is concerned. The most important theory of spectatorship in the past thirty years is Laura Mulvey's "Visual Pleasure and Narrative Cinema." Written in 1973 and published in *Screen* in 1975, the idea of the "male gaze" has become so widely dispersed across so many genres and media that it is worth revisiting some of Mulvey's original points, which have sometimes been lost in translation.

All Mulvey's work focuses on the deep structure of the Oedipus complex, the persistence of fetishism and fascination. Following Freud, she argues that woman signifies castration; man activates voyeuristic or fetishistic mechanisms to circumvent the threat of castration. Cinema is a screen much like the Lacanian mirror, an "imaginary signifier." It is ironic that her essay has taken on a life of its own, dispersed across multiple genres, because it is an argument about *genre*—narrative fiction film in classical Hollywood cinema, with specific emphasis on film noir and Hitchcock: "The place of the look defines cinema. . . . Going far beyond highlighting a woman's to-be-looked-at-ness, cinema builds the way she is to be looked at into the spectacle itself" (Mulvey 1989: 25). Furthermore, many who took Mulvey to task for being "reductive or un-objective," failed to notice that the essay itself belongs to a very specific *genre:* it is a manifesto.[15] Like the Futurist Manifesto and the Surrealist Manifesto, objectivity is hardly the aim! The aim is to incite people to action—*three* actions in particular. First, she wants people to recognize the political usefulness of psychoanalysis, a blind spot for the British Left in the late 1960s and early 1970s, and one that materialist feminists like Mulvey, Juliet Mitchell, and Jacqueline Rose *insisted* on. As Rose points out, despite the publication of Lacan's essay and Althusser's famous article on Lacan in *New Left Review* in 1968, the commitment to psychoanalysis was not sustained even by that section of the British Left that had originally argued for its importance. They ignored its radical anti-empiricist potential—the very potential Mulvey's manifesto exhorts us to recognize (J. Rose 1986: 83–89).

Second, Mulvey wants "to destroy pleasure," but she discusses two distinct pleasures in the essay. First, she uses the word "pleasure" interchangeably with "beauty": "It is said that analyzing pleasure, or beauty, destroys it. That is the intention of this article" (Mulvey 1989: 16).[16] No more pleasure in seeing one part of a fragmented body, no more pleasure in turning woman into "a cut-out or icon" (Mulvey 1989: 20). Put another way, Mulvey wants cinema to *cut out the cuts* that make pleasure possible, for the cuts to women are the unkindest cuts of all. Although some of the male theorists who criticized Mulvey denied that they desired or intended to do this to women, J. G. Ballard frankly confirms Mulvey's hypothesis. He clearly has Freud's theory of fetishism and the castration complex in mind when he confesses what the breast signifies:

> Were [Mae West's] breasts too large? No . . . but they loomed across the horizons of popular consciousness along with those of Marilyn Monroe and Jayne Mansfield. Beyond our physical touch, the breasts of these screen actresses incite our imaginations to explore and reshape them. The bodies of these extraordinary women form a kit of spare parts, a set of mental mannequins that resemble Bellmer's obscene dolls. As they tease

us, so we begin to dismantle them, removing sections of a smile, a leg
stance, an enticing cleavage. The parts are interchangeable. (Ballard 1990:
114)

Enter Orlan. If Orlan hadn't existed, Mulvey might have invented her, for she
deliberately assembles and reassembles her *own* "spare parts." She is a "living
doll" who plays with herself. In so doing, she inverts the "natural" order, revealing (and reveling in) the pornography of science. What do pornography and
science have in common? Both "perverse implantations" rely on repetition and
experimentation. Both isolate objects or events from their contexts in time and
space in order to concentrate on a specific activity of quantified functions. Both
murder to dissect. These are all traits pornography and science share with
cinema, for "the male gaze" freezes the look upon the erotic image. Mulvey
again:

> The presence of woman . . . tends to . . . freeze the flow of action in
> moments of erotic contemplation. . . . Playing on the tension between film
> as controlling the dimension of time (editing, narrative) and film as con-
> trolling the dimension of space (changes in distance, editing), cinematic
> codes create a gaze, a world and an object, thereby producing an illusion
> cut to the measure of desire. (19, 25)

Orlan wants to trace the passage from Nature to Culture, with specific
attention to the cuts along the way. (The three nasty newspaper reviews I cited
earlier, by Dovkants, Fox, and Rosen, each tried to suture Orlan into the regime
of beauty and found her wanting.) Like Mulvey, Orlan reminds us that "the male
gaze" does not spring from *omnipotence* but from *fear:* man assuages his own
fears of castration by projecting those fears onto woman, turning her into an
object of voyeurism and/or into a fetish object. By literally showing how the cuts
are made, Orlan reverses the suturing process of ideological interpellation.
Whereas Mulvey shows how the female star is filmed in such a way that maintains her position in relation to the male subject, in Orlan's work, the male has no
relevance, no paternity or divinity, which is what Orlan means when she proclaims, "I fight against God and DNA!"
     She also thwarts the pleasures of passivity—the final trait she shares with
Mulvey, for Mulvey wants to destroy the pleasure of passivity, a point in her essay
which—along with her wit—is often overlooked today. If Orlan is one of the
"cut-ups in beauty school" in my title, Mulvey is another one, for she made a
spectacle of herself by getting arrested for disrupting the Miss World beauty
contest in London, over thirty years ago. Today, it is more important than ever to
remember: "The Spectacle is Vulnerable." Today, furthermore, it is almost impossible to remember the spirit of camaraderie that accompanied such hijinks. That
is what makes Wendy Steiner's comparison of Mulvey to Andrea Dworkin so

unjust in "The Literalism of the Left," for nothing could be further from Mulvey's mischief making than Dworkin's grim censorship campaign. Dworkin's and Mulvey's leftism, feminism, and intellectualism could not be more dissimilar. Dworkin is a self-proclaimed "radical" feminist; she has declared war on any image that can be construed as "subordinating women." Mulvey is a British materialist-feminist, an early champion of popular culture, and what interests her most about Freud are his metaphors—hardly evidence of literalism! Yet, to Steiner:

> Much more worrisome is the feminist critique of aesthetic pleasure. . . . According to some feminists, the experience of traditional art amounts to a seduction by a beautiful object. . . . Just as feminist extremists invest pornography with an extraordinary power over reality, Mulvey's critique invests the cinema with the power of a Freudian fetish. Hollywood cinema, she says, is a magic realm of wish-fulfillment in which male fears of castration are deflected onto a castrated woman. . . . The only way to control aesthetic pleasure for the dedicated fetish-buster is to destroy beauty. Thus for many artists and theorists, the experience of art is necessarily pornographic, sadistic, and ultimately destructive of women. . . . To see art as enactment of a one-way power relation is adequate neither to women nor to art. (Steiner 1995: 91)

Far from interpreting all art as "victim art," as Steiner claims, Mulvey explores the pleasures of passivity. Far from being a "fetish buster," she is fascinated by the logic of the fetish. Far from taking Freud literally, Mulvey is interested in the ways these master narratives of Oedipus, Pandora, and the like are disseminated over and over in films from *Citizen Kane* to *Blue Velvet*. (It is revealing that Steiner does not support her argument with a cinematic example, but instead cites Toni Morrison's *Beloved*.) Far from exhorting us to ban even the classics, Mulvey merely *analyzes* them, while exhorting filmmakers to consider new strategies in avant-garde filmmaking.

Orlan's performances demand a story, but she withholds the plot, the raison d'etre, and—like Flaubert—an authorial point of view. She does not demand one single "proper response" to her art. She thwarts passivity by shoving spectators' voyeurism down their throats. As Michael Prince observes, "the beauty contest transforms a culture's anxiety about the contingency of its defining values into a spectacular reenactment and overcoming of that very anxiety" (Prince 1994: 279). Those consoling transformations and values are precisely what first Mulvey and then Orlan *thwart*. This is an especially crucial point, because while film theorists in recent years have devoted considerable attention to fantasy, more work remains to be done specifically on *anxiety*.

Not only does the act of cutting create anxiety, but the erasure of origins does too. If Orlan is a model that cannot be copied, she is also a copy that has no single origin. "Orlan"—a synthetic name for a personality composed from what Flaubert called its "idées reçues." Orlan clearly has Flaubert's novel *Bouvard and Pecuchet* in mind: the novel consists of a dictionary of received ideas, or clichés, obsessively recorded by two maniacal copyists. Orlan also mimics *Bovarysme*, which means the act of seeing oneself as others see you, just as Emma Bovary formed a self-image in her mind's eye compiled from Parisian corturiers' catalogues. Flaubert duplicated the clichéd language *and emotions* Emma Bovary borrowed from books (specifically from Lamartine and Victor Hugo). In forming her "Image-repertoire" from books, she is a female Quixote; Orlan is her daughter.

Orlan's performances annotate the body of French literature. She gives new meaning to an "Anatomy of Criticism." She cannibalizes the canon, as if to say, "Let us now lie down in the streets named for famous men." But the idea that one's most intimate emotions are mere copies can be traced back to the celebrated maxims of La Rochefoucauld: "Some people would never know love if they had not heard it talked about." Her performances are forms of literary criticism, not unlike Roland Barthes's *S/Z,* which cannibalizes Balzac's tale of Sarrasine, a sculptor who falls in love with a beautiful opera singer named La Zambinella, who is eventually exposed as a castrato. The slash in the title is the sign of castration. When Zambinella's duplicity is revealed, "she" falls to her knees, eyes raised, arms outstretched. Here is Barthes:

> Derived from a complex pictorial code, La Zambinella here achieves her final incarnation, or reveals her ultimate origin: the *Madonna with Raised Eyes.* This is a powerful stereotype, a major element in the Code of Pathos (Raphael, El Greco, Racine's Junie and Esther, etc.). (Barthes 1978: 169)

Barthes concludes that *Nature copies the Book*—a motto that illuminates Orlan's motives for copying the old masters. But she simultaneously refuses to "Invest in the Divinity of the Masterpiece," to cite the words photographer Barbara Kruger slashes across her reproduction of Michelangelo's Sistine Chapel fresco.

Kruger's protest, like Orlan's, is directed at those who can only conceive of art as an economic investment. She is also challenging the patriarchal lineage from God the Father, "giving birth" to man. Finally, Kruger points to the aura that surrounds the unreproducible work of art and makes it priceless. Kruger also accosts the viewer with the word "You": *you* are complicit in these systems of exchange. Your investments are both social and psychic.

Orlan and Kruger both talk back to Charcot, the doctor who was Freud's mentor, famous for parading female hysterics before his medical students in the amphitheater in his Paris hospital (Augsburg 1995). If Annie Sprinkle's performances are "hysterical" in the sense of being humorous, Orlan's return us to the

Figure 3.4 Barbara Kruger, *Untitled (You invest in the divinity of the masterpiece)* (1982). Photograph 73″ × 47″. Collection: Museum of Modern Art, New York. Courtesy Mary Boone Gallery, New York.

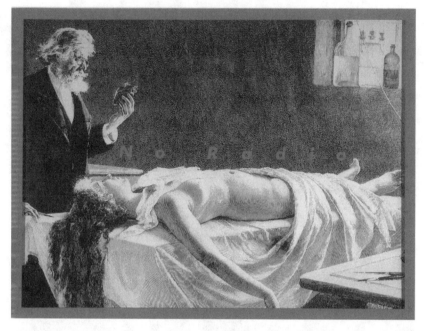

Figure 3.5 Barbara Kruger, *Untitled* (*No Radio*) (1988). Photograph, 51½″ × 68″. Collection: Don and Doris Fisher, San Francisco. Courtesy Mary Boone Gallery, New York.

word's etymology. Medicine's regimes hystericize and cannibalize the female body throughout history, as Kruger's "No Radio" illustrates.

The doctor is holding one of the prone patient's internal organs, probably her heart. As usual in Kruger's work, the text acts as an interdiction, a bar to signification, intercepting the visual image, as if to say, "Don't bother breaking into me, there is nothing left to steal, to appropriate, to dissect." Like Kruger's, Orlan's work trains the spotlight on the drive to frame woman as a collection of symptoms and neuroses—to make a spectacle of her body.

But the spectacle Orlan incites in the *audience* is by far the best part of the show. I first met Orlan at "The Illustrated Woman" Conference in San Francisco in February, 1994. The audience consisted of artists, writers, "modern primitives," the piercing and tattoo crowd, the leather community, gays, lesbians, and transsexuals. Not for academics only, in short. Collectively, they embodied what is becoming known as "The Last Sex," which—like posthuman—signifies how profoundly *conceptual* both gender and sex have become. As Arthur and Marilouise Kroker explain in *The Last Sex:*

> In the artistic practice of medieval times, the privileged aesthetic space was
> that of anamorphosis. The aesthetics, that is, of perspectival impossibility

where the hint of the presence of a vanishing whole could only be captured by a glance at the reflecting surface of one of its designed fragments. . . . Now anamorphosis returns as the privileged perspective of virtual sex, of intersex states. . . . It is that new sexual horizon, post-male and post-female, that we now call the perspectival world of the last sex. (Kroker and Kroker 1993: 18–19)

Anamorphosis defines the mirror stage. The *Oxford English Dictionary* defines *anamorphosis* as "a distorted projection or drawing of anything, so made that when viewed from a particular point, or by reflection from a suitable mirror, it appears regular and properly proportioned; a deformation." One famous example is Hans Holbein's *The Ambassadors:* in the foreground, one sees a blur or a skull, depending on one's point of view or—more accurately—views, for anamorphosis demonstrates that there are *two* moments of viewing: when one concentrates on the worldly objects in the painting, one only sees a blur, but when one looks again, it becomes a skull, radically subverting the smug complacency of the good bourgeois owners of the objects. One must "look awry" to see.[17]

At the San Francisco conference, Susan Stryker, a male-to-female transsexual, read "her" memoir about her operation, fantasizing about seducing the "adorable surgeon" who "flays her awkward little penis; when I lift my hips to meet the knife, he'll see that nothing but my desire brings him here." Another lesbian artist photographed the lesbians in the leather community who were undergoing female to *male* transsexual operations. Not a squeamish crowd, in other words. But their response to Orlan was hostile. When Orlan called herself the first "Woman to Woman Transsexual," only I laughed. Confronted with the graphic video images, the audience groaned and looked away. Many accused her of sensationalism and aggression. Others accused her of maligning the medical profession (merely by exposing its *labor*)! Finally, one member of the audience seemed to "get it." She asked Orlan, "Have we, the audience, adequately performed our role as inquisitors by demanding signs of your suffering, visible proof of your stigmata?" ("Click!")

Orlan smirked.

Now that I have seen this hostility reenacted on two coasts, I realize that it is a reaction to what the audience perceives as Orlan's aggression. But in reality, it is the audience who is projecting aggression; Orlan is merely the object of transference. (One sign that the transference is already working is when the analysand finds faults with the analyst. [Zizek 1989b: 42]). While she lectures onstage with the aid of a translator and someone who signs for the deaf, enormous video screens behind her show the operation in process. The "Before" and "After" photos used to advertise plastic surgery leave an enormous gap where a picture of "During" belongs—that is what one is seeing *for the first time ever* on the screen behind her. As Parveen Adams points out:

The succession of the moments of anamorphosis are presented simultaneously. The gap between the two images empties out the object. It is not that
surgery has transformed her, but that surgery has changed our experience
of the image. Of course this is only one instance of emptying the image.
The space which has opened is radical and has always been there. It is
savagely inconvenient. But it is the space which is new from the point of
view of knowledge. (159)

Ballard had the same space and the same setting in mind twenty-five years ago
when he speculated on all the new technologies that would necessitate the
writing of a new *Psychopathology of Daily Life,* but at the time, the most radical
surgical procedures were Dr. Christiaan Barnard's heart transplants:

A whole new kind of psychopathology, the book of a new Krafft-Ebing is
being written by such things as car crashes, televised violence, the new
awareness of our own bodies transmitted by magazine accounts of popular
medicine, by reports of the Barnard heart transplants, and so on. (Ballard
1990: 157)

If Ballard is the oracle, Orlan is the "Atrocity Exhibition" who fulfills his proph-
ecies. Her exhibition*ism* juxtaposes two temporalities and seems to challenge the
audience: "I am here, I did that, I orchestrated the entire event, everyone capitu-
lated to my will—from the lab technicians to the surgeon to the well-wishers
around the globe." Like Bob Flanagan, she becomes the center of the universe.
Hard to like a woman like that. She is supremely *self-possessed*—a delicious
irony— since what she is doing is emptying the self, revealing that there is
nothing "beneath" the mask.[18]

   The Pandora myth posits femininity is a trap and a mask; female sexuality
is a box that, once opened, lets sin and death loose upon the world. Carolee
Schneemann's question comes to mind: Vulva asks, "Why is cock a thing and
vulva a place?"[19] Pandora is the site of that split between outside/inside, which
becomes synonymous with seductiveness and deceit—a beautiful exterior con-
ceals a pernicious interior. No wonder so many women artists are striving to
make literal the metaphor of "looking inside": their aim is to dispel that myth. In
"Pandora: Topographies of the Mask and Curiosity," Laura Mulvey notes:

The story of Pandora's creation installs her as a mythic origin of the
surface/secret polarity that gives a spatial or topographical dimension to
this phantasmagoric representation of female seductiveness and deceit. . . .
The recurring division between inside and outside is central not only to
understanding representations of femininity in socially constructed fantasy, but also illustrates the uses of psychoanalytic theory for feminism. It is
because of the kind of problem posed by the Pandora phenomenon that

feminist aesthetics has turned to semiotics and psychoanalysis, to transform the work of criticism into a work of decipherment . . . the topography [of] . . . Pandora is an important clue for deciphering the fantasy. And understanding the "dialectics of inside and outside" is a possible point of departure. (Mulvey 1992: 60)

Rather than sealing the lid on Pandora's box, in various ways Kruger, Mulvey, and Orlan turn it inside out, exposing the fears of castration that underwrite misogynistic fantasies, fetishes, and fixations. In different ways, all three women are "cutups in beauty school," dissecting the culture's deep-seated investments— economic and psychic—in woman's "to-be-looked-at-ness."

With Bob Flanagan, Orlan desacralizes our culture's investment in medicine, which she sees as our epoch's religion. The medical amphitheater is our sacred sanctuary. In view of the new medical imaging devices that are transforming artistic practices, something else Barthes once said now resonates with added significance: "the Image always has the last word." By seizing control of the medical apparatus, Orlan strips it of mystique. In so doing, she invokes another epistolary classic, Mary Shelley's *Frankenstein*. Since Mary Shelley's mother died giving birth to her, Mary never lost the uncanny conviction that she had been born of dying parts. Orlan is Frankenstein, the monster, and the Bride of Frankenstein all rolled into one.

I began with the quotation from Flaubert to illustrate that the myth of the inviolate body has been a long time dying. That is what elicited anxiety among Orlan's San Francisco audience, hence their hostility. Finally, someone asks: "Is the point of piercing the skin, showing how the scalpel goes in at the temple and comes out at the neck, to get to the bottom of *interiority?*" "No," Orlan replies, "I don't believe in interiority." (I think again of *Madame Bovary:* "At the pharmacist's request, Monsieur Canivet . . . performed an autopsy, but found nothing." [255]) Therein lies the true scandal, the final cut: Orlan opens herself up and finds nothing.

Notes

1. Gustave Flaubert, Letter to Louise Colet, January 16, 1852, reprinted in Flaubert 1965, p. 309.

2. See the special issue of *Time* Fall 1993, as well as Prince 1994. My thanks to Michael Prince for bringing the *Time* issue to my attention.

3. As a representative of the so-called postfeminist generation, see Wolf 1992.

4. Linda S. Kauffman interview with Orlan, Paris, November 24, 1994; subsequent interview May 18, 1995. All unattributed quotations refer to these interviews.

5. Cited in Hirschorn 1994, p. 13; quoting Keith Dovkants, "Cut Out to Be Venus," *Evening Standard,* March 23, 1994, p. 13.

6. Orlan, "Operation-Réussie: A Performance/Lecture," *The Illustrated Woman* Conference, San Francisco, 5 February 1994. My discussion draws on my interview with Orlan following the conference.

7. I thank Marsha Gordon for bringing this film to my attention; see Gordon 1996.

8. The English translation of Bataille's *L'Erotisme* has Bernini's St. Theresa on the cover.

9. "Virtual Futures" Conference program notes, University of Warwick, England, May 26–28, 1995. My thanks to Clare Brant and Orlan for bringing this to my attention.

10. Orlan belongs to a long line of artists who challenge the relationship between perceptual and sexual contradiction, a line stretching from Leonardo's Mona Lisa (often rumored to be a self-portrait) to Manet's Olympia. See Rose 1986: 226–226 n. 3.

11. As if to suggest the infinite extension of epistolarity in time and space, Orlan's appearance at the First Annual Performance Studies Conference at New York University in March, 1994 provoked a prolonged email debate, which was subsequently published in *TDR* (Fall 1995). Bob Flanagan has also sparked extended email debate on a computer network for people with cystic fibrosis.

12. Artaud 1958, p. 110, and Motherwell 1951, pp. 55–65.

13. Augsburg 1995: 17. My thanks to Tanya for help with translation, materials, and for inviting me to participate on her panel on "Gendering the Medical Body," First Annual Performance Studies Conference, New York University, March 25, 1995.

14. *VST: Revue Scientifique et Culturelle de Santé Mentale* 23/24, Sept.–Dec., 1991. [VST stands for "Vie Sociale et Traitements."]

15. Joanna Freuh is the latest critic to ignore the specific genre of Mulvey's essay, the manifesto, and of its object, cinema, by fallaciously describing "numerous feminist writings mothered by Laura Mulvey's 'Visual Pleasure and Narrative Cinema' . . . [which] denied women the authenticity of their own visual and bodily experiences and have imprisoned women in the accepted reductiveness of the male gaze" (Freuh 1996:149). Robert Ray's opposition to Mulvey is equally misguided, particularly since her own aims serve as dramatic confirmation of several of his major points, particularly regarding the ubiquity of popular culture and the impact of Surrealism—a movement enormously indebted to psychoanalysis in general, fetishism in particular (Ray 1995).

16. Compare Frantz Fanon: "I believe that the fact of the juxtaposition of the white and black races has created a massive psychoexistential complex. I hope by analyzing it to destroy it" (1967: 13). While Mulvey was criticized, no one objected to Fanon's formulation.

17. Lacan discusses anamorphosis and its relation to art (1978: 67–90). See also Zizek 1989a and Zizek 1989b:1–53, as well as Adams 1996: 152–53.

18. Adams 1996: 145. Adams also relates Orlan's work to Mulvey's essay on Pandora.

19. Carolee Schneeman, letter to Linda S. Kauffman, March 1, 1995.

References

Adams, Parveen (1996). *The Emptiness of the Image: Psychoanalysis and Sexual Differences*. London and New York: Routledge.

Artaud, Antonin (1958). *The Theater and Its Double*. New York: Grove.

Augsburg, Tanya (1995). "Private Theaters Onstage: Hysteria and the Female Medical Subject: From the Origins of Psychoanalysis to Feminist Performance." PhD. Diss. Emory University.

Ballard, J. G. (1990). *The Atrocity Exhibition*, ed. Andrea Juno and V. Vale. San Francisco: Re/Search.

Barthes, Roland (1978). *S/Z: An Essay*. Trans. Richard Howard. New York: Hill and Wang.

Bataille, Georges (1957). *L'Erotisme*. Paris: Editions de Minuit; (1986). *Erotism: Death and Sensuality*. Trans. Mary Dalwood. San Francisco: City Lights.

de Beauvoir, Simone (1974). *The Second Sex,* trans. and ed. H. M. Parshley. New York: Vintage.

Byfield, Ted, and Lincoln Tobier (1992). "Television." *Stanford Humanities Review* 2 (2–3): 90–108.

Derrida, Jacques (1980). "La Loi du Genre/The Law of Genre," trans. Avital Ronell. *Glyph* 7: 177–232

Export, Valie (1992). "Persona, Proto-Performance, Politics: A Preface." *Discourse* 14 (2): 26–35.

Fanon, Frantz (1967). *Black Skin, White Masks,* trans. Charles Lam Markmann. New York: Grove.

Flaubert, Gustave (1965). *Madame Bovary,* trans. Paul de Man. New York: W. W. Norton.

Freuh, Joanna (1996). *Erotic Faculties*. Berkeley: University of California Press.

Fox, Margalit (1993). "A Portrait in Skin and Bone." *New York Times* (November 21).

Gordon, Marsha (1996). "Cinematic Body Politics in Peter Greenaway's *The Baby of Macon* and Ngozi Onwurah's *The Body Beautiful*." M.A. Thesis, University of Maryland.

Hirschorn, Michelle (1994). "Orlan: Artist in the Post-Human Age of Mechanical Reincarnation." M.A. Thesis, University of Leeds.

Kroker, Arthur, and Marilouise Kroker, eds. (1993). *The Last Sex: Feminism and Outlaw Bodies*. New York: St. Martin's.

Lacan, Jacques (1978). *The Four Fundamental Concepts of Psychoanalysis,* ed. Jacques-Alain Miller, trans. Alan Sheridan. New York: W. W. Norton.

Motherwell, Robert (1951). *The Dada Painters and Poets.* New York: Wittenborn-Schultz, 1951.

Mulvey, Laura (1989). *Visual and Other Pleasures.* Bloomington: Indiana University Press.

——— (1992). "Pandora: Topographies of the Mask and Curiosity." In *Sexuality and Space,* ed. Beatriz Colomina. Princeton: Princeton Papers on Architecture.

Prince, Michael (1994). "The Eighteenth-Century Beauty Contest." *Modern Language Quarterly* 55 (3): 251–79.

Ray, Robert (1995). *The Avant-Garde Finds Andy Hardy.* Cambridge: Harvard University Press, 1995.

Rose, Barbara (1993). "Is it Art? Orlan and the Transgressive Act." *Art in America* 81(2).

Rose, Jacqueline (1986). *Sexuality in the Field of Vision.* London: Verso.

Rosen, Nick (1993). "The Birth—by Surgeon's Scalpel—of Venus." *Sunday Telegraph* (November 14).

Shulman, Ken (1994). "Peter Greenaway Defends His 'Baby.'" *New York Times* (February 6): H18.

Steiner, Wendy (1995). *The Scandal of Pleasure: Art in an Age of Fundamentalism.* Chicago: University of Chicago Press.

Vale, V., and Andrea Juno, eds. (1991). *Angry Women.* San Francisco: Re/Search.

Williams, Linda (1993). "Second Thoughts on *Hard Core:* American Obscenity Law and the Scapegoating of Deviance." In *Dirty Looks: Women, Pornography, Power,* ed. Pamela Church Gibson and Roma Gibson. London: British Film Institute, 176–91.

Wolf, Naomi (1992). *The Beauty Myth.* New York: William Morrow, 1991; rpr. New York: Anchor.

Zizek, Slavoj (1989a). "Looking Awry." *October* 50: 30–55.

——— (1989b). *The Sublime Object of Ideology.* London: Verso.

4

Deep Skin

William A. Cohen

This chapter originates in a fundamental question about embodiment: What does
the skin cover? Responses to this question are traditionally articulated in two
different registers: the physical and the spiritual. The skin is the integument that
encloses the visceral interior of the body, yet it is also the membrane within which,
mysteriously and ethereally, the human essence is supposed to reside. The outside
surface of the body and its first line of defense against the external world, the skin
is also the psychically projected shield that contains the self within. Both tactile
membrane and enclosure, the skin is a permeable boundary that permits congress
between inside and outside, whether that interior is conceived in material or
metaphysical terms. The skin thus forms the border not only between bodily
interior and exterior, but between psychical and physical conceptions of the self as
well. As a social signifier, moreover, the color, texture, and appearance of the skin
have often been presumed to testify to what resides within or beneath it.

By virtue of its peculiar status as both physical embodiment and psychical
envelope, both a surface projected from inside and a mask immediately comprehensible from without, the skin has crucial, if sometimes conflicting, psychological, spiritual, and social functions. Most materially, as the exquisitely sensitive
seat of tactile perception, capable of fine discriminations on the basis of pressure,
density, texture, and temperature, the skin has physiological functions that situate it at the crossover point between the phenomenal world and all that is
contained inside: the internal organs, the mind, the emotions, the soul.[1] As the
physical embodiment of the imagined boundaries of the self, the skin also gives a
morphological dimension to the ego; its external appearance in turn has shaping
effects on subject formation and self-perception. The skin is the beginning and
end of the body.

The following discussion addresses these issues through three separate but
converging lines of inquiry: literary, theoretical, and historical. My analysis
focuses on a nineteenth-century tale by Anthony Trollope, which dramatizes the
expressive and impressionable capacities of the skin through the story of a body
subject to confusions of gender and race, as well as physical distress. I employ
some insights of Didier Anzieu's psychoanalytic discussion of the so-called skin
ego to think through Trollope's representations and, in so doing, also use Frantz
Fanon's analysis of race to consider how Trollope's work requires revisions of
Anzieu's theory. By situating Trollope's work within a contemporary frame of
racial characterization and urban sanitation, I demonstrate how the literary,
psychological, and spiritual functions of the skin as both enclosure and projection
are historically determined.

Trollope's story "The Banks of the Jordan" supplies an especially incisive staging of the question: *How do we go beneath the surface of the body and reach profound truths within?* The answer, I will suggest, is that, in 1861, one cannot get very far: the narrator of Trollope's tale finds himself perpetually stuck on the surface. Like many nineteenth-century British authors, ranging from Charlotte Brontë to Gerard Manley Hopkins, Trollope confronts the conflict between spiritual and material accounts of human interiority. Whenever these writers aim to portray a transcendent, immaterial spirit, they find themselves compelled to write about the body, which, when they go inside it, presents a profoundly debasing materialism. Trollope's story conspicuously poses the problem of the relation between surface and depth in several different registers: first, through an exotic setting that dramatizes English contact with unfamiliar nationalities and nonwhite races; second, through a plot of cross-gender masquerade; and third, through an extraordinarily evocative depiction of human bodies at odds with a quest for spiritual fulfillment. In each case, the narrative seeks to move from outside to inside, from external form to inner truth, but finds itself blocked: the surface, variously conceived as pigment, clothing, or tactile membrane, is untranscendable, and the confusion induced by penetrating beneath it only reinforces what was already known from without.

Not nearly so well known a chronicler of British empire as Rudyard Kipling, Joseph Conrad, or H. Rider Haggard, Trollope set many stories in overseas colonies, such as Jamaica, the East Indies, and Australia, places with which he was familiar from his extensive travel. "The Banks of the Jordan" (reprinted under the title "A Ride across Palestine") itself serves as a world tour in miniature, with characters that include Bedouin Arab desert guides, a Catholic French dragoman, Austrian sailors, a Polish hotelier, and a collection of Eastern Christian pilgrims.

> It must be remembered that Eastern worshippers are not like the churchgoers of London, or even of Rome or Cologne. They are wild men of various nations and races—Maronites from Lebanon, Roumelians, Candiotes, Copts from Upper Egypt, Russians from the Crimea, Armenians and Abyssinians. They savour strongly of Oriental life and of Oriental dirt. They are clad in skins or hairy cloaks with huge hoods. Their heads are shaved, and their faces covered with short, grisly, fierce beards. They are silent mostly, looking out of their eyes ferociously, as though murder were in their thoughts, and rapine. But they never slouch, or cringe in their bodies, or shuffle in their gait. Dirty, fierce-looking, uncouth, repellent as they are, there is always about them a something of personal dignity which is not compatible with an Englishman's ordinary hat and pantaloons. (Trollope 1861: 114–15)[2]

For all its international cosmopolitanism, Trollope's story performs the usual imperial work of demonstrating British superiority, pluck, and cultivation, expressed through a brutalizing hierarchy of physical appearances and hygiene. Collapsing race with nationality and religion in dismissing all those around him, the blithely imperious narrator feels confident of his own privilege. In the context of British colonialism and the long history of Western racism based on pigmentation, the skin and other outward markers are taken as a wholly reliable register of character. The narrator never doubts his instinctive impression of the people and places he witnesses as dirty, disgusting, and alien. Foreignness here lacks the possibility of a deep identification for the Englishman, such as one finds in other British fictions of empire, in which European characters (like Kurtz, Kim, and Holly) "go native" or meaningfully encounter nonwhites.

The importance this analysis will attach to skin consciousness—and particularly skin-color consciousness—in "The Banks of the Jordan" derives in part from the story's historical context. Such attention is ratified by the pages surrounding the fiction in the *London Review,* the periodical in which it originally appeared in three serial parts, on January 5, 12, and 19, 1861. Prominent in the news during those weeks were the early stirrings of the American Civil War. The leading article in the issue containing the third installment of Trollope's story, for instance, discusses the "Missouri Slave" case, in which Canadian courts had to determine whether to extradite an escaped slave back to Missouri, where he had inadvertently killed a white man who was trying to recapture him. The editorial opines against extradition:

> The law of the British Empire not only does not recognize the status of slavery, but regards it as contrary to human nature. . . . If a negro or man of colour had been pursued in any of the British dominions by persons with the avowed intention of restoring him to slavery, he would be justified in employing all reasonable means to avert the consequences with which he was threatened. . . . The occurrence of this discussion at a period when America is agitated on the question of slavery is most remarkable, and presents the materials for deep reflection to the statesman, the lawyer, and philanthropist. (*London Review* 1861: 54)

This "deep reflection" on slavery, race, and justice might indeed be furthered by turning the page and reading the final part of Trollope's tale, in which colonial condescension toward ignorant, wily, or invidious races is, if mocked with dramatic irony, also implicitly endorsed by a comic smugness indistinguishable from this irony.

Even before arriving at Trollope's story, however, a reader would encounter another editorial, this one at odds with the liberal sentiments expressed in the righteous condemnation of American slavery. Here, the editorial gaze shifts to the opposite end of the British Empire and expresses jingoistic support, in the most baldly racist terms, for the bloody suppression of Maori natives in New Zealand.

The natives of New Zealand are as warlike as savages usually are, but they possess, according to most accounts, a greater degree of natural intelligence than the negro or Red Indian races that have hitherto come most frequently into collision with the Anglo-Saxon and Anglo-Scandinavian races, who are now peopling and subduing the world.

It would, therefore, seem that the task of reconciling them to the inevitable necessity of white occupation of the land, would be easier than with barbarians of less brain, and that their civilization and conversion to Christianity would not be so hopeless as has been the case elsewhere. But, from some cause or other, an idea has got into the heads of these poor people, that it is possible either to expel or extirpate the whole white population, and to re-establish a native sovereignty, and consequently a native barbarism. Leaving all sentiment out of the question, and all merely abstract ideas of the rights of the natives to the lands where they were born, and to the hunting-grounds where their forefathers prowled like wild beasts, and with about as much relish for the flesh of man as the lion or the tiger, it is quite clear that the British and other settlers will not allow themselves to be either expelled or exterminated; that they will not submit to a Maori sovereignty; that they will not give up their farms to men of dusky skins, to be reconverted into wilderness; and that as long as such ideas have possession of the native mind, so long will war, overt or covert, be the normal condition of affairs in New Zealand.

The experience of America and other parts of the world is before us, to prove that in all such struggles the white race must and does prevail; that the aboriginal savage must either conform to the new state of things, and consent to be civilized, or disappear altogether from the face of the earth. . . . The civilization and christianization of the savage will follow in due course, if he be capable, as we believe the New Zealander is, of accommodating himself to altered and superior circumstances. But all attempts to pamper him with exalted notions of Maori sovereignty, or lead him astray by exaggerated estimates of his natural right over lands which he nor his predecessors never knew how to turn to account, and which owe their whole value to white energy, capital, and skill, can but lead to future misery and bloodshed, and to the gradual extinction of his race. (*London Review* 1861: 54)

In the most explicit form, the editorial gives voice to the bloodthirsty racist ideology that justifies colonial conquest—an ideology that, if in comparatively muted terms, equally motivates the national, racial, and religious taxonomies (based on fine discriminations of perceived hygiene and cultivation) by which Trollope's narrator makes sense of his surroundings. The portrait of the Maoris collapses together savagery, degeneracy, cannibalism, paganism, ignorance, and dark skin, relying on both mythical and anthropological stereotypes to justify the conquest. The "dusky skin," set in contrast to "white energy, capital, and skill," is the register of civilization; plainly at stake is a justification for extending imperialism, no matter if genocidal conquest is required. Yet to discover alongside Trollope's story of epidermally coded conflict a news item that repeats so many of its themes is hardly the fantastic coincidence that might be imagined. Rather, it is the very ordinariness of the ideas that deserves emphasis: skin is presumed to be so reliable an indication of the inside that it gets only casual mention in the racist account of New Zealand; one could expect to find similar language in a paper from almost any week in the Victorian period. Trollope's story does, however, give peculiar depth and extension to the theme, amplifying it from racial terms to those of selfhood, gender, spirituality, and, especially, the superficies of physically embodied experience itself.

"The Banks of the Jordan" is told in the voice of an Englishman who adopts the pseudonym Jones and pretends to be a carefree bachelor. He narrates his travels through Palestine at Easter time, where he meets a mysterious fellow tourist, a young man who equally identifies himself with an implausibly generic name, John Smith. Together the two visit holy sites, where they encounter Eastern Christian pilgrims as well as non-Christian natives, all described in characteristically Victorian racist terms of disparagement. As part of his tour, the narrator bathes in the River Jordan and the Dead Sea, only to be horrified at the repulsive desiccation of his skin. A surprisingly homoerotic intimacy springs up between the two strangers, although the enigmatic young man, Smith, exhibits a peculiar anxiety and reticence. All is explained at the story's end, when Smith is exposed as a woman in disguise, and the two are discovered by her guardian, who accuses the narrator of seducing the unprotected young lady. The tale concludes when the narrator reveals to the others that he is himself married, and so cannot mend matters by wedding her.[3]

The tale's most overt theme is deceptive appearances. This is so familiar a convention of literary fiction as to be one of its defining features, however exaggerated it is here by the exotic contexts. "I was taken with John Smith, in spite of his name," Jones states early on. "There was so much about him that was pleasant, both to the eye and to the understanding. One meets constantly with men from contact with whom one revolts without knowing the cause of such dislike. . . . But, on the other hand, there are men who are attractive, and I must confess that I was attracted by John Smith at first sight" (Trollope 1861: 110). The story proceeds by an almost banal logic of the surface hiding a depth that contradicts it: the young man is in fact a woman, the Holy Land is really a squalid tourist trap, the repulsive outward form of the Eastern pilgrims covers a soul no baser than that of the conceited Englishman. One is eventually made to see the narrator's obtuse blindness, on a range of subjects, as the sign of his foolish arrogance and self-absorption. Indeed, rather than focus on the disguised objects, we are finally meant to recognize how the *subject* of perception has distorted vision—be that subject the narrator or the reader (if the latter fails to discern

Smith's disguise before the end). The cross-dressed young woman suggests just such a shift of attention from the object to the perceiver: "[D]o we not know that our thoughts are formed, and our beliefs modelled, not on the outward signs or intrinsic evidences of things,—as would be the case were we always rational,— but by the inner workings of the mind itself?" (126). One sees from the inside out, such a remark suggests: the mind determines what the eyes perceive.

Although the narrator blunders through the story unaware of the young woman's disguise, the reader is amply supplied with clues to her true sex. "I thoroughly hate an effeminate man," he says at one point, "but in spite of a certain womanly softness about this fellow I could not hate him" (128). Or a little later: "I did love him as though he were a younger brother. I felt a delight in serving him, and though I was almost old enough to be his father I ministered to him, as though he had been an old man, or a woman" (134). Jones is unable to see beneath the surface of his companion's male costume, and his humiliation at the conclusion is proportionate to his obliviousness along the way. The device of the cross-dressed woman permits an intense homoeroticism in the story, yet the revelation that explains it is available only retrospectively. After his bathing, for example, the narrator says, "I found myself lying with my head on his lap. I had slept, but it could have been but for a few minutes, and when I woke I felt his hand upon my brow. As I started up he said that the flies had been annoying me, and that he had not chosen to waken me as I seemed weary" (128). For a reader as taken in as the narrator, the retroactive alibi hardly seems adequate to defuse the force of such contact between two characters who both appear to be men.[4] The story's overt narrative of disguised gender identity in an exotic setting, along with its covert implication of male homoeroticism, seems almost designed for queer and postcolonial reading, a critical effort that Mark Forrester has undertaken in a subtle, persuasive interpretation.

Through the cross-dressed romance plot, Trollope ironizes, and thus criticizes, Jones's incapacity to recognize the most obvious sort of deceptive surface— clothing, the second skin. The story's conspicuous emphasis on the narrator's bodily experience of his tour allows the skin both to metaphorize and to literalize the more general theme of deceptive appearances—to estrange it, that is to say, by giving it bodily form. The link between clothing and skin is made deliberately in Smith's unwillingness to strip off "his" outfit and bathe, as to do so would expose the female body beneath ("He did not like bathing, and preferred to do his washing in his own room" [122]). As with the cross-gender plot, the narrator is equally egocentric in the realm of nationality: he is unerringly persuaded of his superiority to the ostensibly barbaric foreigners he encounters, and of the rightness of his perceptions on the basis of their superficial appearance. While this aspect of the narrator's attitude is also gently mocked, however, it is less clear that Trollope intends us to view it as wholly wrong-headed.

Jones's relentless superficiality becomes still more significant when we recognize that, while the story satirizes the vulgar tourism of consumer culture, it takes the *form* of a sacred religious pilgrimage. The narrator supplies no explanation for his presence in the Holy Land at Easter, but as a Christian visitor there, he might be expected to seek spiritual gratification. His attendance at major Biblical sites—the Mount of Olives, the Sea of Galilee, the tomb of the Virgin— suggests such a quest, as, more metaphorically, does his Christlike sojourn in the desert, "those mountains of the wilderness through which it is supposed that Our Saviour wandered for the forty days when the devil tempted him" (107). Yet reach as he might after spiritual revelation, the secular tourist remains just that: set apart from the fervent evangelicalism of Eastern pilgrims, he merely goes through the motions dictated by Baedeker, evincing no enlightenment in religious terms at all. Spiritual interiority is demonstrably vacuous: just as he cannot delve beneath his traveling companion's costume or the alienating appearance of the foreign nationals he meets, Jones is thrown insistently back onto the profane surface of his own body at every moment that he seeks to plumb the depths of a divinely ordained soul. For the tourist (at least) spiritual experience, like gender and racial identity, turns out to be skin deep.

At his visits to religious shrines, the English pilgrim finds his body a problematic intrusion, in part because of the contact he is forced to make with disconcerting foreign objects. First, in his visit to the chapel at the tomb of the Virgin, the narrator reports on nothing but the vaguely horrifying experience of shoving his way through a crowd of filthy "Eastern worshippers," and at British superiority in so doing. Such national differences are immediately linked to bodily form and hygiene:

> How is it that Englishmen can push themselves anywhere? These men were fierce-looking, and had murder and rapine . . . almost in their eyes. . . . Yet we did win our way through them, and apparently no man was angry with us. I doubt, after all, whether a ferocious eye and a strong smell and dirt are so efficacious in creating awe and obedience in others as an open brow and traces of soap and water. I know this, at least,—that a dirty Maronite would make very little progress if he attempted to shove his way unfairly through a crowd of Englishmen at the door of a London theatre. (115)

Absent is any account of what one might see in the tomb of the Virgin, or what such a sight might make a Christian feel. In light of the long history of the English Church condemning the stage, the comparison between the tomb and a theater seems particularly sacrilegious, even allowing for Protestant skepticism about Mary worship. The physical description of penetrating a crowd of fearsomely dirty foreigners lends debased material form to the would-be spiritual quest, whose place it takes.

The account of subjective interiority as dispersed across the surface of the body reaches its climax when Trollope's narrator bathes in the Dead Sea and the

River Jordan. Again he follows the prescription for Christian renewal, bathing at
the very site at which Jesus himself was baptized; again Jones experiences repulsive embodiment, realizing only his own epidermal limits. He seeks to immerse
himself in the water, but it resists him: "Everything is perfectly still, and the fluid
seems hardly to be displaced by the entrance of the body. But the effect is that
one's feet are tripped up, and that one falls prostrate on to the surface. . . . I was
unable to keep enough of my body below the surface. . . . However, I had bathed
in the Dead Sea, and was so far satisfied" (123). Like a figure for himself, the
Dead Sea functions as pure surface: it cannot be penetrated, it seems, but no
matter—whatever depths it holds are irrelevant to his feeling "satisfied." As the
passage progresses, the water then penetrates and revolts *him:*

> Anything more abominable to the palate than this water, if it be
> water, I never had inside my mouth. I expected it to be extremely salt, and
> no doubt, if it were analyzed, such would be the result; but there is a flavor
> in it which kills the salt. No attempt can be made at describing this taste. It
> may be imagined that I did not drink heartily, merely taking up a drop or
> two with my tongue from the palm of my hand; but it seemed to me as
> though I had been drenched with it. Even brandy would not relieve me
> from it. And then my whole body was in a mess, and I felt as though I had
> been rubbed with pitch. Looking at my limbs I saw no sign on them of the
> fluid. They seemed to dry from this as they usually do from any other
> water; but still the feeling remained. (123)

Jones locates phenomenal experience as a surface effect, which, if it reaches past
the cutaneous layer, does so by osmosis, as corrosive infection. Within the narration, the putrid liquid moves in the opposite direction—from inside out—
jumping immediately from palate and tongue to the hand and the full extent of
the skin. The water not only abrades the surface of Jones's body but, as he
imagines, darkens it like pitch as well, to effect a quasi-racial debasement.[5] As
though to reinforce and exaggerate his disgust, the narrator finds himself still
more repulsed by dipping in the River Jordan next. Upon leaving the river, he
states: "I was forced to wade out through the dirt and slush, so that I found it
difficult to make my feet and legs clean enough for my shoes and stockings; and
then, moreover, the flies plagued me most unmercifully. I should have thought
that the filthy flavour from the Dead Sea would have saved me from that
nuisance; but the mosquitoes thereabouts are probably used to it" (125). As he
returns to proper European costume, the story alludes to the Biblical plague, but
in being evacuated of any spiritual content, the experience is again set entirely on
the surface of the body. Beneath the epidermis seems to lie not spiritual depth but
simply more body, ever more capable of physical distress.

The narrative emphasizes not only dirt on the surface of the body but the
pains and pleasures available to the skin as well. A Turkish saddle, for example,

penetrates the surface of the so-called Christian body to reach not its soul but its gore, even as it supplies the occasion for potentially erotic touching. "Of what material is formed the nether man of a Turk I have never been informed," the narrator states, elaborating a fantasy of Eastern male sexuality;

> but I am sure that it is not flesh and blood. No flesh and blood—simply flesh and blood—could withstand the wear and tear of a Turkish saddle. . . . There is no part of the Christian body with which the Turkish saddle comes in contact that does not become more or less macerated. I have sat in one for days, but I left it a flayed man; and therefore I was sorry for Smith.
>
> I explained this to him, taking hold of his leg by the calf to show how the leather would chafe him; but it seemed to me that he did not quite like my interference. (112–13)[6]

To be Western and Christian is thus to have specially sensitive skin. Yet Smith exhibits less discomfort than the narrator predicts, perhaps because her "nether man" does not impede her. "[T]hat confounded Turkish saddle has already galled your skin," he tells her later. "I see how it is: I shall have to doctor you with a little brandy—externally applied, my friend" (118). Even the mildly obscene prospect of rubbing the thighs of his friend suggests a transposition of the remedy (brandy) from its proper location inside the body to the exterior integument. The texture of the surface has both racial and sexual determinants: by contrast with the apparent roughness and dirtiness of the foreigners, Jones perceives the "womanly softness" of Smith's skin: "He then put out his hand to me, and I pressed it in token of my friendship. My own hand was hot and rough with the heat and sand; but his was soft and cool almost as a woman's" (127–28). Such an intimate tactile exchange affects both subject and object; if it touches an emotional interior, its vehicle is the skin. In a similar way, powerfully repellent olfactory sensations reach inside: the pilgrims' "strong smell and dirt" and their "savour[ing] strongly of Oriental life and of Oriental dirt" signify a frightening foreignness that pervades the sensitive nose of the Englishman. By contrast with visual apprehension, which accentuates distance, hierarchy, and difference, the proximate senses, which physically incorporate the outside world into the subject, occur on the sensitive, inscribing surface of the body.

In the narrator's description of Eastern Christian worshipers, distress is again embodied, but pain is also excluded from effecting a spiritual transformation. He witnesses "a caravan of pilgrims coming up from Jordan" (119) who, unlike himself, appear impelled by an abiding religious faith, at which he can only wonder. Like his tourism, however, he portrays their religious exercise as wholly formal, as far as his from modifying any interior essence. Of "these strange people," he says, "The benefit expected was not to be immediately spiritual. . . . To these members of the Greek Christian Church it had been handed down from father to son that washing in Jordan once during life was efficacious towards salvation. And therefore the journey had been made at terrible cost and terrible risk" (120). As unthinkingly driven to go through their religious paces as he is through his sightseeing, the pilgrims seem to suffer bodily pain as an end in itself. Yet among them, Jones witnesses a figure to whom, as Forrester demonstrates, he is particularly drawn, and with whom he vividly identifies:[7]

> Some few there are, undoubtedly, more ecstatic in this great deed of their religion. One man I especially noticed on this day. He had bound himself to make the pilgrimage from Jerusalem to the river with one foot bare. He was of a better class, and was even nobly dressed, as though it were a part of his vow to show to all men that he did this deed, wealthy and great though he was. He was a fine man, perhaps thirty years of age, with a well-grown beard descending on his breast, and at his girdle he carried a brace of pistols. But never in my life had I seen bodily pain so plainly written in a man's face. The sweat was falling from his brow, and his eyes were strained and bloodshot with agony. He had no stick, his vow, I presume, debarring him from such assistance, and he limped along, putting to the ground the heel of the unprotected foot. I could see it, and it was a mass of blood, and sores, and broken skin. An Irish girl would walk from Jerusalem to Jericho without shoes, and be not a penny the worse for it. This poor fellow clearly suffered so much that I was almost inclined to think that in the performance of his penance he had done something to aggravate his pain. Those around him paid no attention to him, and the dragoman seemed to think nothing of the affair whatever. (120–21)

To a point, Jones identifies with and is attracted to this figure, for he stands out among the pilgrims by virtue of his superior bearing and his armed potency. The narrator combines admiration for the pilgrim's self-abasing devotion with disgust at his excess; yet mingled with these reactions is also a sense of sheer bewilderment at the form this piety takes. As the passage progresses, the very connection between spiritual ardor and bodily prostration that Jones reads in the pilgrim's pain effects a *dis*identification with him. Just as his own physical abasement affords no spiritual apotheosis, the penance he here witnesses remains incomprehensible because he cannot himself imagine how altering the surface might affect religious depth. At the moment in which the tale comes closest to representing masochism, it is important that the narrator regards, but does not himself experience, such physical abjection. For masochism, whose gratifications may be religious as well as sexual, depends on a rigorous connection between the surface of the body and an interior emotional, spiritual, or mental entity, in all of which Jones seems to be deficient. As soon as he registers the fullness of the pilgrim's agony and its probable justification, he disavows his initial identification (on the basis of class and appearance) by introducing the otherwise unaccountable allusion to the Irish girl. Even as the comparison distinguishes the refined pilgrim from the stereotyped Celt, it also differentiates him from Jones, both by insidiously feminizing the pilgrim and by relegating him to the status of a colonial subject. Jones's potency and superiority are, though momentarily relaxed by regard of this figure, ultimately reinforced by the distinctions, for he, unlike, the suffering barefoot pilgrim, stays entirely on the surface. He lacks the depth—here conceived of as spirituality, albeit a negated entity—to warrant a masochistic harrowing of the outside.

From the comic and ironic plot through which Trollope presents the relations between the surface of the body and its depth, we can here move to a psychological account of some related material, which the story itself modifies. That the narrative's perplexities about gender, nationality, and religion are projected onto the surface of the body points us to the most sustained discussion of the skin in relation to the psyche, *The Skin Ego* (1985), by French psychoanalyst and theorist Didier Anzieu. Anzieu's work develops the psychical topography Freud outlined in *The Ego and the Id* (1923), at whose center is the proposition that the ego is "first and foremost a bodily ego"—which is to say, precisely mapped onto the surface of the body.[8] Anzieu's theory elaborates for the skin ego "three functions: as a containing, unifying envelope for the Self; as a protective barrier for the psyche; and as a filter of exchanges and a surface of inscription for the first traces, a function which makes representation possible. To these three functions, there correspond three representations: the sac, the screen and the sieve" (98).[9] These "functions" resonate with the depiction of skin in Trollope's story, as both a porous container of, and an entity contiguous with, the narrator's ego. The outer surface of the skin, Anzieu shows, protects the self and situates it in the world, operations that Jones is at pains to reinforce. He must shore up his psychical integrity by securing the surface of his own skin as well as his comprehension of others', both of which seem frequently to be in danger of dissolution. Yet the story departs from the psychological ruptures of the skin ego, on which Anzieu focuses his theoretical and clinical accounts in terms of narcissism, masochism, and castration. The fiction dramatizes such threats—as well as the necessity to reestablish the containing and protecting functions of the skin ego— by making them external, through the narrator's racial and sexual subjugation of others and his inflation of himself. He aims to secure the wholeness of his integument as much for cultural as for psychological reasons.

To Jones's dismay, the outer surface of his body, rather than simply containing him and differentiating him from others, is a permeable barrier. This surface has a double capacity, for even as it holds his insides within, it permits interaction with and intrusions from the exterior world. The spiritual experience from which, as the story shows, he is barred, assumes the form of dermatological trauma: desiccation, contusion, and avulsion of the skin, both experienced and witnessed. Erotic contact with Smith, though suggested, is made impossibly distant, consigned to a comic, seemingly unconscious homoeroticism, which is then recuperated as a heterosexual flirtation, itself made unavailable by the narrator's prior marriage. Like the spiritual quest, exmptied of deep content by its expression as epidermal abrasion, the romance is rewritten as laceration, and so equally relegated to the surface of the flesh. Yet the psychological distress expressed in the skin is compensated to some degree by its cultural valuation, for by comparing the surface of his skin—its color, hygiene, and texture—to those he perceives as fundamentally different from him (by race, nationality, and religion), Jones establishes a sense of his own value and integrity. This is the point at which Trollope's story necessitates adaptation, in cultural terms, of Anzieu's narrowly oedipal frame of reference.

Although psychoanalytic theory in the main attributes psychical formations to developmental experiences, at its roots are physiological processes that orient the psyche. Freud's theory of drives and the development of the ego ultimately finds its basis in the body, an insight Anzieu pursues and expands. While Anzieu focuses on the etiology and pathology of subjects' mental conceptions of themselves in relation to the surface of their bodies, he has nothing to say about the social determinants of the skin: that the skin is a sign of racial classification receives no attention in Anzieu's discussion of the psychical consequences of human subjects being embodied in their flesh. It is easy enough to fault Anzieu for ignoring race, but to suggest that the skin is socially as well as psychologically encoded is not merely to argue for a more culturally attentive account; it modifies the psychology itself, since skin color, in the modern West, contributes at least as much to the constitution of the ego as any of its other attributes.

Within a system of epidermal discrimination, in which rights have been distributed on the basis of pigment, the skin always functions both individually and socially—as a cover and a surface—a fact that the psychoanalytic interpretation ignores. Skin color, as the physical embodiment and visual evidence of (otherwise unverifiable) racial difference, assumes the enormous importance of making moral distinctions between people.[10] In combination with its psychological qualities as "sac, screen, or sieve" (envelope, barrier, or medium), the skin has not only functions but *significations* as well. Frantz Fanon, the preeminent psychoanalytic theorist of race, makes this point by showing how a psychological or phenomenological account of ego formation is inadequate to a subject marked, at the surface of the body, as "colored." He indicates the necessity of supplementing this "corporeal schema" with a historical and political description of a body that operates in the socially delimited world (the "racial epidermal schema"), within which the ego necessarily forms:

A slow composition of my *self* as a body in the middle of a spatial and temporal world—such seems to be the schema. It does not impose itself on me; it is, rather, a definitive structuring of the self and of the world— definitive because it creates a real dialectic between my body and the world. . . . Below the corporeal schema I had sketched a historico-racial schema. The elements that I used had been provided for me not by "residual sensations and perceptions primarily of a tactile, vestibular, kinesthetic, and visual character" [Lhermitte], but by the other, the white man, who had woven me out of a thousand details, anecdotes, stories . . . and above all *historicity*. . . . [A]ssailed at various points, the corporeal schema crumbled, its place taken by a racial epidermal schema. (Fanon 1952: 111–12; emphasis in original)[11]

Using Fanon's analysis of race in combination with Anzieu's notion of the skin ego allows us to see how Trollope's narrator has his internal integrity threatened through the experiences of dermatological abrasion (bathing in the Dead Sea, witnessing the bloody foot and the bruised leg) and yet secures that surface by contrasting its purity and cleanliness with the rough, dark, and dirty skins he encounters on his tour. These are not separate processes—one internal (psychological, spiritual, or erotic), the other external (social or political)—but in fact belong to the same "schema," at once "corporeal" and "racial epidermal," by which the self is constituted at the body's surface and also brought into contact with the world. In giving these processes narrative form, the story parcels them out, but moments like the one in which Jones says he feels *himself* "rubbed with pitch" by his bathing illustrate how the language of racial coloring extends to that of psychological self-perception. Moreover, we can now see that, in narrating the effects of the skin on soul or self, the story connects the gender plot itself to the exotic setting: by portraying abrasions at the surface of the body, the tale provides a vehicle for translating between the realm of racial/national distinction and that of sexual/gender confusion. The distressed skin is a metaphor for each mode of establishing difference, but is also metonymically linked to both, for these distinctions are themselves bodily. The repeated collapse of surface and depth, interior and exterior, enables the valued inside to assume a privileged form (integrity, consistency, purity, and cleanliness) through projection onto the outside.

In this raising of interior qualities to the surface, dirtiness and dark skin are made to stand for each other. That having dark skin is imagined to be tantamount to having dirt *on* the skin suggests, on one hand, the transitive possibility of racial infection and, on the other, the fantasy that racial distinction might be washed away: it is, in either sense, a resolutely superficial phenomenon. The link between dirty and dark skin is not incidental: as Anne McClintock has shown in an analysis of Victorian advertising iconography, the idealized domestic sphere, in which soap prevails, and the fearsome colonial one, in which dirt abounds, are mutually dependent.[12] Trollope's narrator gets dirty, and so fears becoming like one of the savage "dusky" natives described in the adjoining story about New Zealand; at the same time, he witnesses pilgrims from across the Mideast and determines, on the basis of their appearance, that they are ontologically dirty. Perhaps the strangest aspect of this fantasy is that he feels himself to be dirtiest—not in some deep, metaphysical way, but, again, on the surface—when he bathes. Hardly purifying his soul, the double baptism instead threatens to taint or tarnish his skin.

One can appreciate the significance of this oddity when it is placed back in the historical context of widespread (and well-founded) Victorian concerns with dirt and sanitation. Trollope's story was published in a periodical called the *London Review:* with the sweep of its imperial gaze, this journal takes in the whole world, but it derives fundamentally from the metropolitan capital. In that cosmopolitan context, around 1861, the depiction of filthy, infectious water could not but remind readers of the repulsive state of the River Thames itself. By the 1850s, England's urban waterways had become horrifically polluted, and widespread debates about the necessity of installing modern sewer systems ensued. During the summers of the late 1850s, hot, dry weather made the unembanked Thames so putrescent that passersby were overcome and Parliament, situated on the river, nearly had to close. Trollope may be thinking more of England's than Palestine's dirty water in his tale, for similarly disgusting rivers appear in roughly contemporary texts, including (among the best known) Charles Dickens's *Our Mutual Friend* (1864–65), Charles Kingsley's *Yeast* (1848–50) and *The Water-Babies* (1863), Friedrich Engels's *Condition of the Working Class in England* (1845), and Henry Mayhew's *London Labour and the London Poor* (1851). These works uniformly portray dirty water in an urban English context, where sewage gets mixed up with drinking water, threatening disease and social decay. They fully exploit its metaphorical potency, as a sign of infectious circulation among bodies, classes, and commodities.[13]

Trollope's use of the pollution metaphor to link *foreign* brutes and filthy waters is not entirely unprecedented, however: popular reporting about the disgusting condition of London's waterways is frequently drawn to the same equation. In fact, the connection might have seemed inevitable as, in 1858, newspaper stories about alarm over the dirty river ran right beside reports of the Sepoy uprising in India, a serious rebellion against British imperialism and the decisive event in the move to place India under direct control of the British government.[14] An editorial in the *Times* about the repulsive state of the Thames makes the connection explicit:

> The stench of June was only the last ounce of our burden, or rather it was an accidental flash of light which brought a great fact before our eyes. That hot fortnight did for the sanitary administration of the Metropolis what the Bengal mutinies did for the administration of India. It showed us more clearly and forcibly than before on what a volcano we were reposing. It proved to us that the Thames had become a huge sewer, not only figuratively but actually; that we had made it, of the two, rather worse than a regular drain; and that, if we did not set our city in order at once, there was

no telling what might befall us. (July 21, 1858; 9; partially quoted in Halliday 1999: 74)

The comparison suggests that stinking rivers, like violent native uprisings, require powerful, civilizing state intervention, for both threaten the integrity of the white man's body. Both are filthy, frightening, and potentially lethal to the ruling-class population; both threaten to explode (in this heap of metaphors) like a flash of lightning or a long-dormant volcano—the one into mutinous bloodshed, the other into toxic cholera. The military/sanitary analogy serves to taint the colonies with hygienic offense while attributing bloodshed to the river pollution. Other comparisons draw the calamities common to England and India nearer still: *Punch,* in its "Essence of Parliament" of July 10, 1858, reports, "The Thames and the Ganges again divided the attention of the Commons. . . . To which is offered the largest number of Human Sacrifices?" In this implied allegory, urban sanitary degeneration converges on uncivilized religious fanaticism: the ineffectual government of the metropolis is as callously indifferent to human life as barbarians who deliberately sacrifice it. Like the hyperdevout Eastern Christian pilgrims portrayed in "The Banks of the Jordan," the crazed Hindus care only for the deep interior of spiritual life.

Through the coincidence of the Thames crisis and the sepoy uprisings, a local urban problem is displaced onto a connection between filth and foreignness, which makes its way into Trollope's story as a failed spiritual quest: it is no wonder the narrator finds his baptism so utterly unenlightening, for the foul water seems to speak more to English sanitary conditions than to affirming Christian faith. The link between a bathing that dirties and epidermal transformation becomes clearer still when we turn to one further piece of evidence from the period, which shows how the concatenation of mid-Victorian sanitary and imperial administrations necessitates a skin consciousness to keep them distinct. However filthy the metropolis may be, it is still not so bad as the colonies, the logic runs, where dirty subjects require blanching by the British administration. Figurative though it may sound, *Punch* makes this racist imagery altogether literal. The issue of July 17, 1858, contains a mock Parliamentary hearing on the state of the Thames, which parodies legislative paralysis by showing every piece of expert advice to be contradicted by another. At the bottom of the same page, a small item titled "Ineffectual Ablution" reads: "His Highness the Maharajah JUNG BAHADOOR has been created a Knight of the Bath. A similar experiment has been tried before. JUNG BAHADOOR is a gentleman of a dark red complexion. The Bath will not render it white." A corresponding illustration at the top of the page, titled "Washing the Blackamoor White. Sir Jung Bahadoor and His Knights Companions of the Bath," shows the unhappy maharajah plunged in a steaming tub, white men in knights' armor scrubbing him vigorously (see figure 4.1). The items about the maharajah, who was being rewarded

WASHING THE BLACKAMOOR WHITE.

SIR JUNG BAHADOOR AND HIS KNIGHTS COMPANIONS OF THE BATH.

Figure 4.1 *Punch,* July 17, 1858. Courtesy of Special Collections, University of Maryland Libraries.

for his role in suppressing the sepoy rebellion, literally surround the story of Parliament's inaction over the stinking river. This graphic arrangement makes explicit the analogy between the metropolis and the colonies: like disease, dark skin is an impurity requiring violent purgation. The English claim for racial superiority, and the aspiration for whiteness imputed to the purportedly red-skinned Indian, indicate in the idiom of ethnicity how degrading Londoners find it to have reached such an appalling level of sanitary degradation. Such reasoning equates dark skin, the bodily integument of the colonial subject, with the pollution that reaches inside and disturbs the metropolitan one. In this racist fantasy, one is ontologically dirty, visibly stained on the outside; the other is situationally infected by a miasma that carries the putrescence within, making the domestic subject *feel* unclean. The danger for Trollope's narrator is that he, like *Punch's* maharajah, might not be able to scrub off the uncivilizing dirt that adheres to, and threatens to become, his skin.

In the context of Victorian sanitary reform, the tale's ironic desublimation of ritual cleansing seems even more insistently and irreducibly corporeal. In both historical and phenomenological terms, then, the tale's paradoxically defiling baths repudiate a traditional spiritual account of the body as merely epiphenomenal to an ethereal essence. Once the body's visceral depths are revealed—its sexual cravings, its odors and its filth, the gore exposed by macerating saddles and contaminated waters—it too exhibits an interior. Yet this inside turns out to be no less horrifyingly material than the outside, and the narrator's failure throughout the story to move beneath the surface seems, if not wise, then efficient. The reparations of the skin ego, he suggests, can take place only dermatologically, not internally.

The story thus proposes that, while one is foolish to stay on the surface, because it can so easily deceive, there may be nothing *but* surface beneath. The final word on the matter comes at the moment in this desert tale when the epitome of deceptive appearance, a mirage, appears—or rather, fails to appear. "We have often heard, and some of us have seen, how effects of light and shade together will produce so vivid an appearance of water where there is no water, as to deceive the most experienced. But the reverse was the case here. There was the lake, and there it had been before our eyes for the last two hours; and yet it looked, then and now, as though it were an image of a lake and not real water" (Trollope 1861: 121–22). Like the touch of its water, the appearance of the Dead Sea confounds expectations: it recedes when approached, just as it sullies rather than cleansing. While a mirage is an hallucination of an absent object, the phenomenon described in this moment *denies* the material existence of an actual object. A mirage signals desire and imagination; this countermirage indicates negation and distorted perception. Like the cross-dressed young woman, the Dead Sea hides in plain sight; as elsewhere, Jones does not interrogate the smooth exterior before him, just as the physical surface of the sea keeps buoying him up when he tries to dive beneath it. He fails to go below the surface, not so much because of his arrogance and prejudices, which are many, but because, Trollope suggests, there is nothing else: efforts to penetrate result, not in the revelation of deep truths, but in a further gliding along the slippery surface of the skin.

Notes

1. On the physiology and psychology of the skin, see Montagu.

2. References are to the collected edition, but quotations have been slightly emended to conform to the original journal publication.

3. According to biographer Hall, *Cornhill* first rejected the tale because it "was filled with sexual references that Smith and Thackeray felt too explicit for

the magazine" (207). When the story eventually appeared in the *London Review,* readers met it with "disapprobation" and dismay: an editor "wrote to Trollope . . . [and] quoted one of the 'mildest' of the many letters to their editor, this reader speaking of destroying the supplements in which the stories were printed and giving up the paper, while inquiring whether the proprietors meant to appeal to men of 'intelligence & high moral feeling' or those of a 'morbid imagination & *a low tone of morals*'" (208; emphasis in original).

4. In *The Bertrams,* whose early scenes occupy the same landscape as "The Banks of the Jordan," the alienating setting serves more straightforwardly as the site of seduction: the novel's hero, George Bertram, meets and falls in love with Caroline Waddington (the work's self-consciously announced *"donna pri-missima"*) in Jerusalem, proposing to her on the Mount of Olives, while gazing out on "the temple in which Jesus had taught" (Trollope 1854: 120). This is the normative romance, upon which the later story plays, in its disguises and disruptions, as well as in its archetypal names and characters.

5. See O'Connor, ch. 1, which supplies evidence for disease and factory work itself as blackening, and thereby racially degenerating, in Victorian popular imagination.

6. With the allusion to flaying, Trollope's story here converges on the Greek myth of Marsyas (a mortal who inadvertently entered into competition with Apollo and was punished by being flayed alive), which Anzieu places at the center of his analysis of the skin ego.

7. Forrester notes: "While Jones had been disgusted by (and yet drawn to) the filthy masses at the chapel, he is clearly drawn to (and yet repelled by) this solitary, suffering pilgrim. In terms of background and physical appearance, the pilgrim bears striking similarities to Jones (and to Trollope himself), and in that moment of self-reflection Jones begins to acknowledge a masculine (remember his 'brace of pistols') craving for submission and suffering."

8. Freud states: "The ego is first and foremost a bodily ego; it is not merely a surface entity, but is itself the projection of a surface" (16). In an explanatory footnote to this passage added to the 1927 English translation, Freud writes: "I.e., the ego is ultimately derived from bodily sensations, chiefly from those springing from the surface of the body. It may thus be regarded as a mental projection of the surface of the body, besides, as we have seen above, representing the superficies of the mental apparatus." On the embodiment of ego, see also Laplanche, Bersani, and Grosz, ch. 2.

9. Anzieu's is at base a material and biological account, and he elaborates these three functions (later expanded into nine) in greater detail at another point: "Every psychical activity is anaclitically dependent upon a biological function. The Skin Ego finds its support in the various functions of the skin. I shall proceed later to a more systematic study of these. For the moment, however, I shall briefly indicate three of the functions (the ones to which I restricted myself in my original article of 1974). The primary function of the skin is as the sac

which contains and retains inside it the goodness and fullness accumulating there through feeding, care, the bathing in words. Its second function is as the interface which marks the boundary with the outside and keeps that outside out; it is the barrier which protects against penetration by the aggression and greed emanating from others, whether people or objects. Finally, the third function—which the skin shares with the mouth and which it performs at least as often—is as a site and a primary means of communicating with others, of establishing signifying relations; it is, moreover, an 'inscribing surface' for the marks left by those others" (40).

10. On the "economy of visibility," on which race and gender categories rely, see Wiegman, ch. 1.

11. Fanon articulates this largely psychoanalytic account of racial distinction in the terms of Sartrean phenomenology, predominant in the period of the work's composition. See also Silverman, ch. 1, and Seshadri-Crooks.

12. See ch. 5, and Anderson, on the medical representation of human waste in a colonial context (in this case, the Philippines of the early twentieth century).

13. On the relation between spiritual conceptions of bodily waste and Victorian sanitary policy, see Hamlin. For a more theoretical discussion of waste and value, see Laporte.

14. On British representations of the Sepoy rebellion, see Sharpe.

References

Anderson, Warwick (1995). "Excremental Colonialism: Public Health and the Poetics of Pollution." *Critical Inquiry* 21: 640–69.

Anzieu, Didier (1985). *The Skin Ego,* trans. Chris Turner. New Haven: Yale University Press, 1989.

Bersani, Leo (1986). *The Freudian Body: Psychoanalysis and Art.* New York: Columbia University Press.

Fanon, Frantz (1952). *Black Skin, White Masks,* trans. Charles Lam Markmann. New York: Grove, 1967.

Forrester, Mark (2003). "Redressing the Empire: Anthony Trollope and British Gender Anxiety on 'The Banks of the Jordan.'" In *Imperial Desire: Dissident Sexualities and Colonial Literature,* ed. Richard Ruppel and Philip Holden. Minneapolis: University of Minnesota Press.

Freud, Sigmund (1923). *The Ego and the Id,* trans. Joan Riviere. New York: Norton, 1960.

Grosz, Elizabeth (1994). *Volatile Bodies: Toward a Corporeal Feminism.* Bloomington: Indiana University Press.

Hall, N. John (1991). *Trollope: A Biography.* Oxford: Clarendon.

Halliday, Stephen (1999). *The Great Stink of London: Sir Joseph Bazalgette and the Cleansing of the Victorian Capital.* Stroud: Sutton.

Hamlin, Christopher (1985). "Providence and Putrefaction: Victorian Sanitarians and the Natural Theology of Health and Disease." *Victorian Studies* 28 (3): 381–411.

Laplanche, Jean (1976). *Life and Death in Psychoanalysis*, trans. Jeffrey Mehlman. Baltimore: Johns Hopkins University Press.

Laporte, Dominique (1978). *History of Shit*, trans. Nadia Benabid and Rodolphe el-Khoury. Cambridge, Mass.: MIT, 2000.

London Review and Weekly Journal of Politics, Literature, Art, and Society (January 19, 1861) 2 (29): 54.

McClintock, Anne (1995). *Imperial Leather: Race, Gender and Sexuality in the Colonial Contest.* New York: Routledge.

Montagu, Ashley (1978). *Touching: The Human Significance of the Skin.* 2d ed. New York: Harper and Row.

O'Connor, Erin (2000). *Raw Material: Producing Pathology in Victorian Culture.* Durham, N.C.: Duke University Press.

Punch (1858).

Seshadri-Crooks, Kalpana (2000). *Desiring Whiteness: A Lacanian Analysis of Race.* London: Routledge.

Sharpe, Jenny (1993). *Allegories of Empire: The Figure of Woman in the Colonial Text.* Minneapolis: University of Minnesota Press.

Silverman, Kaja (1996). *The Threshold of the Visible World.* New York: Routledge.

Times (London 1858).

Trollope, Anthony (1859). *The Bertrams.* Stroud: Sutton, 1993.

———— (1861). "The Banks of the Jordan." In *Complete Short Stories,* vol. 3: *Tourists and Colonials,* ed. Betty Jane Slemp Breyer. Fort Worth: Texas Christian University Press, 1981. 107–43.

Wiegman, Robyn (1995). *American Anatomies: Theorizing Race and Gender.* Durham, N.C.: Duke University Press.

PART III
RACIAL EDGES

5

Ontological Crisis and Double Narration in African American Fiction
Reconstructing Our Nig

Laura Doyle

Suddenly she saw her hands and thought
with a clarity as simple as it was dazzling,
"These hands belong to me. These *my* hands."
—Toni Morrison, *Beloved*

These hands belong to me. These *my* hands. As Baby Suggs sheds slavery and crosses the border between South and North in *Beloved,* this revelation comes to her in two voices. If we read the first as the "false" white voice and the second as the "true" black voice, we witness here a movement of *recovery:* a lost self found. But we can also read these two voices otherwise, as one voice with two registers, two dialects, speaking *to* each other.

And then we can consider these two possible readings together, understanding the movement from one voice to the other as an effect of what Maurice Merleau-Ponty names the body's "chiasmatic" relation to its own hands, its own voice, its peculiar doubleness. Morrison's syntax shows Baby Suggs entering just this self-relation. This chiasm of the body, as I'll explore below, underlies the political condition W. E. B. DuBois called "double consciousness." That is, what DuBois describes as "a peculiar sensation, this double-consciousness, this sense of always looking at one's self through the eyes of others" will be understood here as a common ontological condition that, however, under the stress of racism, issues excruciatingly in "two souls, two thoughts, two unreconciled strivings . . . in one dark body, whose dogged strength alone keeps it from being torn asunder" (DuBois 1965: 215). Art can redeem this exhausting condition by representing it and, in the process, relaunch, through art's mirror effect, a *productive* corporeal self-relation.

I propose to take this chiasmatic self-relation, its exhaustion, and its artistic regeneration as the frame for understanding one characteristic narrative mode in African American fiction: the doubled narrator. Harriet Wilson's *Our Nig* (1859), the first African American novel published in the United States, initiates a narrative practice in which the narrator tells an autobiographical story but does so partly or mostly in the third person. One might think of this narrator as "cubist" insofar as he/she collapses two dimensions into one view; that is, the front and the side angle or, in this doubled narration, first person and third person. Such a practice creates an apparently incoherent narrator, whose "cubist" eye looks forward while her mouth speaks sideways. Critics have long explored the various forms of masked, dialogical, signifying, or doubled voice in African American writers; and several have focused on the ways *Our Nig* shapes such a voice.[1] I hope to bring a decidedly ontological emphasis to this conversation by reading *Our Nig* as a representation of the unhinging of corporeal self-relation, which finally—*as* representation and in its turn toward an audience—seeks to repair that condition.

While eighteenth- and nineteenth-century ex-slave narrators such as Olaudah Equiano often generated disjunctive styles of self-reference so that, implicitly, several selves narrate their stories, Wilson's novel crafts a more dramatically split voice, one which is later echoed in such writers as Charles Chesnutt, Jean Toomer, Zora Neale Hurston, and Ralph Ellison. I will focus on what I take to be the paradigmatic structure of *Our Nig,* in which the unaligned adjacency of narrator and narrative allows us to feel the *dimensionality* of the body, foregrounded and broken open.

Our Nig tells the story of a biracial woman, born to a white mother and black man in the North, whose mother abandons her at the age of six (after her father's death) to a white family that makes her their "nig." While titles and fleeting references to "I" in *Our Nig* establish that this is the narrator's own story, she approaches herself throughout as "Frado" or "Nig," her own main character. She speaks from a voice located outside of her characterological body. The title page installs this alienated subjectivity immediately:

> *OUR NIG;*
> OR,
> Sketches from the Life of a Free Black,
> *IN A TWO-STORY WHITE HOUSE, NORTH.*
> *SHOWING THAT SLAVERY'S SHADOWS FALL EVEN THERE.*
> *BY "OUR NIG."*[2]

Even as the alternative versions of the title oddly juxtapose "our nig" and "free black," the two references to "our nig" most uncomfortably unsettle our entry into this text. This is the story of *Our Nig* (italicized) written by "our nig" (in quotation marks): the repetition creates two meanings for "our," a semantic situation further shaped by the word "nig" and the history of racism and slavery, of humans *owning* other humans. Who does this "nig" belong to? The title words—*Our Nig*—on one level belong to those who own the author—for *them* is she "ours"—and yet the tale, condemning the "shadows" of such conditions, is written by someone calling herself by this same name, which suggests that even as "they" authorize her authorial act, she condemns them and that, trickily, in this process she counterauthorizes or signifies on their name for her. Moreover, by placing quotation marks around this name, she distances herself from it, stressing her difference from it, but also leaving us with the question *Who is this "her"?* She has effaced any other name for herself (except that, ironically, of "Free Black"); she has allowed us no access to the very voice that speaks from behind this name-in-quotes mask. We are left with no "authentic" voice but only two "our nigs," one telling the sufferings of the other yet also captive to that other self.

This circumstance takes another twist when we realize that the narrator relates her story in the third person, about a girl and a woman—herself—whom she almost never calls "I." Her pronoun evasion makes it difficult for readers, for me in this chapter, to know what to call "her," for Frado is and is not the narrator, the narrator is both Frado and another. The preface and opening chapters establish this equivocal self-relation by slipping some first-person references into an otherwise third-person narrative voice. In the novel's preface, for instance, Frado directly links her life to the story when she uses "my" in mentioning that "My mistress was wholly imbued with *southern* principles" or tells us that "I do not pretend to divulge every transaction in my own life" (Wilson 1983: 3, emphasis in original). Noting the titles of the first three chapters ("Mag Smith, My Mother," "My Father's Death," and "A New Home for Me"), we reasonably conclude that this is a memoir or some sort of autobiographical fiction. We prepare to hear a tale in the tradition of slave narratives, albeit set in the North to show that region's complicity with slavery.

Yet this orientation is immediately disrupted and remains so for most of the story. Except for a final hint in the last chapter, there is no "I" nor "me" nor "my" nor "we," only Frado, our nig, her, and she. Without the titles and the preface, we would have no clue that this story is the narrator's story. On the contrary, within the body of each chapter, the narrator adopts the stance and diction of a third-person storyteller looking on philosophically, not a memoir writer testifying by her own life that the shadows of slavery reach North. She tells a tale that begins when a destitute and depressed white woman, Mag, marries a black man only for his ability to support her. When he dies, Mag and her biracial children move in with his business associate, Seth—until that business fails and the couple decides to abandon the two children, Frado and her brother. What happens to the brother is not explained, but in Frado's case they leave her with a white family on the pretense that it will only be for an afternoon. They never come back. After this white family debates about whether or not they can bear to keep this "nigger," the cruel mother decides that she can use her as a servant. Until Frado reaches womanhood, Mrs. Bellmont works her to the bone and abuses her daily with insults and slaps, sometimes more severe beatings. The name "our nig" is coined on the day Frado arrives, when a Bellmont son who is ostensibly sympathetic to Frado teases his sister and predicts that although the sister feigns disgust at the idea of "keeping" Frado, she will soon be bragging to her friends of "our nig, our nig."

Frado narrates all of this in the novel but she does so as if she were not Frado. I suggest that it is only by such disjunctive narration, with its unresolved juxtaposition of "I" and "she," that the character-narrator can generate a tolerable, perhaps productive self-relation. Via the symbolic dimensionality of language (I and she), she creates a wedge between herself and herself—like the literal wedge Mrs. Bellmont occasionally forces between Frado's jaws. In her narration, Frado pries open a span across which she can touch herself, though only obliquely, and she herein works to undo the colonization of her being by the Bellmont family. It is this narrative wedge that connects her to herself even as in a more obvious sense it obscures herself. Apparently she can experience what Maurice Merleau-Ponty calls chiasmatic being-in-the-body only in this way. In fact, Merleau-Ponty's phenomenology of the body sheds strong light on Frado's narrative self-relation.

When Baby Suggs looks down and sees her hands, she is "dazzled" by the sudden visibility of her own capacity for handling the world, by the appearance for herself and to herself of this handed body, which might now choose to stroke rather than slave. She is pausing to discover the ways that, in Merleau-Ponty's words, "the body . . . is not itself a thing, an interstitial matter, a connective tissue, but a *sensible for itself*" (Merleau-Ponty 1968: 135). She relishes for the first time the possibility that *her* "body is a being of two leaves, from one side a thing among things and otherwise what sees and touches them" (Merleau-Ponty 1968: 137). Within the "circle of the touched and the touching" that Merleau-Ponty describes, it is neither the sameness of the one body nor the difference of the two parts but rather both of these together that open up a world—literally a span of time and space—within this circle (Merleau-Ponty 1968: 143). Like the rhetorical trope of the "chiasmus" in which parallel phrases are inverted, the chiasmatic body folds back upon itself, sensing its sensibleness. Each body, each person is in this sense two bodies, "two leaves"—or a kind of double helix where two opposite sides of one ribbon touch and describe a circle of time and space, a here and a now, an entry into worldness. Thus "when one of my hands touches the other, the world of each opens upon the other because the operation is reversible at will" (Merleau-Ponty 1968: 141).

At will, that is, if one is not enslaved. As we will see, for Frado it is exactly this chiasmatic self-relation that is distorted and threatened. Merleau-Ponty's descriptions of the self-touching body can help in describing the ontological trauma of Frado's condition because it is partly this "reversibility" that such slavery collapses through tactics of fear and torture—and which many African American narrators work to recover.

In this context it is especially important that the hands, in their meeting, touch and are touched *almost* simultaneously, they *almost* close into a perfect circle, but not quite. There is an opening within the circle of the touched and touching that Merleau-Ponty calls the *écart,* the difference or noncoincidence at the heart of the meeting between a body and itself: "If my left hand is touching my right hand, and if I should suddenly wish to apprehend with my right hand the work of my left hand as it touches, this reflection of the body upon itself always miscarries at the last moment: the moment I feel my left hand with my right hand, I correspondingly cease touching my right hand with my left hand" (Merleau-Ponty 1968: 9). At the moment when the body, and the being it yields, verge on closure of the "circle of the touched and the touching," there is what he calls a "brief torsion" (Merleau-Ponty 1968: 7), for "Never does the perception grasp the body in the act of perceiving" (Merleau-Ponty 1968: 9). Always there is a lag or turn in the relation between myself felt from within and myself perceived by me from without. Yet in this torsion there is both decentering *and* possibility: "this incessant escaping . . . this hiatus between my right hand touching and my right hand touched . . . is not an ontological void, a non-being." Instead "if these experiences never overlap, if they slip away at the very moment they are about to rejoin, if there is always a 'shift,' a 'spread' between them, this is precisely because my hands are two parts of the same body, because it moves itself in the world, because I hear myself from both within and without" (Merleau-Ponty 1968: 148). The écart within the chiasm of the body arises from an existential condition in which "I am from the start outside myself and open to the world" (Merleau-Ponty 1962: 456). The slippage moment is the hyphen in self-touching; it is the means by which the self knows itself in the world.

This chiasmatic condition yields both exquisite tenderness *and* slashing abuse in the relations between self and other and self and self. For the racial or sexual Other, it issues in a *tortured* "double consciousness." In coming to oneself from outside one self, coming to the left hand through the right, and not quite arriving, one is vulnerable, exposed. One is left open to painful entry, to domination, and to interpellation by the world. That is, the world can get between us and ourselves, and feed self-directed racism, because we know ourselves only via the medium of that world to which our bodies belong if they are to live. Thus the torsion or the span Frado recreates in her narrative reveals a self-relation so willed and so strained that the two parts of herself threaten to come unstuck, the chiasm gaping like a maw. Yet exactly because her openness to the world and the access of others to her body has brought such violence and pain, she tries in her narrative to imagine another chiasmatic way of being—a form of being in which "our" (as in "our nig") is generated equally by her and them.

Frado reaches, in other words, toward discovery like Baby Suggs's, a reseeing of herself in the wake of slavery's brutalization of self-relation. Baby Suggs's hybrid diction (these my hands; these hands belong to me) at once accomplishes the joining of those two parts—experienced as *my* part and *their* part—and expresses the écart, their noncoincidence, their nonclosure, the slippage between left and right, the disjunction of side and the front viewed together in one plane. While Morrison uses the play of dialect and standard English, Wilson chooses third and first person to show that, like a cubist painting, language can hold the disjunction, make a structure of it, by arcing words in syntax across the écart. In this way while Frado seems to close herself to us, she opens herself to herself in the only bearable way.

Frado's desire for sustaining self-relation takes her, at the start of her story, to her mother, yet in a torsioned mode. In the opening chapter titled "Mag, My Mother," we might expect at some point to meet Frado the daughter—the narrator herself—as an event and presence in the mother's life. But the chapter closes with no sign of Frado, only that of an earlier illegitimate child who died shortly after birth. The strain on our understanding tightens as we realize, moreover, that this daughter-narrator is positioning herself as witness to scenes that predate her birth. She narrates as a kind of time-traveling ghost, guiding us through her mother's early life, which fact becomes further warped when we learn at the end of the next chapter (telling of Frado's birth and desertion) that after age six Frado never again "saw or heard of her mother" (Wilson 23). If, as critics have suggested, Wilson's story gives a "gothic" cast to the mother-daughter relationships of U.S. women's sentimental novels, one of the ghostly features of this relationship is the way the narrator uses a dissociated, third-person omniscience to imagine a continuity of relation with her mother that would otherwise be impossible.[3]

In fact, there emerges within Frado's narration of her mother a weird mixture of identification and disdain; she simultaneously conflates herself with and stands disturbingly remote from this mother in a way that parallels her inside/beside relation to herself. In the Preface, the author had described herself as "deserted by kindred, disabled by failing health" and explains that she writes this book because she is "forced to some experiment which shall aid me in maintaining myself" (3). Similarly, in the first paragraph of the story, we learn that Mag was "early deprived of parental guardianship, far removed from relatives" and so "left to guide her tiny boat over life's surges alone" (3), and eventually she must "provid[e] herself with the means of subsistence" (8). Likewise, just as her mother, Mag, was misled, seduced, and made pregnant as a young woman, so Frado—after her years of servitude with the Bellmonts and at the end of her written text—is misled, seduced, and made pregnant by a man who eventually abandons her. The narrator uses the same phrase in each case: "He left her to her fate" (6,127). Under these circumstances, her mother faced "a sneering world," and likewise Frado finds that "No one wanted her" (128). Because Frado's and her mother's lives mirror each other, the text seems to move in a circle; and in fact it's typical for first-time readers to confuse the mother's and daughter's stories.

Yet the tone and diction of the opening chapters move against this identification of mother and daughter, as does the abrupt surfacing of Mag's racism. First, the darker daughter's literary diction contrasts sharply with the white mother's harsh vernacular speech in a way that is highly unflattering to the mother. From the opening lines of the book, we feel the daughter standing above the mother, at first in a kind of pitying tone: "Lonely Mag Smith! See her as she walks with downcast eyes and heavy heart" (5). The onlooking gaze and the exclamatory mode lack the intimacy we might have expected from the daughter, even as the narrator's sentimental language imbues her portrait with condescension: "As she merged into womanhood, unprotected, uncherished, uncared for there fell on her ear the music of love" (5). She goes on to tell how Mag lost the "priceless gem" of her virginity and then how "her offspring . . . passed from earth, ascending to a purer and better life."

Frado's rhythms of speech and her euphemistic descriptions of the "music of love" and the "gem" of virginity collide in tone with the speech of Mag on the occasion of this first infant's death: "'God be thanked,' ejaculated Mag, as she saw its breathing cease; 'no one can taunt *her* with my ruin'" (6). Mag's abrupt "ejaculation" seems almost to spit upon the euphemistic prose of the narrator; yet the narrator resumes with "Blessed release! May we all respond" as if untouched by Mag's insinuation yet perhaps carrying a quiet note of irony. These equivocations trouble the entire portrait of Mag, as epitomized in her next comment: "How many pure, innocent children not only inherit a wicked heart of their own . . . but are heirs also of parental disgrace and calumny" (6). How do "pure" children "*inherit*" "wicked" hearts of "*their own*"? That is, how is a child born at once pure and wicked? How are children's "own" tendencies also "inherited"? The very confusion of mother and daughter here enables Frado to at once pity and condemn her mother, as it fosters the narrator's strategy of maintaining two selves, two "nigs," one inherited (from the racist mother) and one constructed (to maneuver around and back to that mother). And the undecidable question of inheritance, linked as it is with race, turns out to be at the heart of the matter.

Race comes to the fore in the scenes in which Mag decides to abandon Frado to the Bellmonts. If Mag seemed harsh in referring to the first child's death, she is blatantly hateful toward Frado. After the death of Mag's African American husband and the failure of Seth's business, when Seth suggests they give the children away and get work elsewhere, Mag "snarls" (so Frado tells us), "Who'll take the black devils?" (18). Mag's racism receives no comment from her daughter the narrator.

Yet clearly the matter of race enters joltingly here and intensifies the disjunction of selves in which Frado is caught up. We were earlier introduced to the "races" of her parents when Mag's first husband was characterized as a "kind-hearted African" and we are later told that he thinks of her as "his treasure—a white wife" (14). But little has been made of this mixed-race situation beyond the narrator's brief lecture in which she defends Mag to those readers who might disapprove ("You can philosophize, gentle reader, upon the impropriety of such unions, and preach dozens of sermons on the evils of amalgamation. Want is a more powerful philosopher and preacher" [13]). So when Mag refers to her children as "black devils," the reader is brutally awakened to the poisonous spirit of this family. Yet the narrator stands mutely beside this insulted child-self of hers. She merely reports the ensuing dialogue between Mag and her current white lover Seth in which they coldly decide to leave Frado with the "she-devil" Mrs. Bellmont, interjecting no words of criticism or sorrow (a choice similar, perhaps, to that of the kind but silent Mr. Bellmont in the presence of his wife's cruelty to Frado, a point I'll return to later). Race thus precipitates Frado's loss of self-relation; her body's racial genealogy eases her mother's abandonment of her and leaves Frado exiled from the body born from that mother. Against such a past, "our nig" might indeed express a wish for recuperation—a desire for a self that is theirs, mine *and* theirs, *and* mine.

The desire finds distorted expression in the anecdote Frado interjects just before the moment of desertion. She tells how one night the week before she is left with the Bellmonts, Frado doesn't come home, and during her absence we follow the mother's point of view rather than Frado's, even though it is Frado herself recollecting this story. Mag and Seth, we are told, speculate about Frado's motives (disconcertingly in the narrator's diction—"They thought she had understood their plans, and had, perhaps, permanently withdrawn"[19]), when of course Frado could herself report those motives but would know very little of her parents' speculation. Instead, from within the parents' point of view we eventually learn that Frado and a girlfriend simply lost track of time and place and then couldn't find their way home.

What is important and painful and yet artistically productive here is that Frado is *filtering her story of herself through her mother even at the very moment when her mother is abandoning her.* It is this filtering, strangely, that allows Frado to reimagine her self by reimagining her mother's relation to her. In fact she pictures her mother worrying about and missing her: Mag "could not rest without making some effort to ascertain her retreat" until at one point "Mag felt sure her fears were realized, and that she might never see [Frado] again" (20). Just as the child-Frado in this episode asserts her presence to her mother by making her (inconvenient) absence felt, and she later achieves the same effect in temporarily running away from the Bellmonts, so as adult narrator she now pulls the same trick. She makes her presence felt through her third-person absence; and more specifically she inverts her story's emotional economy: she attributes to her mother the very feelings of love that the mother's abandonment show to be lacking.

This misidentification with and of the mother may well reflect deep denial and thwarted emotional work on the daughter's part; but, as writing, this split between Frado as first-person daughter and our nig as third-person narrator *enables* this imagining of the mother's desire for the daughter. Without the intrasubjective split, the daughter-narrator would be left only with an unreconstructable story of abandonment. Yet, by way of the split, "our nig" can indeed become an omniscient narrator who covertly enacts a self-touching across the chiasm—and so fulfills her desire for a self that is "ours"—hers *and* mine, this "her" referring simultaneously to the mother and Frado. In short, she is reconstructing a "she" for herself that is recognized and desired by an (m)other.

This "she" is uncontainable, excessive, transgressive; she is pure energy, pure opening—the embodiment of a slippage, an écart-ic counterforce to the enclosure and restraint she faces at the Bellmonts and, more deeply and ontologically, to the self-closure and collapse provoked by abandonment. The narrator's first description of herself immediately mentions this energy: "Frado, as they called one of Mag's children, was a beautiful mulatto, with long, curly black hair, and handsome, roguish eyes, sparkling with an exuberance of spirit beyond restraint" (17). She repeatedly emphasizes that, as a young girl, "her natural temperament was in a high degree mirthful" and we hear of her "outburst[s] of merriment" and the moments when her "pent up fires burst forth" (38). Though once again oddly distanced by both the third-person pronoun (which allows us to witness instances of this exuberance from across a field or through a Bellmont brother's eyes rather than from within Frado's own consciousness), we see Frado in clear outline, sometimes moving with self-enjoyment despite the cruelties of the world into which she's been thrust.

Indeed, our narrator fashions the story of *Our Nig* as the battle between Frado's productive, errant energy (her "exuberance of spirit" [17]) and the world's project to "restrain" it or to disconnect it from its source in herself. It is in response to Frado's exploratory adventure with her friend, which reflects the child's capacity for self-delight, that Mag concludes that "severe restraint [at the hands of Mrs. Bellmont] would be healthful" (20). Although with*in* the story Frado exposes how the world restrains and exhausts her and so defeats her, she simultaneously dramatizes in her *narration* a chiasmatic reversal that implicitly exhibits her spirited energy. Via the reversal, *she* not only exercises this energy but she also maintains control over her fictional world and regulates the reading world's access to her story (as when she announces that she has "purposely omitted what would most provoke shame in our anti-slavery friends at home" [4]).

Yet the world does actively restrain her and in the process absorbs her desires into its desires *for her*. During her fifteen or so years with the Bellmonts, Frado is frequently beaten, sometimes gagged, daily worked to the bone, continually insulted. The Bellmonts exhaust her in every sense. In particular the tyrannical Mrs. Bellmont unrelentingly abuses her. Under Mrs. Bellmont's discipline, she must stand when eating, wear no shoes until the first frost, do the work of both field hand and maid. Then, too, "[i]t was [Mrs. Bellmont's] favorite exercise to enter the appartment [sic] noisily, vociferate orders, give a few sudden blows to quicken Nig's pace, then return to the sitting room with *such* a satisfied expression, congratulating herself upon her thorough house-keeping qualities" (66).

The intensity of Mrs. Bellmont's abuse of Frado suggests that Mrs. Bellmont needs and even desires Frado's vivid presence as a prompt to sadistic acts—

that it is through Frado that *she* realizes her intercorporeal and chiasmatic self-relation. Thus on one occasion, after Frado "venture[d] a reply to her command, [Mrs. Bellmont] suddenly inflicted a blow which lay the tottering girl prostrate on the floor. Excited by so much indulgence of a dangerous passion, she seemed left to *unrestrained* malice; and snatching a towel, stuffed the mouth of the sufferer, and beat her cruelly" (82, emphasis added). Mrs. Bellmont here enters a kind of erotic frenzy in which Frado is her desired object.[4] Within this predicament as desired scapegoat and abused servant, Frado becomes a self whose laboring body serves two warring masters, herself against herself. To work is to try to avoid the blows of Mrs. Bellmont and yet to work is to serve Mrs. Bellmont. Disturbingly, the pairing of Frado and Mrs. Bellmont in repeated violent scenes constructs an intimate bondage in the place of—in lieu of—an intimate mother-daughter bonding.

The result is that Frado must become "our nig": she must in some measure identify with the hateful Bellmonts as she did with her hateful mother. The whole of her story as well as its title page reveals how "our nig" filters herself through the Bellmonts in the same way she first filtered herself through her mother. This is the only strategy left to her if she is to overcome the antagonism insinuated into her very self-relation by way of the physical domination of Mrs. Bellmont: she must in some sense see herself through Mrs. Bellmont's eyes. We might say that the story our narrator tells is that of how her mother and then the Bellmonts force Frado to live out this drama of self-antagonism: a civil war, so to speak—or the chiasm in its destructive metamorphosis, when one part (or hand) repulses the other, even as it requires that opposite part, even when it continually reinitiates the looping circuit of antagonism with that other part. We might even understand Frado's experience of self-splitting as a microcosm of a national, equally race-provoked internal contradiction in a nation founded paradoxically on both ideals of liberty and practices of slavery, in effect speaking forward while its eyes look askance, evading its self-contradictions.

Certainly Frado's self-division mirrors the dynamics of the Bellmont family, which is itself organized around an internal split between the sympathetic though silent Mr. Bellmont and the heartless, vociferous Mrs. Bellmont, with other family members ranged on either side. Frado becomes a lightning rod in what she calls the storms of the family and internalizes her function as a ground for opposed forces. It seems she enacts in her writing the split she has witnessed throughout her years with the Bellmonts—and in the land of freedom whose basis in slavery supports families like the Bellmonts.[5] Frado best learns how to make her self-dispossession productive not from any of her apparent family "friends" (the relatively sympathetic brothers and Aunt Abby) but rather through the alienated Mr. Bellmont. Mr. Bellmont gives Frado what turns out to be potent advice: to suffer Mrs. Bellmont silently for the most part, but on rare occasions "when she was *sure* she did not deserve a whipping, to avoid it if she could" (104). He gives license for Frado's acts of evasion and even resistance.

When Mrs. Bellmont soon after takes up a stick to beat Frado for not bringing wood fast enough, Frado shouts "'Stop . . . strike me, and I'll never work a mite more for you'; and throwing down what she had gathered, stood like one who feels the stirring of free and independent thoughts" (105). Mrs. Bellmont "in amazement, dropped her weapon" for "it was characteristic of [her] never to rise in her majesty, unless she was sure she should be victorious" (105). From then on, Frado receives "fewer whippings" (106).

Mr. Bellmont has in effect passed on to Frado his strategy for dealing with his wife: absent oneself in all moments but a few, and in those moments abruptly turn Mrs. Bellmont's fieriness back on her. That is, he makes his presence felt within a pattern of omissions. Frado makes good use of his legacy not only as a young woman in the family but also as the narrator of this story. She borrows from him, it seems, her trick of self-relation through oblique self-presence—a presence that is duplicitous and even complicitous in her own erasure, yet by which she protects herself.

About midway through her story, at the opening of chapter four, our third-person narrator philosophizes about unrealized energies and unfulfilled desire within the span of temporality—a temporality which she, like Merleau-Ponty though in different tones, characterizes as both pregnant and incomplete, moved by a structure of expectancy.

> With what differing emotions have the denizens of earth awaited the approach of to-day. Some sufferer has counted the vibrations of the pendulum impatient for its dawn, who, now that it has arrived, is anxious for its close. The votary of pleasure, conscious of yesterday's void, wishes for power to arrest time's haste. . . .The unfortunate are yet gazing in vain for golden-edged clouds they fancied would appear in their horizon. The good man feels he has accomplished too little for the Master, and sighs that another day must so soon close. Innocent children, weary of its stay, long for another morrow; busy manhood cries, hold! hold! and pursues it to another's dawn. All are dissatisfied. All crave some good not yet possessed, which time is expected to bring with all its morrows. (Wilson 40–41)

Time "with all its morrows": this is the perpetual longing for closure that accompanies a chiasmatic corporeality and ontology. Imminence—the left hand anticipates a moment when the "circle of the touching and the touched" will be consummated with the right. This imminence is the state that the irrepressible Frado inhabits at her own peril, and so it is not surprising that here she makes an implicit comment on the delusion of anticipation, the bitter disappointment of the anticipated touch, the likely collapse of the chiasm's promise. Yet even with her daily life of toil and abuse, she waits expectantly for someone to embrace her, to take her back in; in fact, her driving hope is evidence of both a chiasmatic structure of desire in general and her particularly "exuberant" way of living it. She hopes first for the return of her mother, then for the day the kind brother James will take her to his home, then for the day when brother Jack will. In between these major expectations—none of which is fulfilled—come all those that promise temporary escape—school, church, the departure of cruel Mary or Mrs. B to visit relatives. Her indefatigable waiting extends all her years even into the present in which, prefacing her story, she "appeals[s] to my colored brethren universally for patronage, hoping they will not condemn this attempt of their sister to be erudite, but rally around me a faithful band of supporters and defenders" (preface). She still awaits a protecting embrace.

In fact, the way this tale of Frado's past keeps arriving in the present (in its preface, at its end, and in scattered moments like the reference above to "the consultation which follows") contributes to its disjunctive ontology. Notice that in the above passage each sentence begins in the past and turns toward the present, a present the narrator conflates with *this* present, the moment of narration: "With what differing emotions have the denizens of earth awaited the approach of *to-day*. Some sufferer has counted the vibrations of the pendulum impatient for its dawn, who, *now that it has* arrived, is anxious for its close" (41). These denizens await not the approach of "a new day" or any better day, but *to-day*, this day, the one that brings us and our narrator together as we read these words. It is to-day that Frado awaits the support and approval of her colored brethren. Such turns toward the present become one vehicle by which the narrator involves her audience in her drama. The reader's response to this story has the power to make this day, finally, into *the* day for which Frado has longed all her life. In this way, she invites us to join her across a temporal torsion, to meet her not as her first- but her third-person self. Drawn to her by the desire for an integrated temporal and corporeal dimensionality we can share, we are then bound to her by our felt failure to achieve that integration—a failure felt all the more strongly by twenty-first century readers who know that, after sufering experiences similar to Frado's, Wilson herself died sick and poor and that her book was forgotten for 120 years.

For disintegration is after all the final state of Frado's as well as "our nig's" corporeal being. Her body becomes sickly by the end of her slavery under the Bellmonts and it repeatedly fails her in her post-Bellmont years of life, so that she is even forced to return and live in Aunt Abby's room during a period when she is too weak to do any sewing work. She struggles during the writing of this book to support herself by her bodily labor. One might say that, in turning finally to art as a means to support herself, she gives up the body and hopes to depend on the writing mind, a dissociated mind, for her living.

But this Cartesian dichotomy oversimplifies the matter. Writing no less than sewing requires a body. Instead "our nig" has found in writing an *aspect* of corporeality peculiarly suited to the chiasmatic écart. Language slips in, it seems, where the hands or eyes fail. Perhaps the very différance of language, its delays and detours as understood by Jacques Derrida, expressed here in the conjunction of symbolic "persons" (first and third), are well suited to reconstruct what has been shattered in the self-touching body. Merleau-Ponty already anticipated this inherence in the body of language's *différance;* and he understood, in particular, the centrality of language's literal, linguistic mode of manifestation, for he notes that in speech "meaning is not on the phrase like the butter on the bread, like a second layer of 'psychic reality' spread over the sound: it is the totality of what is said, the integral of all the differentiations of the verbal chain; it is given with the words for those who have ears to hear" (Merleau-Ponty 1968: 155). With this last phrase, Merleau-Ponty emphasizes, furthermore, the dialogical, chiasmatic dynamic of speech as well as being. Language lives on and ramifies that reversible yet incomplete intimacy between the left hand and the right.

In other words, *language takes root within that dehiscent co-formation of the touching and the touched,* the seeing and the visible, the hearing and the audible. Even as words are the joining of sign to sign in a chain of signifiers, so they are also "that certain divergence, that never-finished differentiation, that openness ever to be reopened" (Merleau-Ponty 1968: 153). As audible sound or visible mark, language takes a form *available* to its listener or reader, whose presence both confirms and destabilizes its impact by keeping meaning openended. Therein, and perhaps most pertinent for the narrator in *Our Nig* and for others like her, "the signification redounds upon its own means" just as "the visible takes hold of the look which has unveiled it" (Merleau-Ponty 1968: 154). That is, the palpable text of our narrator testifies to a presence that is at the same time effaced by the substance of her speech, and the two taken together reopen the play of speech. As Wilson thus reveals, embedded in the referentiality of any statement there always lies language's reference to the very possibility of speech, or the possibilities of restraining or witholding speech. The speech act, or its felt absence, coincorporates person and world. It is in seeming to unhinge this self-relation that *Our Nig* reinitiates the person and energy, the doubled ontology, from which it arises.

Such a possibility recasts the importance of literacy within the African American tradition. Slaves', ex-slaves', and subsequent African Americans' valorization of reading and writing has been understood in a number of helpful ways—as the determination to gain that which Blacks were denied under slavery, as the obvious ticket to power in the dominant culture and, more literarily, as a way of constructing a self and community. I would like to add to this list another reason, closely related to the latter: writing is a way of touching and being touched by the body without paining it, without feeling pain. Writing is and is not corporeal, just as I am (not) simultaneously inside and outside myself. Writing is not bodiless abstraction, it is the em*bodi*ment of a gap, a lag, a pivot in the dehiscent, forever-turning body: and so it can occupy the heart of a body yet express that body's pain painlessly. Yet it has its meaning only in reference to the pained body that speaks it.

The closing turn of *Our Nig* stands witness sadly yet productively to this double potentiality of language to speak and yet escape pain, to be and not to be what it names, to embody, finally, the disembodied voice. After appealing once more to her reader for "sympathy and aid," the narrator asks, almost as a challenge, "Do you ask the destiny of those connected with her *early* history?" She summarily, almost begrudgingly, gives details about the Bellmonts—which of them is dead and which still living—and then she closes her paragraph and her book: "Frado has passed from their memories, as Joseph from the butler's, but she will never cease to track them beyond mortal vision" (131).[6] The narrator registers the failure of ontological reversibility between her and the Bellmonts: they continue in their not-seeing of her while she ceaselessly sees them, even "beyond mortal vision." Yet her naming of this failed reversibility undoes the failure insofar as we now supply the part forfeited by the Bellmonts: we the readers see her seeing of them—so her seeing is now, finally, seen. In fact, far from being the obscured one, Frado implicitly steps into the role of an omniscient, all-judging God, who can observe, from above, the Bellmonts' moral-existential failure. And yet she nonetheless makes *our* witnessing of her sight essential to her power, as installed by the question that opens her closing paragraph: "Do you ask the destiny of those connected with her *early* history?" She calls *us* to witness her self-narration through the Bellmonts.

And what we are especially called to witness, beyond her direct question, is its "linguistic *means* of elocution," specifically its disjunctive formation of a voice that speaks from beside itself, an "I" lived by this speaking body as a "she." Signification does indeed "redound upon itself" here and in turn upon us as listeners whose presence inverts her story's meaning, enables her presence to herself. Harriet Wilson thus lays bare, and presages for a tradition, how a text can display a broken body whose breakage on the page revives that body *for its readers* if not for its narrator.

Notes

1. See Stepto, Byerman, Pryse and Spillers, Gates, and Henderson for such approaches to voice in African American narrative. Several critics have specifically called attention to the narrator's disjunctive voice in *Our Nig,* specifically Lindgren, Johnson, Jones, Davis, and Bassard, though none with the ontological emphasis I am pursuing here. Lindgren pays most attention to the first- and third-person narration but without pursuing the implications for the body, and Davis focuses on the body but without linking this issue directly to the narration.

2. Harriet Wilson, *Our Nig* (Wilson 1983). All further references to this work appear in the text.

3. Claudia Tate was the first to give attention to the "complex maternal discourse of desire" (37) in this novel in Tate 1992: 36–50. The attribution of

"gothic" belongs to Julia Stern. For other discussions of *Our Nig* in relation to sentimental fiction, see Henry Louis Gates's introduction to the 1983 edition, especially xxxix–lii; and Ellis 1999.

4. In Katherine Clay Bassard's interpretation, Wilson implies, without stating, that Mrs. Bellmont's sons also impose their sexual desires on Frado. See Bassard 1997.

5. Indeed, as Barbara White has established, Wilson based her story very closely on her servitude with a family that had active abolitionists among its relatives.

6. For a full reading of the Biblical references in the novel, see Bassard 1997. Also see Tate for treatment of Frado's ambivalent relation to Christianity (1992: 43–50).

References

Bassard, Katherine Clay (1997). "'Beyond Mortal Vision': Harriet E. Wilson's *Our Nig* and the American Racial Dream-Text." *Female Subjects in Black and White: Race, Psychoanalysis, Feminism,* ed. Elizabeth Abel, Barbara Christian, and Helene Moglen. Berkeley: University of California Press, 187–200.

Byerman, Keith (1985). *Fingering the Jagged Grain: Tradition and Form in Recent Black Fiction.* Athens: University of Georgia Press.

Davis, Cynthia J. (1993). "Speaking the Body's Pain: Harriet Wilson's *Our Nig.*" *African American Review* 27 (3): 391–404.

DuBois, W. E. B. (1965). *The Souls of Black Folk.* In *Three Negro Classics,* ed. John Hope Franklin. New York: Signet.

Ellis, R. J. (1999). "Body Politics and the Body Politic in William Wells Brown's *Clotel* and Harriet Wilson's *Our Nig.*" *Soft Canons: American Women Writers and Masculine Tradition,* ed. Karen L. Kilcup. Iowa City: University of Iowa Press, 99–122.

Gates, Henry Louis, Jr. (1987). *Figures in Black: Words, Signs, and the "Racial" Self.* New York: Oxford University Press.

Henderson, Mae (1991). "Speaking in Tongues: Dialogics, Dialectics, and the Black Woman Writer's Literary Tradition." *Changing Our Own Words: Essays on Criticism, Theory, and Writing by Black Women,* ed. Cheryl Wall. New Brunswick: Rutgers University Press, 16–35.

Johnson, Ronna C. (1987). "Said but Not Spoken: Elision and the Representation of Rape, Race, and Gender in Harriet E. Wilson's *Our Nig.*" *Speaking the Other Self: American Women Writers,* ed. Jeanne Campbell Reesman. Athens: University of Georgia Press, 96–116.

Jones, Jill (1996). "The Disappearing 'I' in *Our Nig,*" *Legacy* 13 (1): 38–53.

Lindgren, Margaret (1993). "Harriet Jacobs, Harriet Wilson and the Redoubled Voice in Black Autobiography." *Obsidian II* 8 (1): 18–38.

Merleau-Ponty, Maurice (1968). *The Visible and the Invisible,* trans. Alphonso Lingis. Evanston, Ill.: Northwestern University Press.

——— (1962). *Phenomenology of Perception,* trans. Colin Smith. New Jersey: Humanities.

Morrison, Toni (1987). *Beloved.* New York: Knopf.

Pryse, Marjorie, and Hortense Spillers, eds. (1985). *Conjuring: Black Women, Fiction, and Literary Tradition.* Bloomington: Indiana University Press.

Stepto, Robert B. (1979). *From Behind the Veil: A Study of Afro-American Narrative.* Urbana: University of Illinois Press.

Stern, Julia (1995). "Excavating Genre in *Our Nig.*" *American Literature* 67 (3): 439–66.

Tate, Claudia (1992). *Domestic Allegories of Political Desire: The Black Heroine's Text at the Turn of the Century.* New York: Oxford University Press.

White, Barbara (1993). "*Our Nig* and the She-Devil: New Information about Harriet Wilson and the 'Bellmont' Family." *American Literature* 65 (1): 19–52.

Wilson, Harriet (1983). *Our Nig.* New York: Vintage Books, ed. and with introduction by Henry Louis Gates, Jr.

6

Parallaxes
Cannibalism and Self-Embodiment
Or, The Calvinist Reading of Tupi A-Theology

Sara Castro-Klarén

Preamble

The outer frame of this chapter on the limits of the body and the question of cannibalism is the transformative cultural work that conquest and colonization have performed on the formation of Western modernity. The self-fashioning that modernity grounds is intimately connected to the dynamics of cultural battle zones and epistemological entanglements that emerged during the European engagement with Amerindian cultures.[1] The unanticipated presence of Amerindian peoples and civilizations shook the isolated foundations of European theology and political theory.[2] While the debate between Sepulveda and Las Casas in the Spanish Courts (1550–1551) discursively settled the question of the humanity of the Amerindians (they were declared to be human beings), it did not put to rest the powerful mythology already in circulation regarding the strangeness of their bodies and costumes.[3] Declaring the Amerindians human only exacerbated the question of rightful conquest. Charges of cannibalism and human sacrifice became foundational to the process of dehumanizing and othering the conquest required.[4] As a cultural formation that marked indelibly the difference between Europeans (civilization) and Amerindians (savages), the body became the locus for the elaboration of otherness. In this chapter I will focus on our received idea of cannibalism, especially in its elaboration of the limits of the body and the modern constitution of the person. At the core of the chapter I place a genealogical examination of the master text on cannibalism, Jean de Léry's *Histoire de un voyage faite en la terre du Brésil* (1578).[5] My discussion will contextualize the representation of cannibalism within the grid of the Eucharistic crisis that peaked during the Reformation and the Religious Wars in Europe. To think the limits of the body as configured by the trope of anthropophagy, I will engage a comparison between Léry's writing on "cannibalism" and Araweté cosmology in order to show the local origin of the universalizing European fiction.

Having survived the siege and massacre of Sancerre in 1572, Jean de Léry (1534–1613) sought refuge in Geneva. There he returned to writing his account of his 1556 voyage to Brazil. *History of a Voyage to the Land of Brazil, Otherwise called America,* ([1625], 1990) was published a full twenty years after Léry's return from Brazil to France. His treatise on Tupinamba culture—costumes, mores, and beliefs—became, in time, an ethnographic master text. The Calvinist minister authored a work that offered a tightly reasoned description and interpretation of the practice of "ritual cannibalism." The scientific authority of *Histoire* has never been challenged.[6] Marcel Mauss, for instance, relies heavily on Léry's account of "primitive man."[7] Embracing the spirit of human fellowship that permeates Léry's narrative, Claude Levi-Strauss, in his chapter on his own arrival to the bay of Guanabara, evokes Léry's earlier presence and refers to the *Voyage* as the "breviary of the anthropologist" (Levi-Strauss 1963: 85). The veracity and meaning of the man-eating practices associated with the Tupi remain at the core of the cannibal complex. In offering another reading of Léry's cannibalism, my purpose is to return Léry's invention to the matrix of the European imagination on the limits of the body as emblazoned in the mystery of the Eucharist. My empirical point of departure is the fact that Léry took some twenty years to achieve a definitive version of the account of his voyage and that those were the very same years in which the most horrifying acts of anthropophagy were committed in the struggle between Protestants and Catholics (Religious Wars, 1562–1598) over the question of the Eucharist. Anthropophagy was part of Léry's personal, living reality and memory.

Human consumption of human flesh and theophagy—the human consumption of Divine flesh—were doctrinal issues that the Church never really satisfactorily resolved. The Calvinist challenge to the Mass with the Body of Christ at the center of all ritual revived and exasperated the death anxieties imbedded in the doctrine of the resurrection. The Christian promise of salvation as resurrection of the flesh at once set the limits for the discourse on the body and regulated the anxieties springing from the daily challenges to the constitution of the body as an indivisible and impermeable entity in the natural world of the living and, more emphatically, when a cadaver. As a Calvinist and a missionary to the Amerindians, Léry was doubly aware of the problematics of the consumption of other bodies, be these human, animal, or divine. Given the accounts circulating on the customs of Amerindians, Léry fully expected not only to meet anthropophagists but perhaps even, not unlike early Christians in Rome, to suffer martyrdom and pass through the experience of losing his body in the sepulchre of the other's stomach. As he sailed from France, he was fully prepared to be horrified by the ferocity (*feritas*) of the anthropophagy, and yet his actual encounter with the affable and music-loving Tupi made him reconsider. Thus the appearance of the voyage as *reflection* on anthropophagy.

Tracing and analyzing Christian anxiety over the limits of the paradigmatic Christian body—the cadaver—enables us to set the terms for a comparison with Tupi thought on the question of the physical body, its boundaries, and final disposition. The vehicle for this comparison is Araweté cosmogony. The Araweté are a Tupi group who until recently had managed to avoid contact with European culture. In my final analysis I am able to conclude that Léry's descriptions and interpretations of Tupi cannibalism have little in common with Araweté cosmology or practices and much to do with the underside of the Eucharist dispute between Catholics and Protestants, the crucial debate which speaks of the limits of the body as the foundation for the idea of an indivisible and timeless self.

The Body Beheaded, Flayed, Disemboweled, Interred . . .

In 1572, the year of the St. Bartholomew's Massacre in France, the Catholic Viceroy Francisco de Toledo (1515–1582) presided over the beheading of the teenaged Inca, Túpac Amaru, the last descendant of the Cuzco line of Andean sovereigns. The charge against Túpac Amaru was incest rather than human sacrifice cum cannibalism as had been the case in Mexico.[8] In both cases however, the question of human/nonhuman limits, the distinction between inclusion/ exclusion, rested on the normative concepts regulating European body practices. Back on the other side of the Atlantic in the nascent world of Protestant Europe, Jean de Léry (1534-1613) was serving as Calvinist minister in La Charité-sur-Loire. Unlike Túpac Amaru in Cuzco, Léry managed to escape the massacre of his coreligionists. He fled to Sancerre, which was itself a few months later besieged and reduced to starvation by the Royal Catholic forces. In 1563 Léry, while a politico-religious refugee in Geneva, authored a first draft of his *Histoire de un voyage fait en la terre du Brésil*. This draft was lost, and although eventually found, the story of his journey to Brazil was not published until 1578, a good twenty years after his return in 1558 and after personal experiences with mas-sacre and starvation.[9] Ordained a Calvinist priest in 1562, Léry's adult life span-ned both the most heated years of the Religious Wars and the systematic destruc-tion of the Amerindian populations.

The genealogy of Léry's history of his voyage "out there" is important but insufficient if one wishes to understand the fundamental role played by the cannibal complex in the construction of the self-identity rules of the modernity/ coloniality play. A Léry genealogy alone leaves a number of important dimen-sions out of the picture. It reproduces the unidirectional thrust of the European gaze onto the "other." Without taking into account the events taking place in the Amerindian worlds, it constructs a theater in which the lone voice to be heard is the voice of the ethnographer, unaware of the gaze upon him of his own object of study, deaf to discursive systems of that "other." Thus my concern here is to analyze the European discursive *topoi* that were brought together in the con-struction of the now classical scenes of Amerindian cannibalism in order to bring them into convergence with Tupi thinking on the body-person that it purported to represent, and to show the topology of intersection, divergences, and parallaxes that cannibalism entails in both Europe's thinking of the limits of the body and Tupi conceptions of the same question. Stories of cannibalism make good places for thinking the limits of the self for, as in the case of Léry's account, one can find that the displacement of the observed object is due to a change in the position of the observer and not to the objective phenomena themselves.

In 1556, while Léry was training in Geneva to return to France as a missionary of the reformed Gospel, he was called to a truly new mission. He and his fellow Calvinists were to establish a Protestant mission in Brazil. His presence in Brazil was preceded by a French Catholic mission and most especially by André Thêvet, the Franciscan friar, traveler, and author of *Singularités de la France antarctique,* published upon his return in 1556. Thêvet's travelog did much to popularize the image of the Tupi as cannibals, an image of Amerindians that had begun circulating feverishly with the reports that Dr. Chanca issued immediately after Columbus's second voyage and which Peter Martin d'Anghiera disseminated immediately after the second voyage in 1493. Cannibalism as a New World practice was firmly established in Europe's mind by the first quarter of the sixteenth century and became an article of faith with Lope de Gomora's *Historia general de las Indias* (1552). In the specific case of Brazil, Thêvet was critical of the Protestant interaction with Amerindians. He was particularly disturbed by the question of evangelization. He did not see Amerindians as possible subjects of a Christian community. He made his Catholic doubts clear in his *Cosmographie universelle* (1575). In his preface, Léry engages Thevet's critique. Applying his meticulous methods of verification, detailed memory, and tight logic, Léry not only demolished Thêvet's doubts and ethnography but in fact found a breach into the larger site of the dispute between Catholics and Protestants: the question of the Eucharist. His *Voyage* is in fact the place where he engages the fundamental issue then ripping Christianity apart, the emerging frontier between them and us, the insurmountable challenge to the universality of the Christian realm.

It is my contention that the question of the Eucharist—the limits of the human/divine and human/nonhuman body dichotomy—is what precipitated Léry's will to rewrite the lost draft right after the Sancerre starvation-cum-cannibalism episode. The memory of the short stay in the bay of Guanabara emerges charged with hermeneutical possibilities conferred on it by the lived experience of Sancerre. If so, the whole of the anthropological treaties on the Tupinamba is but a meditation on the status of the body in the realm of *feritas, humanitas,* and *divinitas.* In fact one could extrapolate from the case of Léry and view the wide consumption of Théodore de Bry's iconography of his *Grand voyage* (1590–1634) as a reception of a translation of the hotly debated and contested *topos* at the heart of the Reformation and the Counterreformation.[10]

The Calvinist settlement in Brazil failed and Léry lived the last two months of his stay in the bay of Guanabara as a guest of the Tupinamba, who may have considered him a sort of "pet" in the same manner in which they kept parrots. The lasting impact of the writing that was to become the "anthropologists' breviary" can only be measured across the centuries. Its emblem is found in *Tristes Tropiques,* for despite Levi-Strauss's enlightened secular science, he travels to Brazil anxious to find his own affable savages whose cultural meaning can be explained in the imbrication of warfare and cannibalism.[11] With Léry's account of the Tupi in his hands, Levi-Strauss remembers how he sailed, fleeing from Nazi Europe, in trembling anticipation of his "own" perfumed savages.

The classical scene of cannibalism that Léry inscribed does not perhaps achieve all the force of its impact on the European imagination until it is illustrated by the de Bry family. In Latin translation, the text of the *Histoire* became part of the third volume (1583) of the *Grands Voyages,* which circulated widely as part of a publicity campaign to encourage Protestants to colonize America (Léry 1990: 220–21). Of course the most famous version is Montaigne's essay "Des Cannibals" (1580) ["On Cannibals"], which drew on both Thévet and Léry's texts. The cannibalism scene as refined by the French travelers narrates how the Tupinamba eat periodically the barbecued flesh of the dismembered body of a young male warrior. The eating is done after or during a *caouin* (alcoholic beverage) drinking party in which the entire social body participates. According to Léry, the cultural logic of the consumption of human flesh rests on a system of warrior honor and revenge. Wars are staged in order to take captives who are then brought to the village and treated as dear guest (they are incorporated into the designation "we"). Enemy-captive-guests are given wives and every other pleasure. They live in "freedom" until the day of their execution. Bound by a code of honor and revenge, they do not flee, for as they state in their final oration, they have eaten of the flesh of the relatives of those executing them and they will become of the flesh of those who today eat them. This erasure of the line between self and other, between them and us, unconsciously understood but consciously inaccessible, sows fear and disgust in Léry's prose on the Tupinamba.[12]

In Léry's account, what binds this ritual cannibalism is a mistaken code of honor, a materialist view of life and death that has not yet evolved the idea of spirit, much less of resurrection. The horror of Tupi cannibalism is that it does not delimit the body from the soul, or rather that it does not produce a difference between the finitude of the present and the promise of future continuity in body and soul as Christianity does. This othered version of anthropophagy challenges the limits of the Christian self, founded as it is on concepts of the body as "natural" limit. The person, that indivisible seat of individual reason and destiny, becomes tenuous and precarious. Although Léry's description constructs a Tupi cultural logic that reasons this account of events into a ritualized practice, his narrative borders on a logic of alimentary cannibalism.[13] Indeed, the rendition of Léry in the *Grands Voyages* of the de Bry brothers, with but scant titles under the engravings, projects an inhuman silence onto the scenes depicted. Without the logic of war or punishment attending to the "illustrations," the scenes of the dismembered bodies in various stages of cooking and consumption appear nakedly brutal and even banal, for this (other) killing resists assimilation into sanctioned European reasons for the destruction of bodies. It is, of course, de Bry's visual series that will enable a connection between Léry's account of the Tupinamba body of anthropophagy to the culture and controversies of the body in anatomy theaters during the lifetime of the French traveler and the German engraver. But such a study is the subject matter of another essay. For the purposes of this chapter I want to retain my focus on Léry's thinking concerning the consumption of the human body in its dual registers: Christian and Tupi.

Rules of Consumption

While cannibalism offers a meditation on food and Léry is certainly concerned with questions of culinary rules as well as the dangers of pollution by the ingestion of unacceptable foods,[14] I believe that focusing on the question of death and decay of the human body will enable me to show how the discourse on cannibalism and its implicit challenge to the established limits of the body-person activates and disturbs, or better yet *radicalizes,* European fears about the status of the human body as a social and legal construct. In *The Resurrection of the Body in Western Christianity* (Bynum 1995), Caroline Bynum traces the debates over the disposition and status of the dead body in Christian theology, with particular attention to the relation of personal identity and the continuity of the body.[15] This is a concern that cannibalism seems to obliterate with its matter-of-fact attitude toward the disappearance of the body-person into the belly of the other. Another's (digesting) body as sepulchre runs counter to the mystery of the Eucharistic, which avoids the logic of cannibalism, in part, by positing the soul/spirit duality. The ingestion of the flesh and body of Christ is not anthropophagous only by resting on the occlusion of the question of digestion, that is to say, the utter transformation by the body of that which it ingests. How matter—flesh and blood—is spirited by the Christian body into the salvation of soul and body is the paradox that cannibalism does not admit.

Bynum suggests that many of the concerns surrounding the final destination of the body arose in part because of the fear of pain in martyrdom in the Roman circus. Worries that the body would not receive burial and would in fact be eaten by the ferocious beasts in the circus or be left as prey for carrion birds pressed the question further. In other words, martyrdom held within it the prospect of the loss of one's body in the belly of a beast, thus threatening the distinction not only between body and soul but also between self and other. The Church strained to produce a logic that would permit salvation if not of the body, then certainly of the person who was fused with the body. Thus the person appears as something larger than the body itself. The dimensions of the person extend beyond human, material time and space into a realm of entities guaranteed by God himself. When the pagan interlocutor asks the Christian with what body do you rise, the answer holds that bodies can rise just the same as they were in life because things are not lost to God (Bynum 1995: 34). Apologists of the Church such as Tertulian, Irineus, and Justin "spoke of resurrection as God's gift to all bodies but especially to those who experienced suffering and partition in prison or the arena . . . God promised a body both transformed and 'the same', both impassible and identical with the flesh of the earth" (Bynum 1995: 45).

It is clear that resurrection anxiety emerges as a response to persecution. It is not, then, too far fetched to assume that thoughts of suffering, dismemberment, and unholy burial were on Léry's mind when he sailed for his mission among the savages in Brazil and also when he heard of, endured, and witnessed the Catholic sieges and massacres of Protestants. He saw himself as a young Huguenot establishing a colony in a place inhabited by two kinds of bodily enemies: Catholics and cannibals. He knew from personal experience that while Protestant iconoclasts destroyed Catholic statues of the Virgin and the saints, Catholics aimed at destroying Protestant bodies (Eire 1986: 161).[16] Catholics roasted and ate Protestant hearts. They sold the rendered fat from Protestant bodies (Léry 1990: xvii). Léry's imagination was fired up with the events and polemics of everyday life in France and Geneva. Reading the ancient historians together with contemporary accounts of the conquest of America in preparation for his conquest of Brazil, Léry's imagination brought about the convergence of a European archive of thinking on anthropophagy and theophagy with supposed cannibal practices in America. Disparate cultural worlds were conflated, overlapping so as to produce a place for thinking that disavowal which the rising tide of spirit (modernity) over body (coloniality) demanded.

Whether dust or ashes, moisture or smoke, according to the apologists Christian bodies perdure. All bits survive and await reassemblage by God at the end of time. Bynum notes that in these Tertullian arguments the words for destruction are "eating," "consuming," and "digesting." As such they point to a materialist conception of the body that would, in the long run, not only entangle the Eucharist but also devolve on the very question of anthropophagy. As we shall see later in the case of anthropophagy attributed to Amerindian societies, in these discussions among Christian theologians and apologists the paradigmatic body is the cadaver. For Ireneus, for instance, the flesh is what undergoes fundamental organic change (Bynum 1995: 38) and yet it is the flesh that receives life eternal in virtue of the Lord's Supper. For the Bishop of Seville, the flesh is nourished with the blood and body of the Lord. Thus "we are members of His body, His flesh and His bones" (Irineus quoted in Bynum 1995: 39). For Irineus, the proof of final incorruption is not just a reassembling of pieces by the all-powerful God. Incorruption actually occurs in the eating of the God. Furthermore, the very truth of "our flesh is increased and nourished in the Eucharist . . . [and] we know that our flesh is capable of surviving digestion because we are able to digest the flesh of Christ. The fact is that we are what we eat" (Bynum, 39). We become one with Christ by consuming Christ. But the fact that Christ can never really be consumed, brought to end, guarantees that our own consumption by beasts, by fire, or by the gaping maw of the grave is not indeed destruction.

Such logic of man-God mutuality in consumption-digestion and consequent incorruptibility safeguards Christians from complete and utter finitude. Thus the grave is not the disappearance of the body. Death, that is to say rot and decomposition, is made productive via its inversion. It gives birth to its opposite. Death brings forth incorruption, a new wholeness in God, what Bynum calls a "transcendent" cannibalism (1995: 39). Bynum's anachronistic use of the term "cannibalism" attests to the force this idea holds and its capacity to occlude the more historically appropriate "anthropophagy" with its Greco-Christian semantic load. The Christian mindset that will encounter Amerindian societies starts with a fear of material anthropophagy and ends with a transcendental version that both denies and incorporates the materiality of the body and the digestive processes.

The shifting layers that compose the palimpsest of the Eucharist and anthropophagy never really settle down within the heart of Christian theology. The gaps and fractures in Calvin's meditation on the sacrament of the Lord's Supper appear magnified in Léry's meditation in the bay of Guanabara when he anxiously observes that the French Catholic colonists have run out of wheat flower and the materials for the preparation of the Eucharistic host are themselves in question. In Guanabara the Christians argue passionately as to the actual presence of the God in the substitute host (Léry 1990: 35–39). The mystery of the Eucharist, the carefully crafted "transcendent anthropophagy" reaches its own limits in the Bay of Guanabara and this is long before any description or interpretation of Tupi culture has entered Léry's textualization of his encounter with his Amerindian "others." The memory of this crisis will be carried over and layered onto the later anthropophagic experiences during the Religious Wars in France.

If the cadaver constitutes the place for thinking the limits of the body, then burial practices mark with particular emphasis the liminal situation of the body in death. Christian opposition to Roman practices of cremation are in line with the idea of preservation of an intact body for individual identity at the last judgment. But the grave, referred to in Mediterranean funerary practices as the "place that eats," posed also a threat to the integrity of the body. In this vein, both cremation and inhumation, which privilege the bones as the body, can be understood as attempts to deny putrefaction (Bynum 1995: 52–53).

Jews as well as Romans feared the grave. It devoured the departed. Christians, terrified by death in the Roman circus, thus connected ideas of eating with the idea of the sepulchre. The fear of the sepulchre ended, paradoxically, in the practice of the funereal Eucharist. At first Christians opposed the Roman practice of offering a meal at the site of the funeral, but later they adopted it and by "the fourth century the Eucharist was celebrated in graveyards" (Bynum 1995: 55). Once again, anthropophagy was not too far away from the funerary Eucharist for it mixed and matched several topos of the man-eating-God and man-eating-man complex at the heart of Christianity. However anthropophagy, so close at hand, remained a great taboo. It was a commonly leveled charge of inhumanity and incivility by pagans upon Christians and Christians upon pagans (Bynum 1995: 55). For Christians, in view of the necessary integrity of the physical body, the consumption of human flesh became the ultimate transgression. It aroused the deepest horror for it posed the gravest threat to the body's integrity and thus also to the promises of eternal salvation in body and soul. Late antiquity's fear of consumption and digestion posited repeatedly the figure of the famished mother who devours her own baby (Bynun 1995: 111).

The fear of being fragmented, absorbed, and digested throbbed in the multiplicity of genres and cultures of late antiquity. One could say that if there is a common place it is anthropophagy as grave. The figuration of anthropophagy as part of the chewing and salivation of ingesting and the mystery of the digestive processes loomed even more repugnant than the odors, gases, and oozing of the uncontrollable transformation of the body on its way to nothingness in the grave. It combines the threat of the power of the other with the invisible and also threatening cavity of the interior of the body itself.

Bynum observes that the promise of a spiritual body or immutable physicality remained an oxymoron (1995: 57) but it was this very oxymoronic hope that held the earth together in the vision of otherworldly resurrection. The specter of decay moved unresolved right into the Middle Ages and Augustine himself provided a revised foundation for basically the same ideas: resurrection is restoration of the *material* wholeness of the body (Bynum 1995: 95). Incorruptibility, integrity, and perfection were the traits of the resurrected body-person. Augustine even addressed the question of starvation anthropophagy. He held that it did not stand in the way of the reconstitution of the body of the person in life regardless of whether the person's final destiny was heaven or hell. Augustine's thinking is grounded on Luke's own accounting metaphor with which he guarantees the wholeness and integrity of the body-person: "Not a hair of your head shall perish" (cited in Bynum, Luke 21.18). What is more, in Augustine we already see the seeds of the notion of the body as a person's own inalienable right. For him one's body, its wholeness and integrity, constitutes the foundational stone in an economic system of private property. In Augustine's thought, the imbrication of the accounting metaphor with the full restoration of the body via the power of the divinity is foregrounded. It also foreshadows fuller discussion of the sanctity and dispersal of the Christian body:

> For if someone, famishing for want and pressed with hunger, use human flesh as food—an extremity not unknown, as both ancient history and the unhappy experience of our own days have taught us—can it be contended, with any show of reason, that all the flesh eaten has been evacuated, and that none of it has been assimilated to the substance of the eater, though the very emaciation which existed before, and has now disappeared, sufficiently indicates what large deficiencies have been filled up with his food? But . . . all the flesh which hunger has consumed finds its way into the air by evaporation, whence . . . God Almighty can recall it. That flesh, therefore, shall be restored to the man in whom it first became human flesh. For it must be looked upon as borrowed by the other person, and, like a pecuniary loan, must be returned to the lender. His own flesh, however,

which he lost by famine, shall be restored to him by Him who can recover even what has evaporated. (in Bynum 1995: 104–105)

It is interesting to note again that Bynum's translation of Augustine's meditation on anthropophagy employs the translation "cannibalism." Augustine presses beyond Luke's sense of the body as a finite set of particles that bear complete accounting: "Not a hair in your head shall perish." He figures the body as a pecuniary loan whose return in full is guaranteed by God's ultimate restoration. For our present-day discussions of anthropophagy, it is important to note that Augustine's text acknowledges the fact that human consumption of human flesh is a phenomenon considered both a past and present reality. In his own day it took place often enough to cause him to address it not only as a social problem but, rather, as a theological question. The power of the divinity to dispel the horror of the human condition and to offer a supernatural solution to the human conundrum would seem diminished if it could not give a clear answer as to the disposition of the digested body. Augustine's logic on the reversal of decay and digestion holds yet another corollary for establishing the status and the limits of the body in Christian thought: even when partitioned and even in dispersal it remains whole, it holds on to the (visual) form and identity it had when alive. The Christian body is as indestructible as it is holy. The paradigmatic body becomes then the body of the saint. Like all bodies, the saint's body is made not only incorruptible by way of salvation but can indeed overcome the decay of death. It can arrest the flux within it, as well as stop the flow of temporality itself.

Augustine's stress on the recovery of each infinitesimal particle asserts, paradoxically, the idea of the fragment standing for the whole. The metonymic conception of the body eventually facilitated the worship of parts of human bodies as relics. Partition and translocation of bodies may have been quite common in the later part of the fourth century. Records indicate that both Imperial legislation and Christian sermons forbade the moving of bodies into the cities. Dividing and selling them was also forbidden.[17] Despite the fear that mutilation would disempower the bodies of the saints, holy body parts were shipped regularly. It appears that the context of the cult of relics remained tightly intertwined with the discussion of resurrection even up to Calvin's times.[18] Eucharistic anxiety preoccupied minds.[19] Calvin's followers, in their iconoclastic zeal to destroy the "false" objects of Catholic worship, looked with particular disapproval on the relics of the saints (Eire 1986: 179).[20]

Despite serious internal disagreement, scholastic thought did eventually come to a consensus on the composition and identity of the body with which individuals would rise and be resurrected on the day of the final judgment. One of the problems that continued to vex scholastic thinking on the logic of the constitution of the body fit for resurrection was the question of food. While hunger, eating, and wasting remained central problems in the cycles of life and death, food and the modes by which it at once integrated the body and yet expelled its wastes

preoccupied scholastic scatology. The limits of the body assumed to be coterminous with the envelope of the skin did not always hold. Continued growth and
falling out of hair and nails disturbed the idea of wholeness and identity. More
troubling than hair loss were of course the excretions of the body, from feces to
semen. Menstruation and the placenta were not mentioned but one must assume
that they also loomed large in the anxious logic that saw the body as the sum total
of its visible parts. The recurring image of antiquity of the desperately anthropophagic mother devouring her baby seems to have been left behind, even
though the charges of stealing and eating babies remained alive.[21]

It was finally agreed that humans were not necessarily what they ate. And,
as we saw in Augustine, neither could they be conflated with the identity of the
body who eats them. Set apart from the chemistry of digestion, blind to the events
of the interiority of the body as organic function, scholastic thought makes of the
human body nothing less than a *miracle* intended by the divinity as an event
scheduled in the production of individual resurrection (Bynum 1995: 125). The
body's status is reversed: from the indispensable materiality of not losing even a
hair, scholastic thought finds the body's integrity in God's invisible and immaterial plan for salvation. Even in the event of anthropophagy and digestion in the
belly of an animal or another human, human bodies by virtue of divine resurrection remain themselves. By the early twelfth century, Julian of Toledo has gone
full circle. Rather than the body recovered in its full materiality, he imagines a
body totally destroyed, smelted by the fires of Doom, on its way to purification.
Julian reasons that God will recast it into a more beautiful form.[22]

While the question of food in the constitution of the body continues to
draw the attention of Peter Lombard and others, Anselm declares that the
human body rises without any additions or growth gained from food. This
conclusion seems to address the disturbing notion of the anthropophagist himself, who may have from infancy been fed human flesh. As with Augustine, with
Anselm's reassurance one wonders to what extent the contemporary consumption of human flesh was believed to be prevalent. Anselm writes that in the
resurrection the anthropophagist will have a body of his own and "the others by
whose flesh he has been fed will rise in the bodies that were naturally theirs"
(Bynum 1995: 127), thus leaving the task of sorting and restoration to God.
Resurrection gained by humans by virtue of the death and resurrection of the
body of Christ overcomes the conundrum of the food chain. It sets the human
body in a space of its own. The human body, although tied mercilessly to the
cycles of ingestion, digestion, and expulsion of wastes—that is to say to a constant
interaction with otherness—emerged in scholastic thought in denial of its intimacy with its physicality and in full embrace of a constitution that, like Christ's
own, was otherworldly. The idea of the resurrection provided a link of continuity
between the human body and Christ's own resurrected and eternal body in such a
way that it would be later possible for Calvin to envision the pure spirituality of
the individual's identity without having to care about the final or even temporary

disposition of the body, for as Martin Bucer puts it, for Calvin "bones are bones, and not God" (Eire 1986: 91).

Even though one might see the seeds of the Calvinist view of the body in the emphasis placed on resurrection by scholastic thought, it is of course well known that the very same contemplation of the limits and status of the body had another reading. The body's materiality, conceived as an unpolluted physical entity, guaranteed by God himself, remained a central tenet of Christianity. This antagonistic but productive divergence on the limits and status of the Christian body would play a pivotal role in the theological and political struggle between Protestants and Catholics. To my mind it explains why Protestant and Catholic intellectuals and institutions regarded Columbus's and Cortés's reports on "cannibalism" with a very different gaze. The Spanish counterreformation simply continued the Spanish policy of extermination of practices and peoples accused of anthropophagy, while Protestant observers like Léry subjected their "observations" to intense meditation and even a smattering of what later would evolve into ethnography. The "science" of ethnography, a Western discursive complex for looking at its other, has made of the "cannibal complex" one of the centerpieces for its own meditation on the human organization of thought and society and most specially for the development of its disquisition on self-identity. The relationship between "cannibalism" as a place for thinking the "drama of identity" and its ramifications into the constitution of the modern subject has been recently brought into full light by Daniel Cottom in *Cannibals and Philosophers: Bodies of Enlightenment* (Cottom 2001).[23]

Calvin's God, Calvin's Body

The Iconoclastic Movement that sought to end the Catholic cult of images and dead ancestors (the saints and their sacralized bodies) held that the Eucharist should be divorced from the material presence of Christ. In general, Protestant belief sought a separation of the material from the spiritual in the worship of Christ. Catholic beliefs therefore seemed idolatrous because they mixed the two. In 1536 Calvin published his *Institutes* in which the relationship of God to man was redefined.[24] For Calvin the purpose of creation was for man to know God through proper worship. God alone could be glorious—not the Virgin, not the saints. Since finite, man could not contain the infinite God. One now had to conclude, contrary to previous doctrine of the Eucharist, that God was entirely Other. Calvin's God transcended all materiality. He was as different from flesh as fire is from water. Therefore, God's reality turned inaccessible (Eire 1986: 183). Nothing on earth and nothing human could ever metonymically or metaphorically re-present God. God's spirituality did not need any flesh from which to fashion or refashion the human form and likewise there could never be any image or carnal conception of him.

Calvin explains the widespread existence of idolatrous practices by resorting to an evolutionary anthropology. For him the worship of material symbols was part of a cognitive fallen state. Beginning with the adoration of celestial bodies, cultures such as the Israelites passed then from the veneration of idols to divinized mortals, arriving at a pantheon of divinities such as the Catholic Church had done with the saints. In his *Inventory of Relics* (1543) Calvin traced the first fall of Christian worship to the error of having sought Christ in his vestments and other material manifestations rather than having concentrated on the Word. Thus Calvin concluded that materiality in worship represents pollution. Idolatry, like all impure worship, not only displeases God but strengthens Satan (Eire 1986: 213). Calvin thus insisted on a fundamental division between the material and the spiritual: one simply cannot approach the spiritual through the material (Eire 1986: 216). Calvin displaced Catholic cultural reason and worship, recasting it as the product of polluted or false knowledge. In the space emptied out, he instituted a new metaphysics by which the body in its corporeality is not of a piece with the transcendental subject.

In his *Treatise on the Lord's Supper* (1541) Calvin addressed specifically the material/spiritual distinction of his theology with respect to food and the constitution of the Christian body (143–49).[25] God keeps our bodies and feeds us, but the life that has regenerated us, by virtue of Christ's death, is spiritual. Thus "the food for preserving and confirming us in it must be spiritual" (Calvin 1954: 143). Founding his reason on a firm division between body and soul, Calvin stated with respect to the Eucharist: "What is required is not to feed our bodies with corruptible and transitory provisions, but to nourish our souls on a better and more precious diet" (143). The spiritual diet of the world is to be Jesus Christ, or at least his Word, which God has attached as a visible sign to the sacrament of the Last Supper. Therefore for Calvin the mystery of the sacrament of the Eucharist is resolved in metaphorical terms. What to Catholics is a material and literal reality is to Calvin a metaphor, a narrative trope necessary to make visible to humans the indecipherable "language" and knowledge of the Divinity.

To the much-contested question of "How are Christ's words to be understood?" Calvin answers that "two things are present in the Last Supper: Jesus Christ is present as source and sustenance of all good and the fruit and efficacy of his death and Passion" (Calvin 1954: 146). He goes on to clarify that "the bread and the wine are visible signs, which represent to us the body and the blood," but that the name and title of body and blood is attributed to them, because they "are instruments by which our Lord Jesus Christ distributes them to us" (147). Furthermore, in his effort to displace the mass with the sacrament of the Eucharist as its pivotal ritual, Calvin asserts the temporal nature of the Last Supper. Only Jesus Christ could offer such a (self) sacrifice. The very idea of Other's sacrifice is a contradiction. Therefore Jesus Christ's sacrifice cannot ever be repeated, which in turn means that the possibility of transubstantiation is mute. Christ's body never descended from heaven into the host "for if there is any eating which is not spiritual, it will follow that in the mystery of the Supper there is no operation of the Spirit" (Calvin 1954: 279).

Such is the doctrine that inspired Jean de Léry with immense passion to board a ship and sail for the coast of Brazil, the land of the mythological cannibals as already "reported" by Americo Vespucci and Hans Staden.[26] From Columbus to Levi-Strauss and even to modern Brazilian anthropologists, no one ever ventured into the Americas without well-developed expectations of the anthropophagy to be found in the interminable woods and clear brooks of the Amazon basin. To this day, the Western search for scenes of cannibalism among beloved or feared "primitives" has not ended.

Atheology of the Other

In his chapter "What we might call religion" (XVI), Léry both denounces and falls victim to the powerful song of the Tupinamba shaman. The Calvinist unhesitatingly connects the person and the work of the *caraïbes* with what he believes to be the torments of the Tupi soul or spirit, if such names can be brought to bear on Tupi subjectivity. Léry understands the Tupi torment to be caused by their fear of "evil spirits" (Léry 1990: 136). Presenting himself as having gained the trust and confidence of the "savages," Léry reports that with the sweat of anguish beading on their foreheads (a scene reminiscent of Dante's hell) they speak to each other and to him on the nature of their fear. Léry calls these utterances a lament and quotes an unknown Tupi text: "Mair Atouasap, ace-queiey Aygman Atoupave." In Léry's translation the Tupi tell him: "Frenchman, my friend, my perfect ally, I fear the devil" (1990: 136). In a more recent and accurate translation provided by Viveiros de Castro, the sentence reads: "Maneating celestial, my enemy and perfect ally, I fear the evil spirits that devour our cadavers."[27]

With a stroke of the pen Léry misappropriates a whole way of thinking and living. The Aygman, the necrophagic deity, has been translated and translocated into one of the few terms available to Christian eschatology, where the Aygman occupies the place of the devil.[28] Léry's own introduction to Tupi religion was, of course, by "way of the devil," for that is how Christianity formulated the discourse of the shaman, whose knowledge Léry reports and organizes in his treatise. Turning the other's knowledge into the intellectual work of the devil conforms to the general othering operations of Christianity. However, in light of what Léry is to fabulate as the cannibal complex, it turns out that fear of the devil as the foundation of idolatry or false religion fits squarely with Calvin's own evolutionary explanation of a materialist-based idolatry. One must then conclude that Léry's rendition of Tupi fears and anthropophagic practices are indeed none other than an elaboration, *elsewhere,* of Calvin's own explanation for the Catholic complex of Eucharistic practices and beliefs. When it comes to cannibalism we are indeed before the work of a parallax, that process in which the object under observation—the Eucharist—changes position due to a change in the position of the observer—the Calvinist minister in Guanabara.

Léry is greatly intrigued by what he believes is the Tupi conception of "the devil" and their seeming disregard for "the soul." This he takes to mean that the Tupi have failed to have thought about "God," that pure Spirit posited by Calvin. Instead, the portrayal of Tupi cosmology speaks of a straightforward materialism. Léry's fascination increases with every new "discovery" that he makes about Tupi discursivity. He cannot pass up any opportunity to learn more about the Aygman nor about the songs to the ancestors. When he hears reports that the great congregation of caribe is about to take place, he begs the elders into letting him watch the ritual congregation from inside one of the great houses where the women gather to listen to the songs of the shaman and the avatars of the ancestors. Keenly aware of his linguistic limitations, he takes with him one of the Norman sailors who in view of their longer stay with the Tupi offered themselves as interpreters. Léry listens to the shaman's rising songs. Like his hosts, he is soon carried away by the music and singing in a state of ecstasy: "We heard them once again singing and making their voices sound in harmony so marvelous . . . that I wished to watch them from nearby" (141). Against the shaman's prohibition Léry comes out in the clearing and is astonished to see five to six hundred men dancing to the sound of marakas and their own wonderfully pitched voices. He stands there "transformed with delight" (144). He remarks that "although they do not know music . . . their singing transports" him (144).

But Léry's joy is incomplete, for he does not understand the text of the songs of the shaman and his Norman interpreters are of no use. For purposes of authorization of this writing Léry quickly recovers from admission of his linguistic impediment—"since I did not understand their language perfectly at the time" (144)—and moves on to state that in the end the interpreters explained that these songs were a lament for the dead ancestors (144). According to Léry, despite Tupi atheism they nevertheless expressed a measure of comfort in the belief that after their death they would meet their ancestors behind the high mountain (144).

If the Tupi have no concept of the soul or something like it, and if they are given to ritual cannibalism with its total destruction of the body, how can it be explained that they expect, after death, to join their ancestors? What part or in what form is the human entity recoverable after death? What is the status of the body/person in Tupi society and cosmology? What indeed are the limits of the body in Tupi thought? To what extent is their cosmology an ideological formation that corresponds to the organization of their social world, as Protestantism seems to be the expression of a theology in harmony with a political theory of the individual? Should one indeed ask such questions of the Tupi world order? How commensurable or incommensurable were Léry's cultural coordinates with those of the Tupinamba? To some extent and in a different language, Léry's account of Tupi culture attempted to ask and respond to these questions as displaced onto the Tupi by the Calvinist voyage to Brazil. As he constructed the Tupi he enacted many of Europe's own preoccupations on the status of the body. And so it seems fair to say that his construction of Tupi "cannibalism" and the legacy such construction makes to the modern "sciences" of the "other" are indeed the result of a parallax. In order to better appreciate the distance between the Eucharist and the Tupi sense of the person and the "limits" of the human body, I will make a brief reference to Araweté cosmology.

The Araweté are a Tupi society. Up until the last quarter of this century they had managed to avoid contact with the West by means of a constant retreat into the forest. In weighing the truth claims made by Léry, we must pay serious attention to his linguistic impediment. It is only lightly and insufficiently compensated by what he "saw," for seeing is also subject to systems of coding and decoding. We must also keep in mind that the veracity of many an eyewitness report of "cannibalism" in "other" cultures has turned out to be more than questionable.[29] The force and authority of his much-praised ethnographic account on the Tupinamba is predicated on the assumption that what he saw is informed by an irrefutable facticity free of interpretation, a cognitive act that we know is an impossibility. Léry's sustained rhetoric of disinterested observation, as distinct from the rage of the conqueror writing in heat of battle or the bias of the colonizer always justifying his rapacity—his "uncritical" and even admiring or sympathetic tone—bolsters subtly but unflinchingly a key differential and hierarchical fact: he was there and the reader was not. While Lope de Gómora's accounts of life in Mexico and Peru could always be deauthorized by the fact that his accounts were secondhand, Léry's description and interpretations of cannibalism among the Tupi could not be subject to the same doubts because his claims are based on seeing and talking with Tupi "allies." Léry did indeed read Lope de Gómora and he was impressed by his accounts of Aztec and Andean religions. Léry compares the Andean treatment of the deceased body, with its careful preservation and unsurpassed embalming technology, to the Tupi's notion of dissolution in the belly of the other (138). Comparisons of this type strengthen Léry's authority. This is not a report on the fierce enemy. This is an "other" friendly adventure story of survival. Nevertheless, we need to ask ourselves, what kind of access could Léry really have had to Tupi discursiveness, to the cognitive and epistemological structures that bounded their living culture?

Eduardo Viveiros de Castro studied the general Tupi language for several years, then lived for a year with the Araweté. He explains that living with the "affable savages" was easy, but doing anthropology was not. The difficulty arose from the anthropologist's insufficient linguistic ability. Despite his studies Viveiros de Castro found the lack of continuous exposure to Awareté insurmountable. He was overwhelmed not only with the complexity of the discursive system—myth, poetry, cosmology, anecdote—but also with the immensity of the corpus. Moreover the Awareté did not have a time of the day when they recounted myth or the deeds of the ancestors. They did not wait for the great congregation of Caraïbe to occur. Precious stories and episodes of sagas could be recited at any moment. The anthropologist was almost always unprepared to catch his treasure. Even hearing the Awareté was daunting for "its prosody follows a rapid rhythm with a predominance of nasal vocalic and weak articulation" (Viveiros de Castro 1992: 8). Of course this is not to say that the Tupi of the bay of Guanabara spoke the exact same language of the Awareté. That is not the point. What is important is that Léry was there only two short months and that even an anthropologist like Charles Wagley, a man who has worked for a lifetime with the Tapirape, another Tupi group, states that he has always felt that there was a "linguistic haze" separating him from the objects of his search (in Viveiros de Castro 1992: 8).

Such reservations expressed by modern anthropologists who have spent considerable time in Brazil studying the Tupi, the Guarani, and the Gê cast doubt not only on Léry's recollection of any Tupi texts but also on the translations of the Norman mercenaries, Hans Staden's account of his captivity, and on Bishop Thêvet's influential account as well. Viveiros de Castro plainly states that he was "unable to understand the shaman's songs without the help of glosses." For this reason his interpretation of the songs of the Gods and of warfare—central aspects of Araweté culture—is somewhat superficial: "Likewise I was unable to obtain more than fragmentary versions of the corpus of the myths. Araweté mythology operates as a kind of implicit assemblage that serves as an underlying context for the daily proliferation of shamanic songs" (8). As if these obstacles to obtaining a reliable text were not enough, Vivieros concurs with Léry in remarking on the love that the Tupi and Araweté have for irony and all manner of language games. They especially cultivate the sardonic remark for the foreigner who just does not get it. In view of the conditions of ethnographic impossibility imbedded but never before weighed and discussed in Léry's account of Tupi thinking on the limits of the body, or anthropophagy, human or divine, let me now turn to the textualization of the body that Viverios de Castro is able to bring forth in the case of the Awareté as carrier of Tupi culture.

The Awareté say that once the soul of the dead has arrived in the heavens they are devoured by the Maï, or immortals, who then bring together the bones and the skin. After soaking the cadaver in a rejuvenating bath, they resuscitate the body of the deceased who then goes on to join the ranks of the immortals. Death appears as the most transformative event in the life-death cycle of the Araweté. It encapsulates the idea of the person, for one lives to die. Death is the only productive event for the person in as much as human destiny is a process of "Other-becoming" (Viveiros de Castro 1992: 1). Nothing could be further from the Western idea of self-identity. The constant "other becoming" of the Araweté is a flux in which death and life are inseparable: one is the other.

Unlike the Guarani and the Gê, the Araweté do not seem to be enormously preoccupied with making their thought visible in social structures. The reality of their world is highly discursive: "All is word" (2). The Araweté cultivate a passion for speech and song. A great deal of this discursive joy is dedicated to cosmological thinking. Ritual tends to be schematic. Compared to the preponderance of discourse over social institutions, ritual occupies a very small place indeed. There is then very little to observe. And one wonders to what extent any of the episodes that compose the cannibal complex could have actually been seen.

Viveiros de Castro observes that Araweté society presents itself as smooth, unified, and homogeneous in all its parts. However, further probing shows that the lack of internal differentiation is actually but the manifestation of radical difference, of an impulse toward the outside of the self, of a passion for exteriority. Therefore, despite the apparent calmness of the "affable savages," what rages is the torrent of an ever-becoming, the torment of a beckoning outside. Identity is not the product of internal division in preparation of a synthesis that creates a stable and recognizable interiority. Identity is not within but elsewhere. The other is not the mirror of self and of man, rather it is destiny, it is a pull to dispersion (3–4). According to Viveiros de Castro, the Tupi-guarani construct the person through a process of continuous topological deformation in which Ego and Enemy, Living and Dead, Man and God are not opposites but instead are continuously interwoven before and beyond representation (4).

It is thus not far fetched to say that the Tupi universe inverts the Man/God Christian opposition. For the Tupi, becoming is prior to being and that is why death is the only productive event in the cosmos. It is the place where the person, by taking the position of the enemy, the Maï, is actualized. In the "Tupi world the difference between the living and the dead cannot be conceived as an opposition either real or formal" (4). What Tupi thought seeks is a double affirmation: life and death, the self and the other. It cannot conceive of the dialectic of opposition that organizes Christian thought and, therefore, man eating is the duty of the Maï, the enemy, who in devouring the body of the deceased pave the way for man to find his place as an immortal.

In view of the above, the term "cannibal" as derived from the name of the Caribs should now be understood as an unstable construct, a historical representation at the heart of a conquest by a eucharistic religion. To speak of the trope in question we should go back to the more abstract "anthropophagy," which with its Greek roots sounds more scientific and less historically specific. Such rupture is necessary in order for us not to continue the legacy of the voyage to Brazil.

Notes

1. For the inextricable relation between the discovery and invention of the "New World" and the construction of the modern European idea of self as well as a self-centered world history, see O'Gorman 1997 and Rabasa 1993. For the uses of symbolic technology deployed by Europe in the representations of the New World and the self fashioning that thinking the discursive regimes of

human sacrifice, incest, and anthropophagies as "others'" practices made possible, see Greenblatt 1991. For a radical shift in our understanding of the emergence of modernity and its specific and determining relation to Europe's conquest of and struggle with Amerindian societies and discursive territories, see Mignolo 1995. For a more detailed argument on the twin appearance of modernity/coloniality and the emergence of the modern world system in the cradle of the coloniality of power, see Quijano. For a mind-bending discussion of the inescapable paring of modernity and coloniality and its special debt in the formation of the modern system to Latin America's coloniality as its ground and horizon, see Mignolo 2000.

2. For a detailed and deeply thoughtful account of the discursive event that the appearance of Amerindian civilizations occasioned in Europe's intellectual world and its continued repercussion in both Europe's and Spanish America's cultural coordinates, see Brading 1991. For the twists and turns that the construction of the Amerindian peoples and civilizations took throughout Europe's several periods of expansion and conquest of its "others" as nonhuman, noble savages, fierce cannibals, royal subjects, primitives, and objects of ethnology, see Pagden.

3. See the account of the great debate in Brading 1991: 79–104.

4. For discussions based on the critical examination of wide-ranging sources, circumstances, and arguments and the links between the ideology of conquest and charges of anthropophagy, see both Arens 1979 and Hulme 1986. For a detailed account of how charges and descriptions of cannibalism functioned in the very specific instance in the Spanish evangelization and subjugation of the Pijao in modern-day Colombia, see Bolaños 1994.

5. Although I originally read Léry's work in Portuguese, *História de uma viagem feita à terra do Brasil* translated by Monteiro Lobato and published in 1926, the text I use in this study of Léry is the recent excellent translation into English by Janet Whatley (Léry 1990).

6. The concerns found in the work of Lestringant 1994 focus on the colonizing differences between French Catholics and Protestants. While these differences are important they do not bear on the arguments that I intend to develop here.

7. Mauss in 1934 studies the manner in which each society elaborates and imposes on its members particular views, uses, and styles of the body. How the social is projected into the deepest layers of individual self-consciousness leads Mauss to think that little in fact escapes the grid of social coding of the body and its outer limits. In view of this argument, a discussion on the limits of the body under the shadow of both the doctrine of resurrection and the Eucharist is almost an imperative necessity every time we consider Euro-American discourses on "cannibalism."

8. Upon discovery of the mummified bodies of the Incas, the Spanish became aware of the profound implications that the preservation of the cadaver

held for Andean thinking on after-death. The Inca Atahualpa converted to Christianity so that he would not suffer death by beheading, for the preservation of the intact body was paramount for his afterlife. In fact, the myth on Inca-rri, which began with his death and is still alive today in the Andes, holds that Atahualpa's severed head and body, buried by the Spanish, remain in the underground and are growing toward one another. When the unity of the Inca's body is restored, it is believed, the Andean world will rise again and the effects of the conquest will be reversed. Such strong beliefs on the necessary unity of the body were not lost on Viceroy Toledo, who understood the terror implicit in the idea of beheading. See Millones 1990: 331–425.

9. For a detailed discussion of Léry's experiences after his return to France and the avatars of his texts, see Whatley's introduction to *History of a Voyage to the Land of Brazil* (Léry 1990: xv–xxxviii).

10. See Duchet 1987. For a facsimile with color plates see de Bry 1992.

11. Florestán Fernández, the Brazilian anthropologist until recently considered the chief authority on both the historical and present-day Tupi, relies for his data on the texts authored by Hans Stade, Thévet, Léry, and the Franciscan and Jesuit missionaries who took on the evangelization of the Tupi. Fernández, like Levi-Strauss later holds onto the idea that the Tupi practice(ed) cannibalism as a function of warfare, competition, and exchange of economic, social, and psychic energies (Fernández 1949). Maybury-Lewis offers a more nuanced view of cannibalistic practices among the Gê and the Bororo. But in the case of the mostly extinct Tupinamba he cedes ground to the "serenity" of Léry's tone, to his detailed descriptions and thus he leans toward the idea that "[they] did practice ritual cannibalism." See Maybury-Lewis 1992: 19. Lizot reports in an obscure narrative his witnessing of a single individual act of cannibalism among the people with whom he cohabited for several years (Lizot 1985).

12. For the fear of the mother and the erotic phantasms of eating the flesh of the man-husband-father implicit in Léry's cannibalism, see my previous essay "What Does Cannibalism Speak? Jean de Léry and the Tupinamba Lesson" (Castro-Klarén 1992b). There I also argue that the Tupi cannibalistic scene has more in common with the Greek myths on the Bacchea that with any possible alimentary, ritual, or mortuary cannibalism attributed to the Tupi.

13. The most recent report of alimentary cannibalism appears to be the latter-day confessions of Tobias Scheebaum, who claims to have gone native with the Arakmbut in the Madre de Dios territory. While with "them" he regaled himself with sex and open friendships, and one day "they" took him hunting. To his amazement "they" hunted a man, and "they" invited him to savor the feast, which he did. See Zalewski 2001.

14. The washing in hot water, dismemberment, and classification of the gastronomy of the body parts described by Staden and Léry and illustrated by de Bry correspond closely to French techniques of butchering pigs and sheep and the organization of organs, muscle, and bone for cooking. See Boucher 1992.

15. I owe much of the source material to Bynum's careful and generous rendition of the immense material offered in her work. Without her research it would not have been possible to trace the many twists and turns of this singular obsession in European culture (Bynum 1995).

16. For the influential views on idolatry of Heinrich Bullinger, the successor of Zwingli at Zurich, see Eire 1986: 87–95. Eire points out that Bullinger, in *On the Origin of Errors* (1528), traces the history of "image worship among the Jews and the early Christians. He asserts that Christian image worship developed when the bodies of the saints and martyrs began to be revered and places the blame on monastic piety with its emphasis on physical holiness" (87–88).

17. Bynum states that Augustine's concerns with the wholeness of the body become paramount in his later writings. In *The City of God* his concern for the bits of the body appears entwined with his thinking on the dispersal of the bodies of the martyrs and their veneration as relics. The martyrs' parts were being spread throughout the Roman world. The division, selling, and dispersal of the martyrs' bodies intensified during the fourth century. The anxiety of wholeness and resurrection increased concomitantly (Bynum 1995). For further discussion, see Geary 1978.

18. The High Medieval period expresses a fear of mastication. Hell's iconography generally depicts a gigantic mouth that swallows and grinds the bodies of the dammed (Bynum 1995: 307). No wonder Léry thinks that eating the body of the Tupi prisoner is a cruelty beyond punishment. The Christian, Dantesque hell is associated not only with mutilation, cooking, and mastication by the devil and his cohorts but also with nudity, all aspects to be associated with the narrative of cannibalism in the New World. Practices of body partition remain strong and controversial by the year 1300. Bynum notes an "increased enthusiasm for boiling and dividing the holy bodies" so as to ready the relics for quick distribution (1995: 322). Thomas Aquinas's body was boiled sometime between 1303–1304. A Cistercian monk decapitated the corpse in order to retain some of the (holy) remains (Bynum 1995: 323). In the late thirteenth century, in various places in the Northern Alps, royalty and aristocrats had their bodies eviscerated and boiled. Different body parts were buried in different localities (Bynum 1995: 323). Boniface VIII issued a bill in 1299 forbiding this practice. At the same time, it is interesting to observe, dismemberment was reserved as the most severe punishment for the criminal. What is more, some of the bodies of many believed to have died in odor of sanctity were torn apart in order to look for signs of sanctity, stigmata, or incorruptibility in the viscera (Bynum 1995: 323). There is no question that a deep and everlasting anxiety about the body drives a myriad of paradoxical approaches and interests, from the compulsion to see the inside of the body, through the meditation on feeding and digestion, to the preoccupation with partition, dispersal, and ultimate disappearance. These labyrinthine discourses and practices find their way into the trope of anthropophagy elevated to an outside location for thinking after contact with the (nude) Carib and Tupi.

19. In "The Forbidden Food: Francisco de Vitoria and José de Acosta on Cannibalism," Pagden reconnoiters the reasoning that lead both Spanish intellectuals to their fierce condemnation of cannibalism and thus of the American Indian cultures. Pagden notes in the opening of this essay, however, that "Fascination with man eating has a long history. Cannibals—or "anthropophagi," as they were known before the discovery of America—had been a feature of the European imagination since the earliest recorded encounter between men of widely different cultures" (1994: 17). Pagden does not however delve into the question of maneating practices, body dismemberment or boiling holy and or noble bodies in the European milieu in which both Acosta and Vitoria write. Reference and consideration of such practices and discussion has been vacated by both Spanish intellectuals and is not put back into the picture by Pagden, whose essay then reads as is if "cannibalism" at the time were a strictly "American" phenomenon. In "Canibalismo e Contagio: Sull'importancia dell'antropofagia nell'europa pre-industrialle," Pagden discusses the importance of the idea of cannibalism for Christian doctrine: "poneva in questione quale ruolo spettasse all'uomo de la scala naturalle, quali i suoi obblighi di rito, e il delicato argomento dell'elemento fisico dei morte" (541). Here Pagden notes the eating of the enemy during the period of the religious wars but he does not explore the links and the effects that such imbrications can have on eucharist anxiety (544). He concludes that "Nel periodo pre-illuministico, in Europa, l'attitude tenuta nei confronti del cannibalismo era del tutto ambigua" (546). For both essays, see Pagden 1994. For the question of eucharist anxiety in the conquest of Mexico and the reports by Cortés and Bernal Diaz del Castillo, see Greenblatt 1991: 128–39.

20. The Affair of the Placards (October 17–18, 1534) plastered broad sheets condemning the idolatry of the Mass. Religious rebels were called on to bring an end to the worship of martyrs. In Calvin's theology the dead ancestors— saints and even the Virgin—should not be prayed to for they could not intervene before God. The Church had corrupted early Christian burial practices and hopes for resurrection with pagan beliefs. See Eire 1986: 185–97. In *Inventory of Relics* (1543) Calvin denounces relics as fraudulent. The worship of relics is against reason. It is a foolish desire. There is but one reality to be perceived and that is God, pure spirituality. Spirituality cannot be pursued through the materiality of relic worship nor the materiality of the eucharist.

21. For charges of maneating among the pagans, especially during Tertullian's times, see Rouselle 1988: 118–19. During medieval times Jews were suspected of drinking human blood from kidnapped Christians. See Arens 1979: 18–21. Arens writes that the accusations that Jews were cannibals were numerous, persistent, and widespread. He points out that today accusations such as this are "banished from our consciousness . . . they are interpreted as regrettable temporary lapses into prejudice" (19). The same critical position is of course not available when it comes to "reports" of cannibalism among contemporaries of ancient Mexican, Polynesian, or Chaco peoples. See the reproduction of the

fifteenth-century German print depicting the ritual murder of Simon of Trent by Jews for his blood, 20.

22. In the case of those who have been dissolved, those who have been devoured by wild beasts and have therefore been dispersed after digestion and excretion, they too will arise according to God's power and knowledge.

23. Cottom writes that "In the seventeenth and eighteenth centuries human flesh became a new thing, a flesh of sensibility, a surface of stimuli whence all knowing proceeds and against which it must be measured" (Cottom 2001:1). Corporal knowledge was privileged. Cottom contends that to "recognize the unsettling visceral turn within this knowledge, we must attend to bodies not only in their most abstract formulations but also in the popularly reiterated images or tropes that traversed" the period (3). Cannibalism, its metamorphic force, Cottom shows, turns out to be the most powerful trope for the Enlightenment philosophers whose attention turned, as with the Church fathers, toward the interior of things. The "occult" qualities of the body fascinated, paradoxically, the observers of the sensible world of exterior planes and surfaces. Natural philosophy "returned to an emphasis on metamorphosis" (21–25) and the question of anthropophagic ingestion. As if walking over the same path traced in my discussion on the thinking of the limits of the body in Christianity before and after Calvin, in Cottom's account for the seventeenth and eighteenth century we also find that "Bodies in their singularity posed the question of metamorphosis especially through the internal process of digestion and in their plurality especially through the external process of incorporating relations to other lands, behaviors, and beliefs. The inside and the outside of the human body might then become as one in the image of the cannibal, the figure in which metamorphosis can find no beginning or end in nature, culture or spirit" (22).

24. See Calvin 1960.

25. Calvin 1954.

26. See Staden 1919. Hans Staden's story of his captivity among the Tupinamba established the narrative of Tupi maneating. As Arens points out, it is interesting to note that the hero of this adventure story was not eaten. The text is illustrated with woodcuts in which the German sailor appears naked, like his captors, but properly ashamed of his nudity. The link between cannibalism, nudity, and boundless erotic female desire appears already in Columbus texts, but finds perhaps its most delighted report in Americo Vespucci. See Formisano. For Vespucci's and Léry's fascination with the beauty of the naked Tupi women, see Castro-Klarén 1999b: 31–39.

27. See Viveiros de Castro 1992. For the Araweté, once the souls of the dead arrive in the heavens, they are devoured by the Maï, the gods, who proceed to resuscitate them from the bones. Then they join the corpus of immortals. Death is thus a productive event for the Araweté, for death is the place "where the person is actualized" (4) and it is death that articulates the sense of the person in Araweté cosmology.

28. For the deployment of the devil into the discourse and practices of Spanish conquest, see Cervantes. Diabolism had a devastating effect on Indian cultures and bodies.

29. Here I refer the reader back to Arens 1979 and the recent summary article, Osborne 1997.

References

Arens. W. (1979). *The Man-Eating Myth: Anthropology and Anthropophagy.* Oxford: Oxford University Press.

Brown, Peter (1981). *The Cult of the Saints: Its Rise and Function in Latin Christianity.* Chicago: University of Chicago Press.

Bucher, Bernadette (1981). *Icon and Conquest. A Structural Analysis of the Illustrations of de Bry's "Great Voyages,"* trans. Basia Miller Gulati. Chicago: University of Chicago Press.

Bolaños, Alvaro Felix (1994). *Barbarie y canibalismo en la retórica colonial: Los Indios Pijaos de Fray Pedro Simón.* Bogotá: Cerec.

Boucher, Philip (1992). *Cannibal Encounters: Europeans and Island Caribs, 1492–1763.* Baltimore: Johns Hopkins University Press.

Brading, David. A. (1991). *The First America: The Spanish Monarchy, Creole Patriots and the Liberal State, 1492–1867.* Cambridge: Cambridge University Press.

Bry, Theodore de (1992). *America (1590–1634),* ed. Gereon Sievernich, trans. Adán Kovacsis. Madrid: Siruela.

Bynum, Caroline Walker (1995). *The Resurrection of the Body in Western Christianity, 200–1360.* New York: Columbia University Press.

Calvin, Jean (1954). *The Theological Treatises,* trans. J. K. S. Reid. Philadelphia: Westminster.

——— (1960). *Institutes of the Christian Religion,* ed. John T. McNeil. Trans. Ford Lewis Battles. 2 vols. Philadelphia: Westminster.

Castro-Klarén, Sara (1992a). "Viaje y desplazamiento del sujeto: Colón y Léry en los trópicos." In *Crítica y descolonizacion: El sujeto colonial en la cultural latinoamericana,* ed. Beatriz González Stephan and Lúcia Helena Costigan. Caracas: Academia Nacional de la Historia. 49–66.

——— (1992b). "What does Cannibalism Speak?" In *Carnal Knowledge: Essays on the Flesh, Sex, and Sexuality in Hispanic Letters and Film,* ed. Pamela Barcarisse. Pittsburgh: Tres Rios. 23–42.

——— (1999). "Mimesis en los trópicos: El cuerpo en Vespucci y Léry." In *Literatura de viajes. El mundo viejo y el nuevo,* ed. Salvador García and Maureen Ahern. Madrid: Castalia.

——— (2000). "A Genealogy for the 'Manifesto Antropófago': Or the Struggle between Socrates and the Caraïbe." *Nepantla* 2 (4): 295–322.

Colon, Cristobal (1986). *Viajes de Colon,* ed. Martín Fernández de Navarrete. México: Porrúa.

Cottom, Daniel (2001). *Cannibals and Philosophers: Bodies of Enlightenment.* Baltimore: Johns Hopkins University Press.

Duchet, Michèle et al. (1987). *L'amérique de Théodore de Bry. Une collection de voyages protestante de XVI siècle. Quatre études d'iconography.* Paris: Centre National de Recherches Scientifique.

Eire, Carlos M. N. (1986). *War against the Idols: The Reformation of Worship from Erasmus to Calvin.* Cambridge: Cambridge University Press.

Fernández, Florestán (1949). *Organização Social dos Tupinambá.* São Paulo.

Formisano, Luciano, ed. (1992). *Letters from the New World: Amerigo Vespucci's Discovery of America,* trans. David Jacobson. New York: Marsilio.

Geary, Patrick J. (1978). *Furta Sacra: Theft of Relics in the Central Middle Ages.* Princeton: Princeton University Press.

Greenblatt, Stephen (1991). *Marvellous Possessions: The Wonder of the New World.* Chicago: University of Chicago Press.

Hulme, Peter (1986). *Colonial Encounters: Europe and the Native Caribbean, 1492– 1797.* London: Routledge.

Huxley, Francis (1957). *Affable Savages.* New York: Viking.

Léry, Jean de (1980a). *Histoire d'un voyage fait en la terre du Brésil.* Introduction de Sophie Delpech. Paris: Plasma.

——— (1990). *History of a Voyage to the Land of Brazil, Otherwise Called America,* trans. Janet Whatley. Berkeley: University of California Press.

——— (1880b). *Historia de uma viagem feita à terra do Brasil,* trad. Tristão de Alencar Aripe. Rio de Janeiro.

——— (1926). *Historia de uma viagen feita à terra do Brasil,* trad. Monteiro Lobato. Rio de Janeiro.

Lestringant, Frank (1994). *Le Cannibale: Grandeur et décadence.* Paris: Perrin.

——— (1980). "Calvinistes et cannibals: Les écrits protestants sur le Brésil fraçais (1555–1560)." *Bulletin de la Societé de l'histoire du protestantisme frabçais.* 1– 2 (9–26): 167–192.

Levi-Strauss, Claude (1963). *Tristes Tropiques: An Anthropological Study of Primitive Societies in Brazil,* trans. John Russell. New York: Atheneum.

Lizot, Jacques (1985). *Tales of the Yanomami. Daily Life in the Venezuelan Forest,* trans. E. Simon. Cambridge: Cambridge University Press.

López de Gómora, Francisco (1552). *Historia General de las Indias Occidentales.* Saragosa.

Mauss, Marcel (1992). "Techniques of the Body." In *Incorporations,* ed. Jonathan Grary and Sanford Kwinter. New York: Zone, 454–77.

Maybury-Lewis, David (1992). *Millennium: Tribal Wisdom and the Modern World.* New York: Viking.

Mignolo, Walter D. (1995). *The Darker Side of the Renaissance: Literacy, Territoriality and Colonization.* Ann Arbor: University of Michigan Press.

———— (2000). *Local Histories/Global Designs: Coloniality, Subaltern Knowledges and Border Thinking.* Princeton: Princeton University Press.

Millones, Luis (1990). *El retorno de las huacas. Estudios y documentos del siglo XVI.* Lima: Estudios Peruanos.

O'Gorman, Edmundo (1997). *La invención de América: Investigación acerca de la estructura histórica del Nuevo Mundo y del sentido de su porvenir,* 2d ed. Mexico City: Fondo de Cultura Económica.

Ortiz Rescaniere, Alejandro (1993). *La pareja y el mito: Estudios sobre las concepciones de la persona y de la pareja en los Andes.* Lima: Pontificia Universidad Católica.

Osborne, Lawrence (1997). "Does Man Eat Man? Inside the Great Cannibalism Controversy." *Lingua Franca,* 7 (4): 28–38.

Pagden, Anthony (1982). *The Fall of Natural Man: The American Indian and the Origins of Comparative Ethnology.* Cambridge: Cambridge University Press.

———— (1994). *The Uncertainties of Empire: Essays in Iberian and Ibero-American Intellectual History.* Brookfield, Ver.: Variorum.

Quijano, Aníbal (1998). "The Colonial Nature of Power and Latin America's Cultural Experience." In *Sociology in Latin America,* ed. R. Briceño et al. *Procedings of the Regional Conference of the International Association of Sociology.* Venezuela, 27–38.

Rabasa, José (1993). *Inventing America: Spanish Historiography and the Formation of Eurocentrism.* Norman: University of Oklahoma Press.

Rouselle, Aline (1988). *Porneia: On Desire and the Body in Antiquity,* trans. Felicia Pheasant. Oxford: Blackwell.

Staden, Hans (1874). *The Captivity of Hans Stade of Hesse in* A.D. *1547–1555: Among the Wild Tribes of Eastern Brazil,* trans. Albert Tootal, annotated Richard F. Burton. New York: Burt Franklin.

Thevet, André (1568). *The New Found World, or Antarctike.* London: Thomas Hackett.

———— (1941). *Viagem à terra do Brasil,* tradução integral e notas de Sérgio Milliet. São Paulo: Livraria Martins.

Viveiros de Castro, Eduardo (1992). *From the Enemy's Point of View: Humanity and Divinity in an Amazonian Society,* trans. Catherine V. Howard. Chicago: University of Chicago Press.

Zalewski, Daniel (2001). "Once, in the Jungle." *New York Times Magazine* (March 25): 54–57.

PART IV

DIS-ABLING ALLIANCES

7

Making Freaks
Visual Rhetorics and the Spectacle of Julia Pastrana

Rosemarie Garland-Thomson

On December 1, 1854, a Mexican Indian woman named Julia Pastrana was exhibited in New York's Gothic Hall on Broadway. A broadside advertisement for her exhibition described her as a "Marvelous Hybrid or Bear Woman." The theater chronicler, George C. D. O'Dell, who saw her exhibition, called her "somewhat between an human being and an ourang-outang." Although we now imagine such displays as repugnant, O'Dell found her to be a "delight" (O'Dell 1970: 413). Over the many years Pastrana's body was displayed before audiences, she was advertized variously as a "Nondescript," "Misnomer," "Bear Woman," "Baboon Lady," "Ape Woman," "Hybrid Indian," "Extraordinary Lady," and "The Ugliest Woman in the World." Naturalists, scientists, aristocrats, stage fans, and ordinary people flocked to see her and paid to make her famous.

Pastrana was one of many atypically embodied people who were recruited by eager entrepreneurs such as P. T. Barnum for the burgeoning commerce in what the nineteenth century called "freaks," or nature's wondrous whimsies. Since antiquity, congenitally disabled people have been exhibited, interpreted, and studied. Called monsters or prodigies, people with singular bodies— whether dead or alive—were imagined as signs from the gods or omens about the future. Within modern capitalism, displays of ethnically and physically unusual people were a source of profits and entertainment in dime museums, street fairs, sideshows, and the more spectacular exhibitions such as World's Fairs that flourished in the nineteenth century (Bogdan 1988; Dennett 1997; Park and Daston 1981; Rydell 1984; and Wilson 1993).

As the advertisements for her exhibition suggest, Julia Pastrana's body radically violated expectations of how human beings should appear. Her entire body was covered with thick black hair and her teeth were unusually prominent. Today, medical discourse describes her particularities in terms of pathology. Her hirsute body has been retrospectively diagnosed as "congenital, generalized hypertrichosis terminalis" and her enlarged dentition termed "gingival hyperplasia" (Bondeson and Miles 1993: 198). Her departure from human appearance norms is today deemed by the clinical gaze as deformity rather than as delight. Her body is now displayed in medical journals rather than on stages. But in the theatrical nineteenth-century discourse used to hawk monsters and freaks, Julia Pastrana's unusual body generated multiple, sensational narratives of hybridity, wonder, exoticism, and delightful deviance. I focus here not on Pastrana's corporeal particularities, but rather on the operations of the visual rhetorics that were used to interpret her physical singularities. Her bodily differences seemed to challenge established categories that made sense of what her audiences took to be the natural world. The hyperbolic narratives that impelled her viewers to part with their money in order to gaze upon her body reveal much more about the way her audiences understood themselves and their historical moment than they do about this hirsute Mexican Indian woman who so captured their collective imagination.

The history of Pastrana's exhibition is quite remarkable. She appears to have been born in 1834 and belonged to a so-called Root-Digger Indian tribe in the Sierra Madre Mountain region of Mexico. As a young woman, she apparently left the mountains to serve in the household of the governor of the state of Sinaloa, perhaps as a curiosity. By 1854, Pastrana had been appropriated as a profit-making exhibition and was being proclaimed as one of the greatest marvels to be seen on stage. She went on tour in New York, Boston, and Baltimore and made her debut in London in July, 1857, as "the Wonder of the World." Like all people whose bodies were commodities in these exhibitions, Pastrana had a manager who closely regulated her social interactions, controlled the considerable profits, and apparently married her as well. Her manager/husband, Theodore Lent, displayed her throughout Europe in performances where she sang, danced, submitted to examinations, and appeared at staged social functions.

In 1860, while touring in Moscow, Pastrana died shortly after childbirth. Her newborn son, who inherited her hair-covered body died shortly after birth as well. Lent apparently sold both bodies to Professor Sukolov of Moscow University's Anatomical Institute, who embalmed them with his new method. The process was so successful that Lent supposedly repurchased both bodies and continued to exhibit them. By February, 1862, Pastrana's body, along with her baby's, were being viewed again in London. Now billed as "the Embalmed Female Nondescript," her viewers were often those who had seen her live performance only a few years earlier. Pastrana's singular body, now with her son's, continued to circulate on public exhibition in various museums such as the Prater in Vienna, in circuses, before Royal families, and in amusement parks for well over one hundred years. In 1972, Pastrana's body toured the United States with a traveling amusement park called the Million Dollar Midways. Because public and religious objections now make Pastrana's display an embarrassment, her embalmed corpse has been retired to the basement of the Institute of Forensic Museum in Oslo where it is studied by medical experts.

Freaks and Disability Studies

In its broadest sense, the field of disability studies in the humanities analyzes the social practices that invest bodies with meanings—practices like the exhibition of people as freaks and monsters. The display of Julia Pastrana is a part of disability studies because it traces the processes that socially mark human bodies. My analysis centers not on Pastrana herself but rather on the conventions used to display her body and the ideological purposes of her exhibition. Pastrana's exhibition is important to disability studies in two ways: first, because such freak shows were a major site of employment for disabled people before 1930, these performances of disability recuperate the history of disabled people in the public sphere. Second, critiquing the visual rhetorics of Pastrana's display reveals the role of disabled people as spectacles and sources of cultural narrative.

Bodies that depart from social expectations have always been the objects of intense visual interest rooted in a drive to explain and contain the extraordinary. The ordinary is safely anonymous, going unremarked and unnoticeable. But because the unusual invites interpretation, bodies such as Pastrana's became valuable commodities within modernity. The exhibition of freaks and monsters in modernity harnessed the power of the novel in the interest of making money. Pastrana's remarkable exhibition thus imposed upon her body the cultural meanings that her historical moment required. Modernity was a quickly shifting and unstable sign system that made nineteenth-century America preoccupied with appearances and anxious about identity. This phase of modernity fueled the public interest in displays of extraordinary bodies. These exhibitions were a ritualized form of looking that explored the somatic boundaries of what counted as human and as ordinary. The experiment of democracy leveled old social hierarchies and imagined the category of the ordinary person as having new rights, demands, and privileges. Just at the moment Pastrana was being displayed, the terms of citizenship for newly democratized nations were taking shape and being contested. The franchise and the rights it represented had been expanded in Jacksonian America. The drive to abolish slavery forced Americans to consider what being human meant. At the same time, the woman's suffrage movement began pressing for a more universal conception of the citizen. In such an historical context, the stakes of what was included and excluded in the human category were high and under debate. Displays such as Pastrana's were both a manifestation of and an occasion for this debate (Harris 1973). The spectacle of Julia Pastrana compelled her audiences by enacting a complex iconography of self and other that at once created and challenged the borders of human identity.

Pastrana's exhibition presented her as inexplicable, framing her through an extravagant rhetoric of hybridity. Her body was explicated as a boundary violation, a confusion of categories, a puzzlement. Exaggeration, the staple of freak show presentation, heightened the confusion. Pastrana's exhibition intensified the supposed contradictions she embodied, challenging the accepted distinctions that ordered the separation between human and animal, civilized and primitive, normal and pathological, male and female, as well as self and other. Her unexpected body thus threw her viewers' epistemological order into chaos and demanded an explanation to restore order. By teasing and confounding her audiences' interpretive systems, Pastrana's display provoked viewers to place her body into their systems of understanding, producing a kind of anxious delight that kept them buying tickets. While her exhibition made money, it also made meaning. In an age of mechanical reproduction, social instability, and economic transformation, it circulated narratives of human bodily variation that played into the sociopolitical concerns of the historical moment.

The critical context of disability studies frames my analysis of the cultural uses of Julia Pastrana's body. Disability studies is a radical critique that understands the human variations we think of as "disability," not as a natural state of bodily inferiority and inadequacy but as a pervasive cultural system that stigmatizes certain kinds of bodily forms and functions. What we might call the "ability system" produces social subjects by differentiating and marking bodies. The ability system is a comparison of bodies that is ideological rather than biological. While this cultural system is inequitable and oppressive, it also has the potential to incite a critical politics. Disability, then, is a culturally fabricated narrative of the body, similar to what we understand as the fictions of race and gender. Nevertheless, this system penetrates into the formation of culture. It supports an unequal distribution of resources, status, and power; and it creates a biased social and architectural environment. As such, disability has four aspects: first, it is a system for interpreting and disciplining bodily variations; second, it is a relationship between bodies and their environments; third, it is a set of practices that produce both the able-bodied and the disabled; fourth, it is a way of describing the inherent instability of the embodied self. The ability system excludes the kinds of bodily appearances, forms, functions, impairments, changes, or ambiguities that question our cultural fantasy of the body as a neutral, compliant instrument of some transcendent will. Moreover, disability is a broad term within which cluster ideological categories as varied as sick, deformed, ugly, old, maimed, afflicted, abnormal, or debilitated. All these descriptions disadvantage people by devaluing bodies that do not conform to cultural standards. Thus the ability system functions to preserve and validate such privileged designations as beautiful, healthy, normal, fit, competent, intelligent. All these descriptions provide cultural capital to those people who can claim those statuses, who can reside within these subject positions. It is, then, the various interactions between bodies and world that materialize disability from the stuff of human variation and precariousness. Julia Pastrana's exhibition invited her viewers to understand her bodily particularities by way of this representational system based on appearance and ability. This system of representations and assumptions transformed Julia Pastrana from a dark and thickly haired Mexican Indian woman into a freak.

The Human and Animal

The visual rhetorics that governed the display of Pastrana's body questioned the traditional ontological border that divided the human and the animal into opposing and exclusive categories. Narratives such as Genesis, the Great Chain of

Being, and Darwin established a supposedly natural order that elevated "man" above animals and differentiated them absolutely. The dominion Genesis promised to "man" over what he imagined to be the world required a distinct and hierarchical relation between man and beast. The idea of the natural rights of man that animated American democracy asked the question of who should be considered a citizen. Democracy's suggestion that simply being a human being might be the criteria for citizenship threatened the established order by suggesting power sharing among all humans. Consequently, much nineteenth-century science devoted itself to policing the category of the human by questioning the full humanity of women and people of color (Stephen Jay Gould 1981). Science often justified exclusionary practices such as slavery and limited enfranchisement that persisted in a supposedly egalitarian order. Debate raged as abolitionists, suffragists, and Christian reformers equated the human and the citizen to argue for expanded political rights.

Pastrana's exhibition capitalized on this conflicted relation between the human and the citizen by presenting her as a "Hybrid Indian," a creature part human and part beast. Such show sobriquets as "Bear Woman," "Baboon Lady," and "Ape Woman" used her hair-covered body in a fantasy of species fusion (*Curious History:* 1; *Miss Julia Pastrana:* 1). One of the souvenir pamphlets accompanying her show, for example, describes her as having "the face of a Baboon— the body and limbs of a Woman—the skin of a Bear, and other strange formations" (*Curious History:* 1). The unsettling appearance of singular bodies like Pastrana's in a prescientific era was explained as the result of unnatural unions between animals and humans. Indeed, man's sense of being above animals in the natural order was apparently so fragile and a strict boundary between persons and animals was so essential to man's sense of a privileged identity that bestiality—which was thought to produce hybrids—became a capital offense in England in 1534 (Thomas 1983). The sensationalized entertainment conventions that directed Pastrana's exhibition appealed to this earlier, vanished era of superstition and the fabulous by exploiting the once popular suspicion that animals and humans could interbreed, kindling both the anxiety of identity and the wonder of the miraculous in audiences. A souvenir book of her *Curious History* details, for example, "Her Remarkable Formation, and Mysterious Parentage, and how she was discovered in a cave, suckled by her Indian Mother, DWELLING ONLY WITH BABOONS, BEARS, AND MONKEYS" (*Curious History:* 2). This titillating narrative suggests bestiality between the "Indian Mother" and the animals, at the same time that it recruits the excitement and awe of the enigmatic.

Pastrana's exhibition appealed simultaneously to the ancient traditions of the wondrous and to the newest narratives of science as well. Her bodily differences were used to invoke the emerging scientific discourse of evolution by seemingly validating a troubling cousinship between humans and apes. Pastrana's entire tribe ostensibly closely resemble bears and orangutans. One doctor who supposedly examined her gestures toward crude evolutionary thought by testifying, for example, that "from her uncouth gait, it may be conjectured that the mysterious animal moves as if an elongation of the spinal column should have taken place, producing a tail, which in consequence of humanity predominating, has been denied" (*Miss Julia Pastrana:* 2). Hybridity in this account, then, has produced a monster who is abnormal rather than marvelous, one with an "uncouth gait" who is arrested in evolutionary progress between the beast and the human. Pastrana is an early prototype of the abundant "Missing Link" figures, popularizations of Darwinian thought that flourished in exhibits throughout the century (Cook 1996). Under the banner of popular entertainment, the rhetoric of the marvelous, and the authority of the evolutionary, then, the pressing question of who was human enough to be granted the natural rights—rights promised by democracy could be posed.

The Civilized and Primitive

Pastrana's body also occasioned an exploration of the distinction between the civilized and the primitive, an element of racial discourse inflected by science that underpins the then-emergent narrative of self and other we now call anthropology. Because the display of monsters and freaks offended the sensibilities of an increasingly rigid and influential bourgeois respectability, the shows sought legitimacy under the guise of education by invoking the emerging elite discourses of science and medicine (McConachie 1993). One narrative pamphlet assures prospective audiences that "she has appeared in all the principle cities and towns, exciting the greatest curiosity, especially among the medical faculty and naturalists" (*Curious History:* 8). Yet, in the nineteenth century, ethnography and monster displays had not fully bifurcated into high and low culture as they have today. Medical men and naturalists participated in her exhibition and wrote about her in their publications and memoirs. The souvenir pamphlets accompanying Pastrana's exhibition recruited scientific figures to authenticate her and capitalized on the language of ethnology to lend authority to the often fraudulent biographies they offered to explain her unexpected embodiment.

The pamphlets proffered an early racist, proto-Darwinian ethnography of her "semihuman" tribe, the "Root-Digger Indians" that casts them as primitives whose practices are in opposition to those that mark a civilized society. In the authoritative, ostensibly objective language used by nineteenth-century ethnographers, the pamphlets describe her "race" or "tribe" by detailing their supposed diet of "grasshoppers, snails, and wasps," which are elaborately prepared by drying, pulverizing, and mixing them with berry pulp before being eaten. Besides subsisting on gathered foods repugnant to the Western imagination, the "male digger never hunts, but usually depends on the exertions of his squaw" to provide food. Such a practice clearly suggests unmanliness and ineptitude according to bourgeois conceptions of male bread winners. A final testimony to these Indians' uncivilized state is their violation of the middle-class disciplinary codes of labor, thrift, and cleanliness, practices that constitute virtue in the Western self: "They get their food daily, and never lay up anything. They have no cause to labor," readers are assured, and "of all the Aborigines . . . the Digger Indians are certainly the most filthy and abominable." They even eat with their hands while displaying "great relish" (*Curious History:* 6–7). Such ethnographic descriptions simultaneously validated the civility of even the most humble or socially insecure viewer by offering an authoritative, contrasting fantasy of unequivocal primitivity that posited resemblance to bond together citizens both high and low in a comforting vision of equality and shared culture.

In opposition to but along side of ethnographic discourse was the embellished language of wonder as well, perhaps to draw in those readers whose repugnance had overcome their curiosity. Maintaining a balance between intriguing and disgusting the bourgeois sensibility was any freak show's rhetorical challenge. Barnum used temperance and family values; they all appealed to education and science. If the show were to make its audiences more civilized, it had to be careful not to allow them to develop a crude interest in the barbaric. An appeal to myth, wonder, and—most important—progress mitigated the coarseness of the primitive that the show created. Although the Digger Indians in general live a supposed prelapsarian existence of innocence, nakedness, and plenty that may have romanticized the savages, the Diggers' only purpose was to provide a scenic background for the marvelous emergence of Julia Pastrana herself, the figure audiences paid to see. Pastrana is billed as a marvelous anomaly differentiated from the routine pack of primitives: she is "the Extraordinary Lady just imported from the regions of wonder" (*Curious History:* 5).

The narrative of the prodigious Pastrana affirms the march toward evolutionary advancement that Westerners were imagined to lead. The Root Diggers from whence Pastrana sprung are barely differentiated in body and manners from animals in the journey toward civilization. Being "endowed with speech, which no monsters have ever possessed," the Root Diggers are "a kind of link between the man and the brute creation." Pastrana, however, appears as the wondrous exemplar of civilization's sway over the primitive. In a doubled confusion of boundaries, the pamphlets claim that Pastrana is herself a hybrid between the semibrute Diggers and a civilized woman. Having proved "capable of being cultivated and improved," Pastrana differs from her tribesmen physically, intellectually, and culturally because of her exposure to civilization (*Miss Julia Pastrana*). After a detailed description of her simian body, another pamphlet asserts that she is "good natured, sociable, and accommodating," in contrast to her tribesmen, who are "very spiteful and hard to govern." She "can speak the English and Spanish languages—dance, sing, sew, cook, wash, iron—these latter accomplishments being acquired, of course since her introduction into civilized life, having been recovered from a state of nature when she was very young" (*Curious History:* 7). Pastrana's introduction to civilization has also made her larger than her tribesmen and she now "eats the same food as any other person, and speaks the English language" (*Miss Julia Pastrana*). Her ostensibly ultra-primitive hirsuteness and dentition, juxtaposed with her civilized demeanor, make her singular and wondrous. In this narrative of progress toward a state of civilization, then, Pastrana's exploitation becomes a salvation, her colonization becomes a conversion, and her display becomes a testimony.

The Normal and Pathological

The authoritative discourse of medicine, an increasingly elite cousin to science, also framed Pastrana's body as a taxonomical enigma. The entertainment rhetoric, for example, enlisted the authority of medicine, adding a hint of the marvelous, in pamphlets containing Dr. Alex B. Mott's 1854 "Certificate" of Pastrana's examination. "She is therefore a Hybrid," Mott concludes," wherein the nature of woman predominates over the brute—the Ourang Outang. Altogether she is the most extraordinary being of the day," claims Mott (*Curious History:* 8 and *Miss Julia Pastrana:* 3).While the show language tends to blend wonder and science, the medical discourse that defines Pastrana purges all vestiges of awe. Detailed observations expressed in dispassionate, elite, specialized jargon characterize Pastrana as abnormal. Even some of the pamphlets' testimonials use the language of abnormality. One testimony, for example, from Samuel Kneeland of the Boston Natural History Society pathologizes her "anatomical conformation" and "abnormal growth of hair," apparently vouching for her singularity by concluding that "there is no admixture of Negro blood" (*Curious History:* 8). In contrast, the medical discourse banishes wonder and sensationalism in favor of a detached and restrained detailing of her body. The esteemed British medical journal *The Lancet,* for instance, trades the marvelous for the "peculiar" in its delineation of her: "Her face is peculiar: the alae of the nose are remarkably flattened and expanded, and so soft as to seem to be destitute of cartilages; the mouth is large and the lips everted—by an extraordinary thickening of the alveolar border of the upper jaw in front—below, by a warty hard growth arising from the gum" (Laurence 1857: 48). Similarly, the widely published *Anomalies and Curiosities of Medicine,* compiled by the distinguished doctors George M. Gould and Walter L. Pyle, presents Pastrana as having "defective dentition" and "pronounced prognathism" (1897: 229). Gould and Pyle's book has the format and style of an encyclopedia or textbook, even though a majority of the information and illustrations come unacknowledged from freak shows. Thus, the entertainment discourse parades its collaboration with medicine in Pastrana's exhibition, whereas the medical discourse suppresses the fact that doctors were actually attending the shows to examine Pastrana. The increasingly authoritative medical discourse of pathology begins here to eclipse the freak show as the legitimate articulator of the extraordinary body, prefiguring the demise of these shows as the accepted narrators of such bodies.

Pathology transforms hybridity into abnormality. It converts the freak to the specimen. Whereas the spectacle of the freak exhibit tries to expand the possibilities of interpretation through sensationalism and exaggeration, the spectacle of the specimen attempts to contain those possibilities through classification and mastery. The remarkable exhibition of Pastrana's body from 1860 through 1993 illustrates this discursive shift from prodigy to pathology more strikingly than did most of her fellow freaks. After her death in 1860, her embalmed body circulated for over one hundred years as either a medical specimen or a side show, depending upon the context of its presentation. Although the construction of Pastrana as pathological eventually predominated as freak shows became unacceptable to middle-class sensibilities, the narrative of Pastrana as wonder has not been easily subdued.

The most intense pathologizing of Pastrana's body, both discursively and materially, occurred with her actual embalming, along with that of her child, in 1860 by Dr. J. Sokolov of Moscow University and with his accompanying detailed account of that procedure in an article published in a 1862 issue of *The Lancet*. The article contains by far the most comprehensive description of Pastrana's body, including precise measurements and weights of every part of her anatomy, from her little finger to her "pelvicular diameter" (1862: 468). In graphic and repugnant detail, Solokov narrates the complete process of embalming both mother and child, exhaustively noting the colors, smells, textures, and extent of the decomposition against which he raced. In addition, he provides the particulars of Pastrana's difficult childbirth and the subsequent deaths of both mother and child, including diagnoses, dates, times, and names of the accoucheurs in attendance. The report includes as well an indignant explanation of how the American consul and Pastrana's husband/ manager legally procured the bodies, which "well deserved a place among the rarities of the [Anatomical Institute's] museum," affirming that "wherever they may be they have a claim upon the scientific world" (468). Solokov's account is essentially an autopsy report that does not invoke a single trace of Pastrana's or her son's humanity. Both become absolute specimen in this narrative. The only subjectivity that emerges is his pride of craftsmanship in restoring the semblance of life to dead flesh. But no matter how objectifying is this discursive frame, it nevertheless does not reach far enough to contain Pastrana's compelling violation of the order of things.

The embalmed body of Pastrana, with her son on an elevated platform beside her, once again captivated viewers in tawdry side shows, exhibition halls, traveling circuses, and museums as prestigious as the Prater in Vienna. The famous British naturalist Francis T. Buckland, who saw her body exhibited at 191 Piccadilly, reinvokes a vestige of awe by describing her in a section on human mummies in his 1888 *Curiosities of Natural History:* "The face," he notes admiringly, "was marvelous." At the same time, his recollection "of seeing and speaking to this poor Julia Pastrana when in life" restores her semihumanity, her position midway between the human and the other (Buckland 1888: 41).

Gender Distinctions

Pastrana's display violated gender boundaries by calling up and upseting the anxious nineteenth-century preoccupation about distinctions between men and women that supported the ideology of separate spheres. Both the scientific and the entertainment presentations of her body highlight gender transgression. For example, a characteristic medical report detailing her body that appears in the medical journal *The Lancet* depends on gendered traits as a map with which to make sense of her body. She is described as

> a female whose main peculiarity consists in her possessing hairs nearly all over the body, and more especially on those parts which are ordinarily clothed with hairs in the male sex. . . . She has a large tuft of hair depending from the chin—a *beard,* continuous with smaller growths on the upper lip and cheeks—moustache and whiskers. . . . Indeed, the whole of the body, excepting the palms of the hands and the soles of the feet, is more or less clothed with hairs. In this respect she agrees, in an exaggerated degree, with what is not very uncommonly observed in the male sex. (Laurence 1857: 48)

Pastrana's hairiness becomes here not the mark of an ape but the mark of a man. The journal then goes on to juxtapose these signs of the masculine with "other respects" in which Pastrana "agrees with the female. Her breasts are remarkably full and well-developed. She menstruates regularly. . . . The voice is that of a female" (48). The same body that merged the human and animal in one register, here confuses the male and female, as this exaggerated illustration of her suggests. Such a gendered reading of her body casts her as a hermaphrodite figure, a common freak category. Indeed, one medical book combines Pastrana's multiple unusual bodily characteristics into a single transgression of gender: she is "a bearded woman" (Gould and Pyle 1897: 229).

Pastrana's performance visually presented her body as a gender trespass as well. In the onstage part of her exhibition (the offstage portion being medical examinations), she performed the theatrics of femininity by dancing the popular Pepita, doing Highland flings, and singing "Mexican songs in a quiet, sad voice like the Creoles" (Herman 1895: 123). Her costuming included roses, ribbons, elaborate headdresses, and the Russian dancer's dress she wore after being embalmed. Such hyperbolically feminine attire contrasted with her supposedly masculine face to create the disconcerting, illusory visual fusion of male and female.

The naturalist Francis T. Buckland, who examined her in life and in death, summons the language of gender as well to interpret Pastrana as a hybrid of the beautiful, elite lady and the bearded monster:

> her eyes were deep black, and somewhat prominent, and their lids had long, thick eyelashes: her features were simply hideous on account of the

profusion of hair growing on her forehead, and her black beard; but her figure was exceedingly good and graceful, and her tiny foot and well-turned ankle . . . perfection itself. She had a sweet voice, great taste in music and dancing, and could speak three languages. She was charitable and gave largely to local institutions from her earnings." (1888: 42)

Here Buckland is at once attracted and repulsed by Pastrana's seeming fusion of the "hideous" and "perfection itself." Using the gender system as a template to interpret her physical traits, Buckland reads her body as a merger of the male and female that enhances rather than dilutes each identity, producing a figure at once grotesque and compelling.

The visual rhetorics capitalized on this response, heightening the anxious fascination with gender confusion in order to draw customers. The textual presentation of Pastrana challenged the viewers' understanding of what they imagined to be natural and immutable gender differences that structured their own identities as men and women. But if Pastrana's exhibition provoked discomfort, it also assuaged the uneasiness it incited about themselves and their place in the world. One account, for example, of Pastrana's attending a ball in Baltimore provides "a very genteel young man in citizen's dress" an opportunity to demonstrate a kind of heroic civility despite the discomfort that her gender trespass arouses.

The highly embellished—and probably fictional—story presents an ultra-feminized, Cinderellalike Pastrana costumed in "a blue dress, trimmed with silver lace, white kid gloves, black satin slippers, bracelets, watch, and splendid set of Jewellery, including a diamond ring, which had just been made a present to her [sic]." The reader—and prospective audience member—is assured that "had [Pastrana's] face been screened from observation" her femininity would have made her " 'the cynosure of all eyes' " at the ball. The type of bourgeois ladyhood, Pastrana waltzes gracefully and adeptly "by some *natural* intuition," inspiring a "handsome gallant [to run up] to Miss Julia with considerable eagerness." But when the couples face one another to dance, "the young gentleman" is overcome momentarily by "fright or some other undefined emotion . . . and exhibits a degree of embarrassment strangely at variance with his character." Nevertheless, he recovers in a "creditable manner" and the ball proceeds gaily with him as its hero (*Curious History*: 9).

The story leaves the source of his discomfort unnarrated, stressing only the severity of his response to Pastrana's transgressive face and his "genteel" recovery. This vignette assures the reader that he can maintain bourgeois decorum and self-control, literally in the face of this shocking violation of what he imagined as a world discretely ordered into male and female. Pastrana's exhibition, then, becomes a kind of test of the (male) spectator's capacity to absorb the instability of categories that structure self and world, to create "an enchanting occasion," mastering his insecurity despite the "fright" and discomfort such ambiguity kindles (*Curious History*: 9–10). This narrative of spectatorship thus instructs the viewer how to respond to the assault on his worldview Pastrana represents. So while Pastrana seems to be the focus in the dynamic of gazing, closer scrutiny of this encounter reveals that the rhetorical purpose is to verify the viewer's vision of himself.

The Sentimental Economy of Self and Other

This affirmation of the viewer produced by Pastrana's exhibition is nowhere more evident than in the sentimental rhetoric of self and other her display mobilized to establish a relation between Pastrana and her viewers. In this relational choreography, the response Pastrana elicits from her onlookers defines them, ultimately placing them in the order of things that she seemingly so upsets. Coached by the promotional material, the spectator could expect to move through a thrilling, even delightful, excursion consisting of a disintegration and reintegration of his sense of self within the social order in Victorian America. This is perhaps what the audience was paying for. As I have already suggested, Pastrana's presentation as semihuman legitimated the status of her onlookers as fully human and thus potential citizens in a democratic order. Yet, the sentimental discourse of self and other deployed in Pastrana's display established precisely what kind of citizen her viewers might be. In short, the exhibition of Pastrana was an occasion on which spectators could verify their position in the class hierarchy that was solidifying in nineteenth-century America.

Sentimentality was one element in the nineteenth-century discourse that increasingly differentiated the bourgeoisie from the working classes. The sentimental was part of a rhetoric of upward social mobility registering the refined sensibility, genteel manners, and sense of stewardship that characterized emergent middle-class respectability (Thomas 1983; Tuan 1984). Public exhibitions such as Pastrana's were effective vehicles for sentimentality, which rescued what the solidifying middle class took as the vulgar and offensive practice of exhibiting monsters from its slide into low culture and transformed it into the burgeoning business of freak shows and dime museums in the second half of the nineteenth century. In terms of bourgeois taste, such exhibitions moved from the crude to the refined and back again to the vulgar on exactly the same historical trajectory as the prevalence of sentimental discourse. By the 1860s Barnum was courting Queen Victoria and charming the world with Tom Thumb, but by 1923 one writer condemned him for the "complete indifference to the semi-humanity or sub-humanity of the horrible creatures that he often exhibited," insisting that "a nature with a shred of sensitiveness would have recoiled from the public display of these monstrosities and the sickening morbid curiosity they fostered" (Bradford 1923: 216). What made spectacles such as Pastrana's exhibition acceptable and profitable was their suitability to sentimental discourse, the exercise of which was a major marker of bourgeois status in Victorian America.

Sentimentality was the production and demonstration of a certain affect that structured a social relation between the person who could show fine feeling and the one who could induce it (Ellison 1999). Pity, the primary sentimental affect, is the genteel response that often characterized relations between the bourgeoisie and the poor, the disabled, and the primitive. Pity is repugnance refined: the other becomes sympathetic rather than brutish in the service of cultivating a bourgeois self. The sentimental relationship is nonreciprocal as it elevates the self to a position of stewardship over the other. Pity thus defines its object even as it depends on that object for its enactment. In other words, pity needs an incitement to which it must respond. Julia Pastrana's immense popularity, along with that of her fellow freaks, may be explained by her function as an anchor for the respectable sentiment of pity that the newly solidifying middle class needed to display and that its aspirants needed to perfect.

Such an appeal to the ennobling emotion of pity is rather shamelessly exploited in the promotional material for Pastrana's exhibition. One account of her display insists that "there is nothing in her appearance in the least calculated to offend the sensibilities of the most fastidious, whether viewed, socially, morally, or physically. A feeling of pity, rather than of repugnance or antipathy is generally experienced in the bosom of all who pay her a visit" (*Curious History*: 12). Here pity keeps the onlookers "fastidious," delivering them from an interest in the lurid and from the "morbid curiosity" that such shows were often later accused of pandering to.

Similarly, Otto Hermann, who saw Pastrana's embalmed corpse on display in Vienna after interviewing her in life, vows in his memoir, "I felt tremendous pity for this thing who could no longer see or hear, feel joy or pain, or my sorrow. I remembered her smiling face saying [of her manager/husband] 'He loves me for my own sake.'" (Herman 1895: 125). The basis for Herman's pity is his fantasy that Pastrana has the capacity for the same human emotions he feels. Even though he recognizes that "poor Pastrana was known for her ugliness," Herman's interest in her transcends any fascination with the disturbing differentness of her body or with its violation of the gender order. Indeed, Herman differentiates his look from both the medical gaze, which he says "was fascinated with Julia," and the vulgar gawk:

> To the world, she was nothing more than an aberration, something grotesque that was paraded before others for money and trained to do tricks like circus animals. For those few who knew her better, she was a warm, thoughtful, capable being with a big heart. They knew her sorrow at being on the fringe of society, not part of it, of not knowing the normal joys of family, home, love. (Herman 1895: 123–24)

Herman uses sentimental rhetoric to suggest here that the state of total otherness Pastrana's "grotesque" bodily "aberration" creates for "the world" could be inflected and thus redeemed by affective properties imagined as "normal, "as exclusive to the self, such as "a big heart" and being "warm" and "thoughtful." Herman thus envisages Pastrana as pitiful rather than repulsive because she is similar to him emotionally if not physically. By projecting the self onto the other in this manner, Herman finds verification of his own humanizing sentiments in Pastrana. His ability to pity Pastrana makes him more sensitive and cultivated, more bourgeois, than the other base spectators who comprise "the world."

Sentimentality thus hybridizes the self and the other by positing an exchange of feeling so that the other inspires elevating and humanizing sensibilities in the self which then projects those sentiments back onto the other. This sentimental economy merges identification through pity with differentiation through otherness to produce Pastrana as the hybrid construct of the sensitive monster, whose role it is to instruct, edify, and thus construct the middle-class canonical self. Her viewers become better people, citizens higher on the ladder of bourgeois respectability, through looking at Pastrana.

Sentimental discourse, like the others discussed here, leashes spectator and spectacle together in a performance of identity that compels, delights, troubles, and affirms by confusing categories and blurring boundaries. Yet, the ritual and highly stylized quality of that performance seals it off from ordinary experience, and the commercial nature of the encounter demands that it serve the viewer nostalgic affirmations of the normative perspective. Finally, despite the ambiguity these visual rhetorics introduce, they are conciliatory, almost nostalgic. Even though Pastrana's display upset established categorizes, it confirmed the boundaries that organize the order of things: "Go and see Julia Pastrana, the Nondescript," a souvenir narrative instructs, "and learn wisdom, subdued by becoming humility. Go and endeavor to realize where man's bestial attributes terminate and where those that are *Divine* begin!" (*Curious History:* 12). Perhaps this at once sentimental and titillating suggestion that one might be able to determine a line between the "bestial" and the *"Divine"* self drew viewers to Pastrana. Yet, her startling body invariably exceeded the visual rhetorics that attempted to contain her bodily particularities. Ultimately, her exhibition was less about her, and more about who her spectators imagined themselves to be.

References

Bondeson, Jan, and A. E. W. Miles (1993). "Julia Pastrana, the Nondescript: An Example of Congenital, Generalized Hypertrichosis Terminalis with Gingival Hyperplasia." *American Journal of Medical Genetics* 47: 198–212.

Bogdan, Robert (1988). *Freak Show: Presenting Human Oddities for Amusement and Profit.* Chicago: University of Chicago University Press, 1988.

Bradford, Gamaliel (1923). *Damaged Souls.* Port Washington, New York: Kennikat.

Buckland, Francis T. (1888). *Curiosities of Natural History,* vol. 4. London: Bentley, 40–43.

Cook, James W., Jr. (1996). "Of Men, Missing Links, and Nondescripts: The Strange Career of P. T. Barnum's 'What Is It?' Exhibition." Rosemarie Garland Thomson, ed., *Freakery: Cultural Spectacles of the Extraordinary Body.* New York: New York University Press, 139–57.

Curious History of the Baboon Lady, Miss Julia Pastrana, pamphlet, Harvard Theater Collection.

Dennett, Andrea Stulman (1997). *Weird and Wonderful: The Dime Museum in America.* New York: New York University Press, 1997.

Ellison, Julie (1999). *Cato's Tears and the Makings of Anglo-American Emotion.* Chicago: University of Chicago Press.

Garland-Thomson, Rosemarie, ed., (1996). *Freakery: Cultural Spectacles of the Extraordinary Body.* New York: New York University Press.

Gould, George M., and Walter L. Pyle (1897). *Anomalies and Curiosities of Medicine.* Philadelphia: Saunders, 229.

Gould, Stephen Jay (1981). *The Mismeasure of Man.* New York: Norton.

Harris, Neil (1973). *Humbug: The Art of P. T. Barnum.* Boston: Little Brown.

Herman, Otto W. (1895). *Fahrend Volk.* Leipzig: Weber, 123; my translation.

Laurence, J. Z. (1857). "A Short Account of the Bearded and Hairy Female." *The Lancet* 2 (July 11): 48.

McConachie, Bruce A. (1993). "Museum Theater and the Problem of Respectability for Mid-Century Urban Americans." Ron Engle and Tice L. Miller, eds., *The American Stage: Social and Economic Issues from the Colonial Period to the Present.* New York: Cambridge University Press, 65–80.

Miss Julia Pastrana, the Misnomered Bear Woman, pamphlet, 1855, New York City Public Library.

Odell, George C. D. (1970). *Annals of the New York Stage,* vol. 6, 1850–1857 (rpt.). New York: AMS.

Park, Kathryn, and Lorraine Daston (1981). "Unnatural Conceptions: The Study of Monsters in Sixteenth- and Seventeenth-Century France and England." *Past and Present: A Journal of Historical Studies* 92 (August): 20–54

Rydell, Robert W. (1984). *All the World's a Fair: Visions of Empire at American International Expositions, 1876–1916.* Chicago: University of Chicago Press.

Sokolov, J. (1862). "Julia Pastrana and Her Child." *The Lancet* 1 (May 3): 447–49.

Thomas, Keith (1983). *Man and the Natural World.* New York: Pantheon.

Tuan, Yi-Fu (1984). *Dominance and Affection: The Making of Pets.* New Haven: Yale University Press.

Wilson, Dudley (1993). *Signs and Portents: Monstrous Births from the Middle Ages to the Enlightenment.* London: Routledge.

8

Critical Investments
AIDS, Christopher Reeve, and Queer/Disability Studies

Robert McRuer

Introduction: The Limits of the Queer/Disabled Body

For two decades, as Paula Treichler has famously suggested, people living with HIV and AIDS have faced not only "an epidemic of a transmissible lethal disease," but also an "epidemic of signification" (1999: 11). This epidemic of signification, which is "readily apparent in the chaotic assemblage of understandings of AIDS that by now exists" (11), has most often contained or controlled people with HIV/AIDS. Demonized at worst, patronized, desexualized, or tolerated at best, people with HIV/AIDS have repeatedly faced attempts to deny them autonomous voices or subjectivities; the dominant meanings of the syndrome have cast them as passive objects or blank slates onto which the fantasies of those who would like to imagine themselves as "immune" from the epidemic could be written. Moreover, as Treichler and numerous others have shown, this epidemic of signification has often had particularly detrimental effects for people of color, gay and bisexual men, and women, as preexisting racist, homophobic, and sexist fantasies have been redeployed and thus reinvigorated in and through the AIDS crisis.[1]

From virtually the beginning of the epidemic, however, people with HIV/ AIDS have responded by actively, and even promiscuously, *participating* in the epidemic of signification. Providing what Treichler calls an "epidemiology of signification—a comprehensive mapping and analysis of these multiple meanings" (39), they have shaped their own subjectivities, spoken in their own voices, and wrenched control of discourses about AIDS away from those who would contain them. As early as 1985, for instance, the framers of what came to be known as the Denver Principles announced, "We condemn attempts to label us as 'victims,' which implies defeat, and we are only occasionally 'patients', which implies passivity, helplessness, and dependence upon the care of others. We are 'people with AIDS'" (PWA Coalition: 148). The National Association of People with AIDS, likewise, insisted, "We do not see ourselves as victims. We will not be victimized. We have the right to be treated with respect, dignity, compassion, and understanding. . . . We are born of and inextricably bound to the historical struggle for rights—civil, feminist, disability, lesbian and gay, and human. We will not be denied our rights!" (qtd. in Grover 1987: 27). Statements such as these attempted to make the lives of people living with AIDS and HIV readable within discourses of civil rights and social justice as opposed to discourses of pathology.

Queer activism/theory has not always been centrally concerned with AIDS, but I would argue that the cultural theory about AIDS that has been shaped by academics and activists during the past two decades represents queer theory at its best.[2] "Queer theory" at this point describes a diverse array of projects that explore the construction and shifting contemporary meanings of sexuality. Premised on the idea that our current division of the world into heterosexual/homosexual is historical and contingent, queer theory considers how power is temporarily fixed and permanently contested around that binary opposition and how desires and identities do or do not fit neatly within such a model. Although this premise would seem to locate queer theory as always centrally concerned with what Michel Foucault called "the deployment of sexuality" (1978: 75–131), the conceptual center of queer theory has, in actuality, continually shifted as its practitioners have attended to the multiple ways in which difference has been produced and managed. Indeed, as Eve Kosofsky Sedgwick suggested in the early 1990s, "a lot of the most exciting recent work around 'queer' spins the term outward along dimensions that can't be subsumed under gender and sexuality at all: the ways that race, ethnicity, postcolonial nationality criss-cross with these *and other* identity-constituting, identity-fracturing discourses, for example" (Sedgwick 1993: 9).

AIDS activists have been at the forefront of developing queer theory precisely because "identity-constituting, identity-fracturing discourses" criss-cross virtually every aspect of the epidemic. The AIDS epidemic, more than many other contemporary crises, demonstrates not only the fluid and contradictory nature of identity, but also the ways in which the division of "us" from "them," in all of its manifestations, is institutionalized. Contemporary systems of power are structured to shore up—or "immunize"—dominant fictions of identity and to secure thereby the privileges that accrue to those not stigmatized by queerness, deviance, or pathology. AIDS activists/theorists have worked to expose these processes: when members of the AIDS Coalition to Unleash Power (ACT UP), for instance, demonstrated outside the Trump Tower in New York City in 1988, their point was that Trump's luxuriously "housed" existence (the Trump Tower luxury apartments were made possible by tax cuts granted to developers in New York City) literally depended on others living in the streets, often with HIV/AIDS (apartments that could have provided affordable housing were warehoused by the city, and funding for hospice care and AIDS services was repeatedly delayed or denied) (Crimp and Rolston 1990: 122–29). Some might argue that the heyday of this particular brand of deconstructive queer/ AIDS activism has passed, yet it has often reemerged in unexpected and productive locations.[3]

At the same time that AIDS theory and queer theory, and AIDS theory *as* queer theory, have developed, the disability rights movement and the academic field that has come to be known as disability studies have mobilized similar insights. Disability activists and theorists have argued, for instance, that disability should be understood as a minority identity, not simply as a "condition" of lack or loss to be pitied or "overcome." This minority identity has been forged through the common experience of able-bodied oppression—although nothing "naturally" links people with mobility impairments to people with cognitive disabilities to those who are deaf or blind, a common disability identity has been claimed across such experiences and in opposition to able-bodied hegemony. At the same time that this minority identity has been shaped, however, theorists/activists have also argued that the division into two neat categories (able-bodied and disabled) is ideological, more about maintaining a particular system of power than about accurately describing reality; they have insisted that, in fact, all of us inhabit different kinds of bodies and have a range of bodily experiences. Disability studies has not only critiqued the able-bodied stereotypes, metaphors, and ideologies that sustain this false division, but has also launched a widespread interrogation of the idea of "normalcy." Activists/theorists have critiqued the medicalized model of disability and hence demanded that people with disabilities be understood as subjects, and not just passive objects, of knowledge. Both the disability rights movement and disability studies have attempted to provide a far-reaching reconceptualization of how contemporary cultures function according to models (of ability, productivity, efficiency, flexibility) that privilege non-disabled (and docile) bodies and identities. Identification of the ways in which able-bodied ideas are figuratively and literally built into contemporary society helped secure passage of the landmark Americans with Disabilities Act (ADA) in 1990, and the concomitant revaluation of a range of corporealities currently sustains vibrant activist and intellectual communities concerned with the development of alternative disability identities and cultures.[4]

Given that disability studies has explicitly critiqued the limitations imposed on people with disabilities by an able-bodied society, and given that queer theory and activism have explicitly probed the limits of the hetero/homo binary (drawing attention to the perhaps *unlimited* possibilities unleashed by queerness), it might seem problematic to concern myself in this introduction with "the limits of the queer/disabled body." One could, in fact, quite easily define disability studies as a field exposing the limits of the able body and queer theory as a field exposing the limits of the straight body.

Through my invocation of "the limits of the queer/disabled body," however, I mean to call attention to what David T. Mitchell and Sharon L. Snyder call "methodological distancing." Mitchell and Snyder write:

As feminist, race, and sexuality studies sought to unmoor their identities from debilitating physical and cognitive associations, they inevitably positioned disability as the "real" limitation from which they must escape. This methodological distancing was necessary because identity studies resignified cultural beliefs grounded in material differences, real or imagined. . . . [B]iological inferiority had to be exposed as a construction of

discursive power. Formerly denigrated identities are "rescued" by understanding gendered, racial, and sexual differences as textually produced,
distancing them from the "real" of physical or cognitive aberrancy projected onto their figures. (1997: 2–3)

In other words, members of marginalized communitiees in effect identify an
even *more* marginalized group in order to resist the stigma imposed by a dominant culture: gay men and lesbians insist that homosexuality is not "really" a
mental disorder, feminists insist that female bodies are not "really" biologically
inferior, and so forth. As Mitchell and Snyder make clear, disability of some sort
is invariably identified as the "real" aberrancy. They complicate this insight,
however, by suggesting that methodological distancing takes place *within* disability communities as well, most obviously as people with physical disabilities
distance themselves from those with cognitive disabilities. I would extend their
complication further, however, suggesting that queerness or "perversion" also
often functions, within processes of methodological distancing, as the "real"
aberrancy. People with physical and mental disabilities who are *perceived* as a bit
queer can demonstrate that such a difference is textually produced by distancing
themselves from the "real" queerness or perversion (embodied by those who are
not straight).

The processes that Mitchell and Snyder delineate, in fact, seem particularly
pronounced, in both directions, with AIDS. An emphasis on *living* with AIDS
has at times been less about resistance to HIV negative, AIDS-phobic ideas and
more about identification of the supposedly more abject or ill—those, indeed,
who are "really" disabled. Conversely, despite the National Association of People
with AIDS declaring that the AIDS activist movement is "inextricably bound" to
the struggle for disability rights, and despite the central role played by AIDS
activists in the passage of the ADA, people with other disabilities have at times,
over the course of the epidemic, distanced themselves from the concerns of
people with AIDS.[5]

The basic premise that undergirds this chapter is thus that critical insights
from disability studies and the disability rights movement should be incorporated
into queer activism and cultural theory about AIDS and vice versa. The central
thesis of the chapter will be considering, in other words, why an alliance that is
already implicit should be made explicit. I call for critical investments—an
investment in disability theory on the part of cultural workers concerned with
AIDS, an investment in AIDS and queer theory on the part of disability activists.
The title "Critical Investments" is thus not meant to invoke simply the economic
investments of capitalism, where a single-minded focus on individual returns
invariably obscures collective interests. Returning to the Latin root for *invest*—
to clothe, or surround—the critical investments advocated for here would en-
tail continually focusing on a queer/disabled collectivity, surrounding AIDS
theorists with a larger disability community and vice versa. As will be clear, I

am in fact critical of investments made according to the individualistic terms of an economic system that has well served neither people with HIV/AIDS nor people with disability; I seek instead to theorize critical practices that move beyond the limits of queer/disabled bodies—critical practices, that is, that refuse methodological distancing in order to further systemic critique and coalition building.[6]

Disability, Aids, and Superbowl 2000

Neither AIDS nor disability activists/theorists have expressed much interest in football, so the Superbowl—a location that would appear to have very little to do with AIDS or disability—might seem an unlikely location to begin forging disabled/queer critical alliances. From one perspective, in fact, the Superbowl is a site that (like most other sporting events) could be understood as a showcase for able-bodied performance. From another, however, because of the ever-present threat of catastrophic injury, it is a site where the absolute contingency of able-bodied identity is made manifest. Disability always circulates threateningly around the performance at sporting events, even though it is ultimately *always* subordinated to able-bodiedness: games stop momentarily when there is an injury, but the narrative perspective itself doesn't shift to one identified with disability. Even if significant concern is expressed, it's unthinkable that the production site would move to the hospital or, even more desirably, any future locations through which the person with a new disability might move. You don't follow his career from this point on; it's generally assumed that he doesn't have one.

Despite how endlessly fascinating (and troubling) the play of domination and subordination around ability and disability might be in terms of the Superbowl itself, however, like a significant portion of the viewing audience in January 2000, I'm more interested in the commercials. I'm particularly interested in the ways the crisis of ability/disability always circulating somewhere around the game itself was in the year 2000 more clearly circulating around the ads. One commercial, in particular, garnered an unprecedented amount of media attention—the four-million-dollar ad for the Nuveen Investment Corporation. The events represented in the commercial take place sometime after 2006, although no exact date is given. A speaker announces that, in 2004, the "tide was turned against AIDS," and that, two years later, major breakthroughs were seen in the fight against cancer. The announcer speaks before an audience in a large auditorium, but clips of New York City indicate that he is also being heard on radio and television. The New York City skyline looks slightly different, but is still recognizable, and Christopher Reeve—who plays the central role in this commercial—looks about the same age as he did in the late 1990s. In other words, the Nuveen commercial is set in the very near future. The group in the auditorium appears to have come together to "celebrate a remarkable break-through in spinal cord injuries," and Reeve is one of the "very special guests" who will present the award to the scientists and researchers responsible. As the music swells, Reeve gets up from a chair, then walks slowly to the podium, where he stands with others who have supposedly been "cured." Over the applause, and as the audience in the auditorium gives Reeve a standing ovation, another male voice addresses the viewers of Nuveen's ad directly: "In the future, so many amazing things will happen. What amazing things can you make happen?" A father watching the events on television takes his son in his arms, and the commercial ends with the captions, "Invest well. Leave your mark. Nuveen Investments."

The representation of disability in popular culture has rarely been discussed, in mainstream venues, as widely as it was in the days following Super-bowl 2000. In the ensuing mainstream media coverage, Christopher Reeve was often described as "Superman." In the disability media, Reeve is rarely described as "Superman," except very ironically—"point/counterpoint" articles by disability activists following the controversy, for instance, included a representation of the Superman symbol with a question mark in the place of the famous S. Despite the lack of irony in the mainstream media, however, some positive arguments *were* articulated in the aftermath of the Nuveen advertisement.[7] Coverage was given on the *Today* show, for instance, to Jan Garrett of the Center for Independent Living in Berkeley, who said that her organization could cer-tainly use the four million dollars it cost to produce the commercial, and *some* limited mainstream media space was even given to a few basic tenets of the disability rights movement and disability studies. Although they were by no means the dominant messages emerging from the controversy, arguments were made that the problem is not individuals but an able-bodied society that refuses to accommodate disability, that there are multiple forms of embodiment and that disability is a minority identity more than it is a medicalized/pathologized iden-tity, and that some people with disabilities are not simply waiting for a cure—that, in fact, some people would not even *want* to be "cured."

These critical points, however, were nonetheless overshadowed by the dominant construction of the "controversy": people with disabilities were gener-ally represented as either "fooled" by the commercial (with reports pointing out that organizations for people with spinal cord injuries had been flooded with calls for more information about Reeve's "cure") or as having given up "hope" and, for that reason, as critical of Reeve for not facing "reality." "Hope" or "no hope" for the represented "cure" were the two most widely available positions in mainstream media coverage, and an official statement issued by Reeve, which was read on the *Today* show, only secured those options:

> The reason I participated in the Nuveen Superbowl commercial was be-cause research is advancing at a remarkable pace. Scientists tell me con-

stantly that the only thing slowing down the progress towards a cure is not enough funding. But all of them agree that a cure for spinal cord injury paralysis can be achieved in the foreseeable future. *It is time that we create positive images about the miracles that scientific research can bring.* Americans crave this hope. Negativism or dashing hopes never cured a disease, whether it's conquering AIDS, breast cancer or spinal cord injury paralysis. My hope is that people will be energized by the power of the story in this commercial. It is a vision of what can actually happen.

Reeve also thought it appropriate that Nuveen was the sponsor for the ad, since—as he told Diane Sawyer in a *Good Morning, America* interview—"what we need is more intelligent, more thoughtful investment."

With his argument about the need for "positive images about the miracles that scientific research can bring," Reeve positions miracles as under attack. What I call elsewhere a "critically disabled" perspective, however, would quickly point out that such a construction of scientific miracles is precisely the *dominant* ideological message circulating around disability (McRuer 2002: 12–15). John Nguyet Erni identifies two fantasies through which the popular imagination understands AIDS, and these fantasies are, not surprisingly to those in the disability rights movement or who work in disability studies, the same fantasies through which disability generally is understood: the fantasy of morbidity and the fantasy of control and containment. The control/containment fantasy structure, according to Erni, "proclaims the immense curative power of medical science to fight AIDS through a paradigm of hyperrationality" (Erni 1994: 53), while the fantasy of morbidity reads people with AIDS as basically already dead (or worse, secretly wishes that they were). A similar structuring is at work in the Reeve controversy, and what is most troubling is that these two fantasy structures function so seamlessly as truth effects, as messages that hardly need to be sent because the message has already been received, that even critically disabled perspectives are relegated to one of these two limited possibilities: either one can "talk about miracles," or one has given oneself up, in a sort of death-*like* move of resignation, to "spending the rest of your life in a wheelchair." In the interview with Diane Sawyer, Reeve announced, "The biggest problem actually is people who have been in a chair for a very long time, because in order to survive psychologically they have had to accept 'Okay, I'm going to spend my life in a chair.'" The disability rights movement would undoubtedly stress that "the biggest problem" is an able-bodied society systemically structured to privilege certain bodies and deny access to others, and would *never* say that individuals themselves who "have been in a chair for a very long time" are "the biggest problem." Such points tend to be lost, however, in an able-bodied media culture caught between the ideological options of cure or elimination.

As numerous cultural critics have pointed out, queer identities and public spheres are currently under attack.[8] None of these critics have expressed, particularly, a disability perspective, even though it is possible to understand the pro-scription of disability perspectives, identities, and communities, as exemplified in the Reeve controversy, as linked to the proscription of queer cultures and public spheres. Moreover, the critical queerness that has been shaped, collectively, to resist the economic and cultural forces that would contain queerness is remark-ably similar to critically disabled perspectives that have been shaped by activists and scholars to counter able-bodied ideologies.

The containment and control of queerness has taken many forms over the past decade. In New York City and other urban locations, privatization has encouraged development policies (such as those supported and implemented by New York Mayor Rudolph Guiliani) that have eliminated multiple public sites where queer identities were produced and nurtured. The dominant gay rights organization, the Human Rights Campaign (HRC) has pursued programs of privatization *and* normalization: for instance, at the Millennium March on Washington for Lesbian, Gay, Bisexual, and Transgendered Rights in April 2000, which was centered on "family" issues such as the right to marry, the HRC *fenced in* several blocks of Pennsylvania Avenue for a "public" street festival (as a friend suggested to me later, HRC's move might be summed up as "out of the closets and into the designated street-like areas"). The five-dollar admission fee to this street festival, according to a banner at the entrance that was filled with corporate logos, was dedicated "to the future." Highly visible and highly paid gay neocon-servative writers such as Bruce Bawer or Andrew Sullivan, meanwhile, in books such as *Virtually Normal, A Place at the Table,* and *Beyond Queer,* have cham-pioned "normalcy" and stigmatized queerness. In such an embattled position, queers have found it both easy and imperative to lash out at Giuliani, the HRC, and Bawer, Sullivan, and their allies.

However, questioning Reeve's motives (as I'm clearly doing in this chapter) is different from attacking Bawer or Sullivan, not (certainly) because Reeve deserves more pity, but rather because of how he functions in complicated ways for a range of communities: he is the most famous person with disabilities in the world and as such has brought an incredible amount of attention to disability—lobbying, for instance, for bills that would raise insurance caps and extend services. Simply attacking Reeve threatens to obscure that complex and con-tradictory position. I do, however, want to link Reeve's positions to the neocon-servative discourses that are currently threatening queerness, since his positions similarly capitalize (both figuratively and literally) on a demand for normalcy that ultimately works against many forms of embodiment and desire, and conse-quently against the queer/disabled identities that have been shaped around those forms of embodiment and desire. I want, in short, to critique the investments Reeve makes because of the critical perspectives and alliances that such invest-ments foreclose. Indeed, I'll confess to a certain amount of nostalgia here: at the beginning of the last century the most famous person with disabilities in the world, despite her participation in an "overcoming" narrative, was a socialist who understood that disability disproportionately impacted workers and the disempowered; Helen Keller knew that blindness and deafness, for instance, often resulted from industrial accidents.[9] At the beginning of this century, the most famous person with disabilities in the world is allowing his image to be used in commercials for Nuveen Investment Corporation. That's progress for you! But in some ways that is precisely my point—able-bodied notions of a progress tied simply to science, supposedly divorced from culture, mystify the economic forces driving both scientific research and the demand for normalcy and the actual experiences of many people with disabilities. In the end, such limited notions of "progress" make it difficult to recognize the ways in which people with disabilities are forging coalitions with other oppressed minorities and demanding access to, and a broadening of, the public sphere.[10]

Although I feel differently about Sullivan and Bawer, my point here is not so much to attack Reeve personally but to point out how the able-bodied discourses he perpetuates obscure and actually rescript perspectives shaped by and in the disability rights movement. Beyond that, in order to return to the signification of AIDS through disability and disability through AIDS, it is important to note how various disabilities are used together in the Nuveen ad (and, I would argue, ultimately against each other). As with spinal cord injuries, the Nuveen ad thoroughly *manages* what can or cannot be said about AIDS. In the commercial, in the name of "science" and miraculous "progress," viewers hear about a string of "successes": cures for AIDS, cancer, and then, of course, triumphantly, spinal cord injuries (and I do mean to stress that we *hear* about those successes, as the ad was one of the thirty-some Superbowl ads that was not closed captioned—after four million dollars, the two hundred extra dollars must have seemed too much of a bite). From the string of successes on to the climax on the Reeve image *and* the ensuing controversy, the commercial only serves to reinforce commonsense (highly problematic) notions about AIDS. Because in the dominant imagination AIDS and cancer so *easily* fit within a cure narrative, Nuveen can easily slide to spinal cord injuries. Once there, talking about the problems with cure discourse as it pertains to AIDS and cancer and about the possibility and necessity of coalitions between people impacted by AIDS and cancer and people with disabilities more generally, is effectively blocked (coalitions and a more accessible public sphere aren't really necessary if science has this all under control). A focus on "cure" of the spinal cord injury thoroughly solidifies that "cure" is the only way to think about AIDS and contributes to the ongoing two-decades-long blockage of conversations activists have tried to advance—conversations about how HIV positive and HIV negative, disabled and nondisabled, people are all implicated in the epidemic and the systems of power that sustain it, about how people with AIDS are not passive observers who are simply waiting for a cure, and important conversations about the range of sexual and drug-using practices individuals and communities (again, HIV positive or negative) engage in.

Queer cultural theory has positioned us as activists and theorists to make these points about the representation of HIV/AIDS but it has not yet positioned us to make the necessary linkages to cultural theory about disability, which is why my central argument is that a disability perspective needs to be incorporated into our thinking about AIDS, and named as such. The contradictory understanding of AIDS as, according to Erni, "at the same time curable and incurable" (1994: xi), allows it to function within the same arena as other disabilities that are conceptualized only according to a logic of elimination or scientific miracle (and it's worth pointing out that this logic arguably structures many current representations, in the mainstream media, of the global epidemic—the flip side of "miracle" drugs in the West [the fantasy of cure/containment] is countered by "death of a continent" scenarios in reporting on Africa [the fantasy of morbidity]). A queer/disability perspective helps us see how the cultural management of AIDS is of a piece with the cultural management of disability. If such a perspective is not acknowledged, it is easier for ideological understandings of AIDS to be deployed to secure ideological understandings of disability and vice versa.

Managing Queerness/Disability: *In the Gloaming*

By stressing cultural management, I am suggesting not only that AIDS and disability are linked through their similar movement around the two poles of cure or elimination, but also that people with disabilities and people living with AIDS are *used* (and even "tolerated") in productive ways by a culture seeking to secure the dominance of able-bodied and heterosexual perspectives and identities. This management is evident in a range of cultural texts, including some texts produced by people with disabilities or queers. In 1997, for instance, HBO broadcast *In the Gloaming,* a film directed by Christopher Reeve. Despite the aura of the miraculous that haunts the film, it is primarily a story about the main character, Danny (Robert Sean Leonard), coming "home" to die. Firmly located within the fantasy structure of morbidity, Danny can still be *used* to shore up the heteronormative, able-bodied family he leaves behind.[11]

Danny performs this function most obviously in one of the closing shots of *In the Gloaming.* I examine this scene at length in conclusion in order to extend my observations on how AIDS and disability are deployed in the Nuveen Investments commercial. Although one representation (*In the Gloaming*) would seem to focus on death and the other (Nuveen Investments) on life, they nonetheless serve remarkably similar ideological functions. It would be possible to argue, in fact, that the closing caption for the climactic scene of *In the Gloaming* should *also* be "Invest well. Leave your mark." No voice-over informs viewers that "amazing" things will happen in the future, but an able-bodied future is again secured through the elimination of the disabled body. *In the Gloaming* indicates more clearly than the Nuveen ad, however, the ways in which that dream of an able-bodied future is always thoroughly intertwined with the heterosexist fantasy of a world without queers.

In the climactic scene, Danny and his mother Janet (Glenn Close) are sitting outside the family's massive New England country home. Janet and her husband Martin (David Strathairn) have a relationship that, while not hostile, is decidedly distant. Danny's sister Anne (Bridget Fonda), who is married and has a child of her own, is also depicted as somewhat distant from her parents. Danny, in his final scene, lays the foundation for a healing of these rifts within the nuclear family. Since disability and queerness have been positioned throughout the film as largely responsible for those rifts, however, they must ultimately be eliminated from the narrative after the character who embodies them has been both domesticated and, paradoxically, used to alleviate the crises endemic to domesticity.[12]

The scene opens with the soft Gaelic music that plays in the background of most of *In the Gloaming*. The scene is also shot at dusk—it is both the end of the year (November) and of the day. Dusk, shot with soft pinks and blues of sunset, in many ways provides the backdrop for the entire film, both literally (since key scenes occur then) and symbolically (since the title invokes the Scottish word *gloaming*—the time in between day and night that Janet identifies as a time of longing and mystery). As the Gaelic music fades, the laughter of Danny and Janet becomes audible and the camera moves from shots of the pond behind the family home and the pink sunset to a close-up of mother and son:

DANNY: What did you want to be when you grew up?
JANET: Well, I was brought up to be a perfect wife and mother.
DANNY: Mmm . . . and what did you . . . um . . . dream of being?
JANET: A perfect wife and mother.

Janet's last line is delivered with a wistful, longing look that underscores the importance of these ideas.

Danny and Janet begin to laugh together about what she has said, however. For a moment, it is as though the ideological demands of the family, particularly for women, are ridiculous. Such demands are rarely stated so explicitly, and Danny and Janet's laughter is partly, perhaps, a nervous discomfort with the explicit articulation. Whatever the reason for the laughter, the fact that the role of perfect wife and mother is partially deflated on the level of the dialogue does not keep it from being reinstated on a functional level. Indeed, the partial deflation in fact mystifies the degree to which *In the Gloaming*'s subject is precisely the reinstatement of hegemonic notions of marriage and family.

It hurts Danny to laugh, and he begins to have trouble breathing. Suddenly, the accouterments of disability are made visible. The wheelchair in which Danny is sitting, which has not been obvious prior to this moment, is more clearly discernible, and Janet brings an oxygen mask to Danny's face, saying, "Okay,

okay, here you are, here you are." The scene's shift plays out two overdetermined narratives—Janet as mother (and, by extension, mother as nurturer/caretaker) and Danny/person with disabilities as helpless. These two overdetermined narratives obscure the cultural work that is actually being performed: the heterosexual and able-bodied family is in crisis and the queer/disabled figure must be recruited to repair it. This time, there is no laughter at how ridiculous or untenable that demand for the normative family might be.

The next lines in fact suggest, without explicitly acknowledging it, that in the end Janet, Martin, and Anne represent Danny's *real* family, even if in the past there have been queer alternatives. Danny declares (in reference to the lover he left behind in San Francisco before coming "home"), "I miss Paul." For many gay men, of course, a more "realistic" narrative would position the queer/disabled figure as rejected by the nuclear family and embraced by a supportive gay community.[13] Not surprisingly, however, *In the Gloaming* tells a different story. Janet, with apparent dignity that covers over the fact that she never bothered to integrate Paul into her family, says simply, "I'm sorry, sweetheart." The Gaelic music swells again, and the camera focuses yet again on the sunset.

At this point, the conversation seems to meander, but Danny quickly pulls it back to the nuclear family that is, in fact, at the center of the story. The "mystery" that Janet notes is merely the context in which Danny's "healing" of that family will take place:

> JANET: It's here. Oh, I can remember your grandfather talking about it—that time of *longing* between day and night. That mystery. He said it was the only hour that you could see the face of God. He at least was a good talker . . .
> DANNY (sudden shift): Why do you think Dad grows all those tomatoes . . . when he doesn't even eat them?
> JANET (smiles and laughs quietly): I don't know.
> DANNY: I think he grows them for you.

An extreme close-up on Janet's face suggests that Danny's words have affected her profoundly—that, in fact, she is suddenly understanding her relationship with her husband (a relationship she has neglected) anew. This is the climax of the film, and *In the Gloaming* can now move rapidly to its conclusion. The scene moves from this climax to an easily recognizable popular culture AIDS death. Janet asks, "Do you want to go in now?" After a pause, she says, slowly, "Danny?" We have had more than a decade to learn these conventions, and in fact they are conventions that were built upon much older, fully intact conventions for eliminating disability from the story. We know, in short, even before Janet does, that Danny has died. All that remains for *In the Gloaming* is the removal of the queer/disabled body (Danny's coffin is taken out of the house in the next scene) and the tearful reconciliation between Janet and Martin (a three-minute scene that paves the way for more Gaelic music and shots of the sunset as the credits roll).

To many critics of popular representations of AIDS, *In the Gloaming* unfortunately presents us with a familiar, and extraordinarily resilient, story. A full ten years earlier, Simon Watney had written the following about the made-for-TV movie *An Early Frost:* "The closing shot . . . shows a 'family album' picture. . . . A traumatic episode is over. The family closes ranks, with the problem son conveniently dispatched, and life getting back to normal" (114). In many ways, in fact, *An Early Frost* is more challenging than *In the Gloaming,* since the main character with AIDS does not die within the film itself, even if he is removed from the picture to allow for a return to normalcy. The removal preceding the return to normalcy in *In the Gloaming* occurs via death, despite the fact that in the 1990s America has supposedly learned what Cindy Patton calls "the national pedagogy" (1997: 7): the idea that we're all *living* with AIDS. After miraculously mending the rifts between his parents, the actual person living with AIDS in this film is eliminated from the narrative.

Interesting to me about *In the Gloaming,* though, are the ways in which it was packaged in the media, focusing almost solely on Reeve's direction.[14] News clips and reviews of the film tend to focus on Reeve from the first sentence, sometimes omitting entirely any discussion whatsoever of the actual *content* of the film: "In an herculean effort far more inspiring and dramatic than anything offered on the screen, Reeve makes his directorial debut, his first professional outing since his accident," "Christopher Reeve must have incredible capacity to buck up and carry on. Turns out he attended the premiere Monday of *In the Gloaming,* his directorial-debut, with a broken arm." The intense focus on Reeve's body in these accounts directly contradicts the frame the producers provide for understanding Reeve's direction: in a special HBO news report, for instance, one producer compares Reeve to Franklin Roosevelt and insists that Reeve can direct because "you never see the wheelchair."

The particular ways in which the disabled body is made visible and then invisible around *In the Gloaming* coincides not only with the simultaneous scrutiny and elimination of the person living with AIDS onscreen but also with many other contemporary representations of queer/disabled bodies, including the Superbowl ad for Nuveen Investments. *In the Gloaming* represents AIDS, queerness, and disability as crises both for other individuals and for contemporary social institutions, particularly the heteronormative institution of the family. In response to these crises, two kinds of queerness/disability are inscribed in the text and onto the body of the person living with AIDS. The first is an unruly disability/queerness that would disrupt the family and unsettle the identities of others; it is this queerness/disability that is made invisible and indeed eliminated, primarily (in the text of the film) through a discourse of domestication. The second is an exoticized queerness/disability that solidifies the family and secures the identities of others (this is most evident both in Danny's "healing" of the family and in the problematic representation of Reeve as the director who brings "you" to the point where you don't see the wheelchair). Ultimately, in the narrative, this disability/queerness too is eliminated, but only after it secures a heterosexual and able-bodied epiphany for the other characters (and for the audience—which is clearly not imagined as actually using wheelchairs or living with AIDS).

I draw attention in closing to these two kinds of disability/queerness in order to redirect attention, continuously, to the unruly sort. The critical investment in disability that I am suggesting cultural theory about AIDS should articulate would direct our attention back to those productively unruly bodies. In evidence at the margins of controversies such as the Nuveen commercial, even as it is silenced by the very able-bodied and heteronormative ideologies that produced it, a critically disabled perspective, like a critically queer perspective, resists domestication, especially when that domestication is imagined as bringing disability "home" to die, and instead demands access to public spaces and conversations currently configured to reproduce only the limited perspective of the able body.

Notes

1. The essays included in Douglas Crimp's groundbreaking *AIDS: Cultural Analysis, Cultural Activism* still serve as a good introduction to AIDS cultural theory; see also foundational works by Patton, Treichler, and Watney. More recent studies that attend to the intersections of class, race, nation, gender, and sexuality in the AIDS crisis include Browning, Cohen, Roman, Stoller.

2. Consider, on this point, David Halperin's assessment of the distinction between the AIDS Coalition to Unleash Power (ACT UP) and Queer Nation:

> The only thing that need be said about Queer Nation in this context is that it is significantly less *queer,* in the sense in which I am using the term, than, say, ACT UP, whose style of direct-action politics and activist glamor Queer Nation has attempted to replicate. . . . [ACT UP] draws in members of all the constituencies affected by the AIDS catastrophe, creating a political movement that is genuinely *queer* insofar as it is broadly oppositional; AIDS activism links gay resistance and sexual politics with social mobilization around issues of race, gender, poverty, incarceration, intravenous drug use, prostitution, sex phobia, media representation, health care reform, immigration law, medical research, and the power and accountability of "experts." (63)

3. When gay writers such as Gabriel Rotello began to suggest in the late 1990s that gay marriage and domesticity might serve as an effective prophylactic against AIDS, for instance, activists and theorists associated with the group Sex

Panic! in New York City produced a sharp critique of the ways in which such neoconservative arguments not only redoubled the stigmatization of those already living with HIV/AIDS but also proffered, by offering the illusion of safety and proscribing larger public discussions of safe sexual activity, what Cindy Patton would call "fatal advice." See Rotello's *Sexual Ecology: AIDS and the Destiny of Gay Men* and Patton's *Fatal Advice: How Safe Sex Education Went Wrong*. Eva Pendleton's "Domesticating Partnerships" provides a good overview of these conflicts.

4. Michel Foucault develops his theory of "docile bodies" in *Discipline and Punish: The Birth of the Prison* (135–69). Some of the foundational work in disability studies that expands on much of what I have detailed in this paragraph includes Davis, Garland-Thomson, Linton, Mitchell and Snyder.

5. For information on the role of AIDS in passage of the ADA, see Joseph P. Shapiro's overview in *No Pity: People with Disabilities Forging a New Civil Rights Movement* (136–37). Shapiro discusses how activists addressed conservative resistance to the inclusion of HIV/AIDS in the ADA directly, refusing to compromise this portion of the bill. This refusal to compromise is an example of the "critical investment" that I call for in this chapter.

6. I am indebted in this chapter generally, and in this introduction particularly, to Judith Butler's essay "Critically Queer," in which she is critical of the exclusions perpetuated by queerness even as she simultaneously positions queerness as theoretically and politically critical (in the sense of crucial or necessary). See my discussion of "Critically Queer" in *The Queer Renaissance: Contemporary American Literature and the Reinvention of Lesbian and Gay Identities* (149–53). In "Compulsory Able-Bodiedness and Queer/Disabled Existence," in an attempt to develop a theory of "critical disability," I extend Butler's idea of critical queerness to disability studies.

7. Reeve was pictured beside the caption "Superman" on the August 26, 1996 cover of *Time* magazine; the story that accompanied that cover—Roger Rosenblatt's "New Hopes, New Dreams"—is a good and early example of the ways in which the mainstream media has reported on Reeve following his May 27, 1995 accident. The Point/Counterpoint articles, by Danny Heumann and Lolly Lijewski, appeared online in HalfthePlanet.com-The Disability Source ⟨http://www.halftheplanet.com/departments/vote/article5.html⟩. For coverage of the Nuveen controversy, I have drawn from the following articles (and headlines): "When 'Superman' walks, does it raise false hopes?" (Associated Press, Jan. 31, 2000); "Some Criticism of Reeve Walking Ad" (Associated Press, Feb. 1, 2000); "Reeve's 'walk' disturbs doctors and disabled" (*Seattle Times,* Feb. 14, 2000); "Reeve Ads Can't Work Magic" (*San Francisco Chronicle,* Feb. 13, 2000); "Hope or Hype? Christopher Reeve's 'Super Walk' Disquiets Doctors, Disabled" (*New Orleans Times-Picayune,* Feb. 7, 2000); "Reeve takes flak over TV ad" (*Montreal Gazette,* Feb. 3, 2000); "Reality, virtual or not, is that Super Bowl commercials were false" (*Atlanta Journal and Constitution,* Feb. 2, 2000); "No, Mr. Reeve's Not Walking—Yet" (*Columbus Dispatch,* Feb. 2, 2000); "'Walking'

Reeve Ad on TV Shakes Up the Disabled" (*New York Daily News,* Feb. 2, 2000).
Reeve appeared on *Good Morning, America* on January 31, 2000; a transcript of
Diane Sawyer's interview, "Reeve on Superbowl Ad," is available at ⟨http://
abcnews.go.com/onair/goodmorningamerica/transcripts/gma000131_reeves
_transcript.html⟩. The *Today Show* debating the controversy aired on NBC on
February 2, 2000; a transcript of that program is available from Burrelle's Information Services. The Nuveen commercial itself can be viewed at ⟨http://www.
adcritic.com⟩.

    8. For some of the work in queer studies attentive to and critical of the
ways in which queer public spheres are being dismantled by development, com-
modification, and normalization, see Chasin 2000; Dangerous Bedfellows 1996;
Delany, Duggan and Hunter 1995; Munoz 1999; Rofes 2001; Schulman 1988;
Warner 1999.

    9. On Helen Keller's socialism, see Dorothy Herrmann's *Helen Keller—
A Life,* especially chapter 12, "A Fiery Radical" (1998: 171–79).

    10. For example, WinVisible, a group for women with visible and invis-
ible disabilities, participates in global women's strikes and repeatedly makes
connections to a range of progressive movements:

> We are joining the strike to press governments and society to acknowledge
> that in an inaccessible world, all people with disabilities already have to
> work hard just to survive, let alone have a life. Much of disability and ill-
> health is caused by poverty, pollution, war and the arms trade, industrial
> accidents and job injuries, and other deadly effects of a world economy
> which prioritises profit over people's needs. Those who get the lowest
> wages internationally and have the worst working conditions have the
> highest rates of disability: women of colour and immigrant people. (Win-
> Visible 2001)

    11. In "Portraits of People with AIDS," Douglas Crimp identifies Stashu
Kybartas's 1987 video *Danny* as

> one of the most powerful critiques that exists to date. . . . Danny accom-
> plishes this through one overriding difference: the formulation of the
> relationship between artist and subject not as one of empathy or identifica-
> tion, but as one of explicit sexual desire, a desire that simultaneously
> accounts for Kybartas's subjective investment in the project and celebrates
> Danny's own sense of gay identity and hard-won sexual freedom. (Crimp
> 1992: 126)

Although it is unlikely that the producers of *In the Gloaming* were aware of the
existence of *Danny,* it is ironic that "Danny" is recruited ten years later for a
normative role that effectively blocks the critical investments Crimp invokes.

12. In "Capitalism and Gay Identity," John D'Emilio notes that a shift from an economy based on household production and interdependence for survival to a "free labor" economy brought concomitant shifts in ideologies of the family and domesticity. As the world of work was consolidated as "public," domestic space was consolidated as "private" and the (heterosexual) family was reconstituted as the entity that could provide intimacy, happiness, and emotional satisfaction. However, this emotional satisfaction was (and is) often illusory given that capitalism produced social and material instability. In D'Emilio's analysis, gay men, lesbians, and feminists became the "scapegoats for the social instability of the system" (1992: 12).

13. Such an embrace has, of course, not been universal in gay communities. I am thinking of the communal practices of queer communities at their best here, as detailed in studies such as David Roman's *Acts of Intervention: Performance, Gay Culture, and AIDS*. See especially Roman's first chapter, "Acts of Intervention," which discusses some of the collective practices developed by gay men and their allies even in the early days of the epidemic (1998: 1–43).

14. The news report on production immediately follows *In the Gloaming* on the HBO video. For reviews of *In the Gloaming,* I have relied on the following sources: "Reeve Breaks Arm" (E!Online News, ⟨http://www.eonline.com/News/Items/0%2C1%2C935%2C00.html⟩); "Paralysis didn't hinder Reeve in directing film" (*Lubbock Avalanche-Journal,* April 4, 1997); "Reeve goes behind the camera" (*Boston Globe,* April 20, 1997); "In the Gloaming: Christopher Reeve Turns First-Time Director with New HBO Drama" (*The Buffalo News,* April 20, 1997); "A Debut with Resonance, a Family with a Problem" (*New York Times,* April 19, 1997); "'Gloaming' proves Reeve has a director's vision" (*Houston Chronicle,* April 18, 1997); as well as the film notes for *In the Gloaming* from beproud.com's gay video collection ⟨http://www.beproud.com/gay-video/in-the-gloaming.htm⟩.

References

Bawer, Bruce, ed. (1996). *Beyond Queer: Challenging Gay Left Orthodoxy.* New York: Free Press.

——— (1993). *A Place at the Table: The Gay Individual in American Society.* New York: Touchstone-Simon and Schuster.

Browning, Barbara (1998). *Infectious Rhythm: Metaphors of Contagion and the Spread of African Culture.* New York: Routledge.

Butler, Judith (1993). "Critically Queer." *GLQ: A Journal of Lesbian and Gay Studies* 1 (1): 17–32.

Chasin, Alexandra (2000). *Selling Out: The Lesbian and Gay Movement Goes to Market.* New York: St. Martin's.

Cohen, Cathy (1999). *The Boundaries of Blackness: AIDS and the Breakdown of Black Politics.* Chicago: University of Chicago Press.

Crimp, Douglas, ed. (1987). *AIDS: Cultural Analysis/Cultural Activism.* Cambridge, Mass.: MIT.

——— (1992). "Portraits of People with AIDS." *Cultural Studies,* ed. Lawrence Grossberg, Cary Nelson, and Paula Treichler. New York: Routledge.

Crimp, Douglas, and Adam Rolston (1990). *AIDS DemoGraphics.* Seattle: Bay.

Dangerous Bedfellows, eds. (1996). *Policing Public Sex.* Boston: South End.

Davis, Lennard J., ed. (1997). *The Disability Studies Reader.* New York: Routledge.

——— (1995). *Enforcing Normalcy: Disability, Deafness, and the Body.* London: Verso.

Delany, Samuel R. (1999). *Times Square Red, Times Square Blue.* New York: New York University Press.

D'Emilio, John (1992). "Capitalism and Gay Identity." *Making Trouble: Essays on Gay History, Politics, and the University.* New York: Routledge, 3–16.

Duggan, Lisa, and Nan D. Hunter (1995). *Sex Wars: Sexual Dissent and Political Culture.* New York: Routledge.

Erni, John Nguyet (1994). *Unstable Frontiers: Technomedicine and the Cultural Politics of "Curing" AIDS.* Minneapolis: University of Minnesota Press.

Foucault, Michel (1977). *Discipline and Punish: The Birth of the Prison,* trans. Alan Sheridan. New York: Vintage-Random House.

——— (1978). *The History of Sexuality,* vol. 1, trans. Robert Hurley. New York: Vintage-Random House.

Garland-Thomson, Rosemarie (1997). *Extraordinary Bodies: Figuring Physical Disability in American Culture and Literature.* New York: Columbia University Press.

Grover, Jan Zita (1997). "AIDS: Keywords." Crimp 17–30.

Halperin, David M. (1995). *Saint Foucault: Towards a Gay Hegiography.* New York: Oxford University Press.

Herrmann, Dorothy (1998). *Helen Keller—A Life.* Chicago: University of Chicago Press.

In the Gloaming (1997). Dir. Christopher Reeve. Perf. Glenn Close, Robert Sean Leonard, and David Strathairn. HBO.

Linton, Simi (1998). *Claiming Disability: Knowledge and Identity.* New York: New York University Press.

McRuer, Robert (2002). "Compulsory Able-Bodiedness and Queer/Disabled Existence." *Disability Studies: Enabling the Humanities,* eds. Brenda Jo Brueggeman, Rosemarie Garland-Thompson, and Sharon Snyder. New York: MLA Publishing.

——— (1997). *The Queer Renaissance: Contemporary American Literature and the Reinvention of Lesbian and Gay Identities.* New York: New York University Press.

Mitchell, David T., and Sharon L. Snyder, eds. (1997). *The Body and Physical Difference: Discourses of Disability.* Ann Arbor: University of Michigan Press.

——— (2000). *Narrative Prosthesis: Disability and the Dependencies of Discourse.* Ann Arbor: University of Michigan Press.

Munoz, Jose Esteban (1999). *Disidentifications: Queers of Color and the Performance of Politics.* Minneapolis: University of Minnesota Press.

Patton, Cindy (1997). *Fatal Advice: How Safe-Sex Education Went Wrong.* Durham: Duke University Press.

——— (1990). *Inventing AIDS.* New York: Routledge.

Pendleton, Eva (1996). "Domesticating Partnerships." *Policing Public Sex: Queer Politics and the Future of AIDS Activism,* ed. Dangerous Bedfellows. Boston: South End, 373–93.

PWA Coalition Portfolio. Crimp 147–68.

Rofes, Eric (2001). "Imperial New York: Destruction and Disneyfication under Emperor Giuliani." *GLQ: A Journal of Lesbian and Gay Studies* 7 (1): 101–109.

Roman, David (1998). *Acts of Intervention: Performance, Gay Culture, and AIDS.* Bloomington: Indiana University Press.

Rotello, Gabriel (1997). *Sexual Ecology: AIDS and the Destiny of Gay Men.* New York: Dutton-Penguin.

Schulman, Sarah (1990). *Stagestruck: Theater, AIDS and the Marketing of Gay America.* Durham: Duke University Press.

Sedgwick, Eve Kosofsky (1993). *Tendencies.* Durham: Duke University Press.

Shapiro, Joseph P. (1994). *No Pity: People with Disabilities Forging a New Civil Rights Movement.* New York: Time-Random House.

Stoller, Nancy (1998). *Lessons from the Damned: Queers, Whores, and Junkies Respond to AIDS.* New York: Routledge.

Sullivan, Andrew (1995). *Virtually Normal: An Argument about Homosexuality.* New York: Knopf.

Treichler, Paula (1999). *How to Have Theory in an Epidemic: Cultural Chronicles of AIDS.* Durham: Duke University Press.

Warner, Michael (1999). *The Trouble with Normal: Sex, Politics, and the Ethics of Queer Life.* New York: Free Press.

Watney, Simon (1989). *Policing Desire: Pornography, AIDS, and the Media,* 2d ed. Minneapolis: University of Minnesota Press.

——— (0000). *Practices of Freedom: Selected Writings on HIV/AIDS.* Durham: Duke University Press.

WinVisible (Women with Visible and Invisible Disabilities) (2001). "Women with Disabilities." Web Page in Support of Global Women's Strike. 28 Mar. ⟨http://womenstrike8m.server101.com/English/women—with—disabilities.htm⟩.

PART V
LIMINALITIES

9

The Inhuman Circuit

Jeffrey Jerome Cohen

"You know that the body is a hot topic," a friend recently confided, "if even the medievalists are studying it."

Contrary to the expectations of some scholars who conduct their work primarily in contemporary-oriented materials, medievalists have long been engaged in the study of the body, since the occidental Middle Ages were, on the whole, just as obsessed by the flesh as we moderns.[1] The theorization of corporeality has therefore proceeded in medieval studies with the same vigor that has animated the exploration of the body elsewhere, but (if I may make the broadest of generalizations for a moment) medievalists have been immediately and acutely aware of the body's limits as they invite recent discourse on the subject to travel distantly back in time with them. Indeed, this collection of essays is to some degree built around a progress narrative that medieval studies never quite bought into: that "the body" has until recently been assumed to be a bounded object, and is only now beginning to be examined as a dispersed phenomenon, especially in light of recent technological advances. True, most medievals had an experience of bodiliness dissimilar to the one provided by the postindustrial, postcapitalist, postmedicalized West. Medieval bodies were caught between gravitational forces that pulled them at once toward a fantasy of impossible completeness (for medieval Christians, the sacred body that existed beyond the limits of life and death) and at the same time confronted them with a daily spectacle of the flesh dissolving into pieces, of bodies composed of metamorphic humoral fluids, of the corporeal as the scene for the staging of magic, holiness, perversity, wonder. Bodies were, quite simply, caught in a process of eruptive becoming.[2]

The chapter that follows examines a limit case of the body as *human*. Through an analysis of chivalry, a medieval code of masculine embodiment the effects of which are still being felt on gendered relations in the West today, I argue that the European Middle Ages could be antihuman in a way associated in contemporary writing with cyberculture and postmodernity. Deploying the collaborative insights of the philosopher Gilles Deleuze and psychoanalyst Félix Guattari, I detail the permeability of the medieval species barrier. The perfected manhood that chivalry represented was enabled only through the loving dispersal of selfhood across and into the body of a horse. This assemblage, which commixes the animal and the human, the organic and the inorganic, illustrates well the limits of the body for the medieval and the postmodern period, and underscores along the way a possible shortcoming of queer theory, a mode of analysis central to much contemporary writing about bodies and their limits.

Queer in Theory

Allen J. Frantzen closes *Before the Closet: Same-Sex Love from Beowulf to Angels in America* with a poeticized account of his body's awakening to selfhood and to pleasure. The passage is beautiful, and worth quoting at length:

> I remember another night one summer on the farm when I was in high school. For some reason, I was home alone, a rare event; I seldom felt unwatched. The moon was full and my room was bright with its light. I got up, took off my pajamas and walked down the stairs and outside, where I stood on the porch in the warm silence. Then I ran to an old swing that hung from a huge elm tree by the garage. I jumped on the seat, surprised at how smooth the old wood felt under me, and began to swing as fast as I could, leaning back, legs spread, sailing naked through the night and the warm air, hearing only the creak of the rope and the wind rushing past me. Eventually I saw headlights in the distance, surely from my parents' car. . . . As the gravel crunched and my father's Impala pulled into the driveway, I fell into bed. There I lay, heart pounding, scandalized, sweaty, thrilled. I never wrote about that experience. Neither boy nor man shared it. . . . It was a moment of awakening to the nearness of forbidden pleasure, to danger, darkness, mystery, and to the possibility of feeling at home in my body, which was, just then, in every sense and for once, my own. (Frantzen 1998: 308)

At first glance, the narrative is a straightforward account of a young man's discovery of his sexuality, consonant with learning how to inhabit ("feel at home in") his body. Like all epiphanies, the story is structured around the coming into awareness of something already present but not previously realized; that is to say, "sexuality" and "body" are assumed to be discrete and timeless objects.

As a sexual coming-of-age narrative, the story is joyfully onanistic, its pleasures shared with "neither boy nor man" (at least until Frantzen narrates them in 1998). The naked swing through a moonlit night is so poetically rendered that it is impossible not to share in its exuberance, an intersubjective moment where author meets audience for the making public of what had been solitary enjoyment. The vignette seems to depict a self-enclosed world where the limits of the body are unproblematically visible: individuality and embodiment are coterminous, even if one has to *learn* how to feel at home within the flesh. On closer reflection, however, somatic boundaries are more porous than Frantzen would seem to allow. The adolescent would not be able to awaken to his corporeality without the sensuous impingement of warm moonlight, smooth wood, sonorous ropes. The act of disrobing, the caress of nocturnal air, the rising and falling of the swing are as much a part of the experience of embodiment as naked skin, spread legs, limbs in motion through the night. At home by leaving the house: the discovery here is perhaps not so much of a preexistent, "individual" body that was always with Frantzen, if previously estranged from him, but rather of a haptic series of alliances formed with a wide natural world outside the walls of his home (the place he must temporarily leave in order to experience a bodiliness which is nondomestic, nonfamilial, unsocialized). Before the reinstatement of boundary precipitated by the arrival of the paternal Impala, the limits of Frantzen's adolescent body do not necessarily form a second circumscribing "house" within which he must learn to dwell. Sexuality and corporeality are in fact dispersed across an exquisite summer night.

I open with this extended examination of the closing paragraph of Frantzen's important book because *Before the Closet* argues nostalgically for a return to the certainties of the "history of sex" over the "lack of critical rigor" inherent in contemporary queer theory (1998: 15–25). If sex, sexuality, embodiment are as dispersed as both Frantzen's moonlit swing and queer theory make them out to be, however, speaking of the "history of sex" or even the "history of the body" is quickly going to bring us up against the messy, uncertain limits of both categories. With Frantzen I will argue that contemporary queer theory has limitations, especially when applied to prepostmodern culture and texts. Unlike him, however, I contend that queer theory can usefully become *more* queer, not less. To do so I will read a series of medieval texts in which masculine embodiment functions only within what, following Gilles Deleuze and Félix Guattari, could be called an inhuman circuit. This dispersive assemblage has much to offer both to those who, like Frantzen, reject queer theory, and to those who are its most ardent proponents.

Queer theory's strength is its insistence on the historical instability and the mutability of epistemological categories, especially those involving sexual identity. Recent work by medievalists has therefore insisted on the queer's deconstructive effect. Glenn Burger argues that "in contrast to the stabilizing categories of identity politics, the term 'queer' would resist nominalization . . . stressing epistemology rather than ontology" (Burger 1994: 156). Carolyn Dinshaw gives the queer an inherently unruly definition:

> Queerness works by contiguity and displacement, knocking signifiers loose, ungrounding bodies, making them strange. . . . It makes people stop and look at what they have been taking as natural, and it provokes inquiry into the ways that 'natural' has been produced.[3]

Something in the queer prevents its full reintegration into whatever matrix of identity it arises to challenge with its perversity, its excess, its defiant joy. Its "disillusioning" force is certainly an "insistent reminder . . . of heterosexual incompleteness" (Dinshaw 1995: 92), but it is also something bigger: the discomfiting limit of any circumscriptive system (of space, of time, of identity) that parcels the world into discrete phenomena and impossibly immobile categories.

Dinshaw's limitation is perhaps in applying queerness exclusively against hetero-normativity. Recent work by Claire Sponsler and Robert Clark applies queer to race in the Middle Ages, while Steve Kruger and Karma Lochrie have queered medieval religion and ethnicity.[4] The queer, in my understanding, involves sexuality without being reducible to it.

Affirmative and refreshingly utopian, queer theory would seem to be the logical place from which to launch any inquiry into the limits of the body. David Halperin's *Saint Foucault* is an influential book that sanctifies a founding father of queer studies in order to (among other things) advance queer theory against academic "complacency" and "monolithic, homogenizing discourse" (Halperin 1995: 113). Just as Jean-Paul Sartre once transformed the criminal-artist Jean Genet into *Saint Genet,* into existentialism made flesh, Halperin attempts to embody an activist notion of "queer" in the life and writings of Michel Foucault—an admirably perverse project, considering how much of Foucault's scholarly energy was given over to demolishing Sartre's brand of humanism. "Queer," Halperin writes, is "identity without essence," "positionality" rather than "positivity."[5] He argues persuasively that "Queer politics, if it is to remain queer, needs to be able to perform the function of emptying queerness of its referentiality or positivity, guarding against its tendency to concrete embodi-ment, and thereby preserving queerness as a resistant relation rather than as an oppositional substance" (Halperin 1995: 113). The danger is that "queer" has already begun to function as an institutionalized and therefore inherently nor-mative category, forfeiting its power to challenge, resist, and unsettle—becoming "an unproblematic, substantive designation for a determinate subfield of aca-demic practice . . . signifying little more than what used to be signified by 'gay and lesbian studies'" (113). Halperin insists that the queerness—the alterity, the irreducibility to some other thing—has to be returned to "queer theory," so that it functions again as an effective catalyst to desubstantiation.

Surprisingly, then, Halperin's queer is haunted by that very "tendency to concrete embodiment" he so strongly condemns elsewhere. In discussing the transformative ascesis of bodybuilding, he argues that "queer muscles are not the same as straight muscles" (116), for they "produce a physique" that destabilizes heteronormative masculinities. A page later, he writes that because they activate desire and are not produced "by hard physical labor" (that is, because they originate in the gym, and are not an occupational byproduct) "gay muscles do not signify power" (117). There are all kinds of problems with the two versions of this statement (an astonishing class bias, an un-Foucaultian insistence that an "object of desire" somehow cannot "signify power"), but what I find most re-markable is the slippage of "queer muscles" (116) to "gay muscles" (117) via the materiality of the human body. It is as if queer as a resistant, antiontological category can exist in theory—and only *as* queer theory—but when the queer manifests itself "in the flesh," the stability of those categories it was supposedly undermining returns, concretely embodied—and usually embodied in an overtly, if not excessively, male form. The human body and the queer of theory seem to be radically at odds, like the flesh and the spirit of some medieval theology.

Queer theory is undoubtedly the most radical challenge yet posed to the supposed naturalness of sexual identity, but it seems strange that a critical movement predicated on the smashing of limit should content itself with the small contours of human form, as if the body could be contained within the porous embrace of its skin. Perhaps the reason Halperin's articulation of queerness falls back into the essentializing materiality which it professes to discard is simply because the queer theory he advances has jettisoned the notion of an atemporal, inherently natural sexuality without taking the next logical step (a step Foucault himself took, in distinction to Sartre): abandoning the humanism on which such a claim is founded. The body is not human (or at least, it is not only human); nor, as Frantzen's narrative has already suggested, is it inhabited by an identity or sexuality unique to or even contained fully within its flesh.[6]

Two Deleuzoguattarian Horses

How could the body and sexuality be thought outside of reductively anthropomorphic, humanist terms? Gilles Deleuze and Félix Guattari, postmodern philosophers of identity, compatriots and friends to Foucault, have offered in their diverse writings a toolbox full of instruments useful for constructing the posthuman, antihumanistic body. Deleuze and Guattari are singularly uninterested in essences. Of a body they never ask "What is it?" but "What can it do?"

> We know nothing about a body until we know what it can do, in other words, what its affects are, how they can or cannot enter into composition with other affects, with the affects of another body, either to destroy the body or to be destroyed by it, either to exchange actions and passions with it or to join with it in composing a more powerful body.[7]

When Deleuze and Guattari discuss Freud's famous case of Little Hans, for example, they argue that Freud went wrong when he tried to interpret the boy's fascination with a horse being whipped by invoking a master narrative of identification and discrete subjectivities. Psychoanalysis, they insist, has always erred in interpreting animals as anthropomorphic symbols rather than as points of movement within a larger assemblage [*agencement*] of identity. Freud argued that the beaten horse represented Little Hans's father ("blinders are the father's eyeglasses"), provoking Deleuze and Guattari to complain that Freud says nothing about the larger world within which Hans and the horse are interconnected: "not one word about Hans's relation to the street, on how the street was forbidden to him, on what it is for a child to see the spectacle" (1980: 259). The boy's desire toward the horse has nothing to do with sympathy, imitation, or fantasy, but is instead a "becoming-horse," which offers Hans an escape from the blockages of forced, familial identifications (258). Whereas psychoanalysis insists that Little Hans's "problem" can be solved simply by reference to the oedipal triangle, the authors argue that the identity machine Hans constructs exceeds the suffocating confines of domestic space to connect "his mother's bed, the paternal element, the house, the café across the street, the nearby warehouse, the street, the right to go into the street" (258). Like the adolescent Frantzen on his nocturnal swing, Hans moves within *un agencement machinique* ("machinic assemblage," 1987: 257, 314) that makes of the body an exploded site of possibility and desire rather than a circumscriptive, delimiting "home."[8]

Children and masochists, observe Deleuze and Guattari, have always viewed bodies in such energetic, Spinozist terms.[9] In *A Thousand Plateaus,* for example, they describe how a masochist transforms his body via bridle, whip, spurs, and rider-dominatrix into *un circuit d'intensités* ("circuit of intensities"), which constitutes a "nonhuman sexuality" (1987: 233, 285):

> PROGRAM . . . At night, put on the bridle and attach my hands more tightly, either to the bit with the chain, or to the big belt right after returning from the bath. Put on the entire harness right away also. . . . If the animal should display impatience or rebelliousness, the reins will be drawn tighter, the master will grab them and give the beast a good thrashing. (1987: 155–56, 192–93)

Through a *participation contre nature,* a series of forces are brought into explosive contact (258, 315). Identity and form do not reside within any single point within this strange assemblage, which is itself constituted only through the movements uniting corporealities, text, affects, and objects as they mutually transform each other. The masochist's desire circulates within a heterogeneous alliance that commingles the desires of fragmentable human bodies (each organ of which could have its own desires), the desires of an animal body (the horse that the masochist is intent on becoming, who "transmits" its forces to tame and "over-code" the human body), even the desires of the sharp whip, the constricting bridle, the cold spurs, the binding contract. "Little by little," the masochist writes, "all opposition is replaced by a *fusion* of my person with yours ... you will give me the imprint of your body as I have never had it before and would never have it otherwise" (156).[10] There is no possibility of "concrete embodiment" here: where is the horse? the woman? the man? The best analysis can only map the movements and becomings such an inhuman circuit makes possible. If we ask of this assemblage, "What is it?" we can answer only with inadequate, dismissive categorization ("It is perversity," "It is pornography," "It is a silly man [literally] making an ass of himself") If we ask "What can it do?" however, we can perhaps see that it gathers at least three bodies into a dispersive assemblage of forces without totalizing them, without insisting on anything but the combinatory power of fragments and the plural autonomy of desire.

The Chivalric Circuit

With its origins in childhood fantasy and recurrent intimations of B&D, this deleuzoguattarian *equus eroticus* may at first seem far removed from the Middle Ages, a time period more commonly associated with ecclesiastical injunctions to celibacy and a cultural obsession with virginity. Yet the inhuman circuit has an unexpected analogue in that rigorous training of the male body which is chivalry, a medieval technology of the self that relies on a similarly complex assemblage capable of catching up human, animal, objects, and intensities into what also might be called a nonhuman body.[11] A brief scene from a wildly popular fourteenth-century romance makes this point about chivalric dispersedness emphatically. Originally composed in Norman French, *Beves of Hamton* was eventually translated into English, Italian, Welsh, and even Yiddish. During one particularly intense battle against a fierce giant, the hero chides his monstrous opponent for slaying his steed: "'Oh!' said Beves, 'You committed great villainy when you spared my body, and on my account killed my horse!' (1890–93; translation mine). The declaration that Beves values his own life less than that of his horse may seem puzzling to modern readers, but medieval knights were nothing without their mounts, as the etymology of the French and German words for knight (*chevalier, Ritter*) suggests.[12] Chivalry is a code of masculinity that is, at its linguistic and cultural base, predicated on a mutually constitutive relationship between men and their horses.

Beginning in the eighth century, a widespread European dissemination of the stirrup coincided with an increase in the martial utility of cavalry during combat.[13] Through a downward shift in the force their bodies could assert, mounted combatants were seated with greater stability in their saddles, allowing more complicated battlefield maneuvers. At the same time, this enlargement of corporeal possibility affected the horse, enabling it to become more responsive to its rider within an augmented tactile syntax between equine and human flesh. Both bodies were changed in this encounter mediated by some leather and metal. Traditional methods of keeping bodies discrete do not work very well here. It is not as if the horse is a passive vehicle and the knight its all-controlling driver (another version of the tedious body/mind split, with the human as pure intentionality and the animal as passive materiality). There is nothing inanimate about stirrup, which is neither "social" nor "technological," but is instead "neither object nor subject," a "thing that possesses body and soul indissolubly":

> The object, the real thing, the thing that acts, exists only provided that it holds humans and nonhumans together, continuously. . . . What we are

looking at is not a human thing, nor is it an inhuman thing. It offers, rather, a continuous passage, a commerce, an interchange, between what humans inscribe in it and what it prescribes to humans. It translates the one into the other.[14]

If it is true that the equine body learns a new type of control through the changes that the technological engenders, it is just as true that the human body likewise must submit to a new regimen of training and corporeal response, a reconfigured experience of embodiment. Without a disciplinization of the flesh predicated on the instantiation of an *intersubjective* docility, horse and rider are not going anywhere in the cavalry charge except to a quick death. Steed and warrior and accouterments become simultaneously active and receptive points of force in a transformative assemblage. Agency, possibility, and identity are mobile, the product of relations of movement rather than a static residuum contained in discrete bodies (horse, man) and objects (saddle, stirrups, spurs, armor, sword).

This alteration in the distribution of forces between horse and man allowed the "shock charge" with a long spear couched under the rider's shoulder to become possible.[15] In the words of Maurice Keen, the "horse, rider, and lance are thus gathered together into what has been called a 'human projectile'" (Keen 1984: 24). This assemblage catalyzed changes to the materiality of social and somatic reality. A saddle-bow had to be added to prevent unseating of the knight at contact. Since lances so easily punctured flesh, shirts of mail became necessary for knights in order to survive battle, and armor integral to their mounts. Men's bodies had to adapt to this increase in armaments through a more rigorous development of the thighs, chest, shoulders, for the full gear of an armed knight was composed of fifty pounds of iron (Bartlett 1993: 61). Early in the Middle Ages horses were rather diminutive by today's standards, but over time they were bred to be larger and more muscular in order to support the growing weight of their own armor, their rider's armor, and perhaps their rider's increased average body mass.[16] The necessity of a good warhorse, remounts, and squires to assist in arming pushed knighthood farther along the path of aristocratic privilege that it had long been tracing—for very few men outside the aristocracy could afford these proliferating accouterments.[17] Because of the complicated skills the new tactic demanded, men's and horse's bodies had to be trained extensively to foster endurance and coordination, to implant in both animal and human flesh the corporeal knowledge of how to embody the charge.[18] Tournaments became essential as an efficient public means for producing the requisite man-animal alliance by providing a forum for practice and training. By encouraging heavily armed men to aggressive acts, however, tournaments were also dangerous events. The promulgation of a code of chivalry that valorized control and subordination thus became an increasingly important way of altering embodied masculinity, of producing a male body as docile at court as it was deadly on the battlefield.

In his *Livre de chevalerie* [*Book of Chivalry*], a kind of recipe book for producing proper chivalric subjects, the renowned knight Geoffroi de Charny describes how the "most perfect" form of knighthood comes to be embodied.[19] As soon as they reach the "age of understanding" [*des lors que cognoissance se commence*], certain boys with a natural instinct (read "select aristocratic youth") enjoy listening to men describe deeds at arms, looking at knights in armor, and gazing upon "fine mounts and chargers [*beaux chevaux et beaux coursiers*]" (Kaeuper and Kennedy 1996: 100, 101). The ardor [*tres grant volenté*] triggered by these auditory and visual stimuli increases as they approach adulthood, so that as adolescents they desire "to ride horses and bear arms" (100, 101). The originary power of this catalytic *volenté* for horsemanship is acknowledged once more in Charny's description of the knighting ceremony, where the first symbolic gift conferred on a new knight is two gilded spurs (168, 169).

Although treatises on chivalry like those by Charny and Ramon Llull are important documents for the study of Western European aristocratic male identity, narrative was likely the primary technology for the implantation of medieval chivalric desire. The transformation of the world via the assemblage formed by knight, horse, and equestrian objects can be seen most vividly in secular, vernacular works known as romances and *chansons de geste,* both of which abstracted and idealized the material realities in which they intervened, forming with them a new circuit (knight-warhorse-equipage-chivalric text). Of the chansons, for example, Maurice Keen has observed that their protagonists are "cavaliers, skilled in the new art of fighting in the saddle with the couched lance" whose heroism is predicated on "the possession of a war horse and a knowledge of how to handle it" (Keen 1984: 103–104). Their knightly possessions are so central to their identity that these objects take on a numinous aura, agency, even a humanizing name (Roland's sword is called Durendaal, his horse Veillantif). Keen is content to leave his investigation of the contingency of chivalric identity with this brief acknowledgment, but it is worth noting that this mutual dependency between the heroic and the equine finds vivid and extended expression in the chansons. In the *Song of Roland,* for example, Roland's corporeal rebuke to the pagan knight Chernubles involves the Saracen's horse as much as it does the enemy's abjected body:

[Roland] breaks his [foe's] helmet with its gleaming carbuncles,
Slices off his coif and his scalp,
As well as slicing through his eyes and his face,
His shining hauberk and close-meshed mail
His whole body right down to his crotch,
And right into his saddle which is of beaten gold;
His sword comes to rest in the horse itself.
He slices through its spine, seeking no joint,
And flinging them both dead in the meadow on the lush grass.[20]

In the chanson *Aliscans*, Guillaume d'Orange likewise cuts pagans and their horses to pieces. At the same time, he is also quick to acknowledge the passionate ties that unite him to his own charger, Baucent. Overwhelmed by Saracens, Guillaume worries that his horse will be seized, a misfortune he would not be able to endure ("Si en Espaigne es des paiens menez, / Si m'aist Dex, moult en serair irez").[21] Baucent listens like a man ("ausi l'entent com s'il fust hom senez") as his master promises that he will feed him richly, bathe him, and have him clothed in noble blankets if he can gather his courage and get them both to Orange; the horse then joyfully obliges. The eponymous hero of *Ogier le Danois* finds himself happily ensconced in a strange domesticity with his beloved steed Broiefort. Besieged by the French while immured at Castelfort, he tends his oven, bakes bread, cares for his animal. In an inspired moment he snips hair from Broiefort and fabricates bearded mannequins who frighten away his attackers. As Sandra Hindman has observed, Ogier inhabits a world without women: "simultaneously brutish and clever, with only a horse for his companion, . . . [he] moves in an exclusively male world of epic adventure" (Hindman 1994: 154). That "male world" literally originates for Ogier in the body of his mount.

Romance, the genre of medieval writing most ardently invested in the formation of properly self-regulated knightly bodies, continuously links knightly adolescence with equine and martial desire. The proper training of the body which is chivalry is conveyed textually with a reverence that solicits the desire of the young knights who compose the genre's object of address, teaching them how to desire what the proper chivalric subject must desire. Chivalric romance pays special attention to the affectionate relationships young knights formed with their horses and, to a lesser extent, their greyhounds and hawks. These animals are something more than pets. A horse under the complete control of its rider was the public signifier of a knight's internalized discipline, of his self-mastery; the horse functions like the boy in Foucault's *The Use of Pleasure,* as a body with which one forms an alliance as a means to self-transformation, as part of an "art of existence" or "technique of the self."[22] Having fled a long imprisonment and disguised as a poor palmer, Beves of Hampton is restored to his true self only when his beloved horse Arondel hears his master's name spoken, breaks his own chains, and rushes to be with him. When the knight mounts the steed, the princess Josian recognizes her lover and they are joyfully reunited (2147–2208). After Arondel kills a thieving king's son, Beves decides to go into exile with his horse rather than see it killed—leaving behind Josian, now pregnant with twins. Much later in the dilatory narrative, when Arondel is stolen, Beves's foster father Saber dreams that Beves is badly wounded—exactly the same dream he had when Beves once lost Josian; in this romance horse and wife are both integral to knightly identity. At the end of the romance Beves discovers Arondel dead in his stable. He returns home to Josian, embraces her, and they expire together (4539–4620).

In the medieval romances that promulgated the chivalric code, as well as in numerous manuscript illustrations, the process of becoming a knight was enacted in miniature through a youth's domesticating relation to his horse. The dominion that the knight learned to exert over his animal companion paralleled the controlled responsiveness he taught his own flesh. A pivotal moment in Chrétien de Troyes's *Li Contes del Graal* occurs when Perceval, a young man who has been raised in rural Wales and denied knowledge of his chivalric heritage, trades his rustic hunting horse (*chaceor*) for the slain Vermillion Knight's warhorse (*destrier*). Rather naïve (*nice*) because of his unfamiliarity with the knightly world, Perceval is slowly indoctrinated into proper masculine comportment as the narrative unwinds.[23] Mentored by the accomplished knight Gornemant de Gohort, Perceval is shown proper comportment atop his mount, how to spur and check and guide (*poindre, retenir, mener*) the animal (1416, 1438). The horse's great value derives from its tractability combined with its strength ("que nus plus volantiers n'aloit / plus tost ne de graignor vertu," 1424–25), words that exactly describe the body of young Perceval. The youth learns quickly from his instructor; like the horse with which he forms his alliance, Perceval's body is a site of possibility rather than of simple utility.[24] Having trained his flesh and his horse's flesh, Perceval is finally given his knightly spur and armed with a sword symbolic of culturally sanctioned chivalry, "the highest order that God had set forth and ordained" (1615–16).

For Yvain, another of Chrétien's knights, the self-regulation that produces the proper chivalric subject is synonymous with maintaining a series of intersubjective relationships: with his cohort, with a wild lion, with his wife. *Le Chevalier au lion* is a romance of heterosexuality. The narrative valorizes domesticity over errancy, so that when Yvain is repudiated by his spouse for continuing after marriage to inhabit his prematrimonial, homosocial world, the knight loses his identity completely. After wandering the woods as a wild man, Yvain slowly returns to his humanity and to his proper chivalric identity through the agency of his animal companion, a lion he has rescued from death. Taming the exotic beast is really the process of domesticizing his own selfhood, rendering identity relational rather than individuated. *Le Chevalier au lion* promulgates the figure of the husband-knight, an identity inhabitable only through what might be called the matrimonial circuit—and by this I mean not just the "invention" of the heterosexual, monogamous couple, but the enabling of the couple's coming-into-being by the animal who teaches the knight to become a man.

The Middle English romance *Octavian* illustrates well the multiple desires that unite chivalric and animal bodies, conjoining them in a productive, dispersive alliance. An empress is wrongfully accused of adultery and exiled with her twins. One of the baby boys is quickly abducted by a lioness, the other by an ape. A knight encounters the latter animal with its captive and seizes the child; the knight is then waylaid by outlaws and the child is abducted again (this is, indeed, a romance). These men sell the baby to a merchant named Clement, who names him "Florent" (a kind of coin). All Clement's attempts to indoctrinate Florent into the middle class fail, however, as the boy proves incapable of assigning anything but absolute values to the animals, which for his father are negotiable, marketplace commodities. Spotting a falcon for sale, Florent immediately trades the family's oxen to possess the aristocratic bird. While carrying money to Clement's brother, Florent comes across a steed "whyte as any mylke," which so visually enthralls him that he immediately purchases it for more than the asking price. The forty pounds Florent spends on the horse is exactly the sum his foster father paid to purchase him from the robbers, setting up an equivalence between the two bodies in their potentiality. Eventually Clement realizes that noble blood is exerting itself in the child, bestows armor on his adopted son, and allows the newly purchased horse to pull Florent out of his bourgeois enchainment and into a chivalric world of exorbitant enemies and absolute values.

Whereas contemporary biographies are apt to mark the entrance into adult identity through an epiphanal narration of the "awakening to sexuality" (it goes without saying that Frantzen rehearses a familiar script in the passage from *Before the Closet* discussed earlier), the chivalric movement from youth (squiredom) to maturity (knighthood) is more likely to involve a lesson about horses. The life of the twelfth-century knight William the Marshall is unusually well recorded, and includes just such a moment. During his first military encounter, William's warhorse was killed, and he found himself in the humiliating position of being unable to afford a new one.[25] The chamberlain of the lord of Tancarville (under whom he was then serving) chose not to provide the young knight with a new steed in order to teach him a lesson: in battle a disciplined warrior captures the horses of other knights in order to force them into the position William was now enduring. By selling the symbolically charged mantle he had worn when recently dubbed a knight, William was able to secure a baggage horse to transport his equipment, but he was made to suffer the indignities of horselessness until the advent of an important regional tournament, when the chamberlain relented and provided a new mount. William's first tournament was a resounding success. Not only did he spectacularly demonstrate his horsemanship and strength, he defeated three knights and seized their equipment (arms, armor, and four kinds of horses). William always remembered this lesson in his chivalric dependence on equine possession: "never again did he neglect to capture good horses when he had the opportunity" (Painter 1982: 23).

The aristocratic fighting class was not the only social group to depend on horses for the public performance of their identity. Bede recounts the love of horses that animated young Anglo-Saxon clerics, a scene unimaginable as part of clerical identity later in the history of the Church.[26] The portraits in Chaucer's General Prologue to the *Canterbury Tales* often describe the type of mount a pilgrim rides to convey essential aspects of personality, just as a contemporary writer might indicate a model of car in order to embody in external form a character's interiority. Yet the bond uniting knight to horse was of a more intense order than these other examples: linguistically, culturally, physically, there could be no chivalry without a disciplinary relationship of mutual desire between men and their horses.

The Limits of the Body

It may seem that in counterposing David Halperin's erotically charged "queer muscle" with this examination of the chivalric assemblage I am valorizing what is ultimately an apparatus of normalization. That is not my intent at all. First, such an assemblage—simply *because* it normalizes—cries out to be queered in the traditional way: Isn't there an erotic charge between man and horse, and doesn't the knight encounter the horse only within what would have to be called an affectionate, corporeal, same-sex relationship? Isn't that why the horse, following the practice of Alexander the Great, always bears a male name, a male personality? Could the passionate nature of the relationship the chivalric circuit precipitates be why medieval medicine held that excess horse riding led to the practice of sodomy? Why should the queer stop at the boundaries of the human? Why can't it, in the Middle Ages, include the horses, hawks, greyhounds that are so integral to knightly and aristocratic identity? What can we say about Beves's pleasure in Arondel, or Florent's desire for an ideal body that draws him out of his bourgeois captivity through the somatic gravity of falcons and warhorses? Isn't the relationship Yvain enters into with his lion a queer one? (The lion thinks that his master is dead and attempts to commit suicide by throwing himself at a sword a la Pyramus and Thisbe, those mythic [heterosexual] lovers) What kind of threesome is created by the corporeal triangle of the mentor William, his eager-for-discipline student Rainoart, and the horse the page so ineptly rides?[27]

Second, and more importantly, it is not simply that human flesh, in order to receive its chivalric imprinting, its domestication, becomes for a while animal flesh; animal flesh becomes transubstantiated through the same assemblage into human flesh (the mount receives an anthropomorphizing name, as well as a subjectivity). Objects lose their materiality to become conduits and agents. All are transformed (at least for a little while, at least when divorced from their restrictive teleology), all become posthuman hybrids. The horse, its rider, the bridle and saddle and armor together form the Deleuzian "circuit" or "assemblage," a network of meaning that includes the inanimate and the inhuman. No single object or body has meaning within this assemblage without reference to the other forces, intensities, affects, and directions to which it is conjoined—and within which it is always in the process of becoming something other, something new. The Deleuzian assemblage indicates the limits of the human as a conceptual category, and demarcates a new terrain for the queer: a wide expanse where identity, sexuality, and desire are no longer constrained by ontology, "muscle," or lonely residence in a singular and merely human body.

This dynamic *intermezzo* is close to the "provisional, tenuous, mobile" and fluid sexuality that Elizabeth Grosz suggests can resist restrictive corporealizations and take up the challenge that queer once posed.[28] If a normalizing apparatus can be broken (and what apparatus cannot be broken?), if its "hierarchical and systematic whole" can be "realigned in different networks and linkages," then

> the subject's body ceases to be *a* body, to become a site of provocations and reactions, the site of intensive disruptions. The subject ceases to be a subject, giving way to pulsations, gyrations, flux, secretions, swellings, processes. . . . Its borders blur, seep, so that, for a while at least, it is no longer clear where one organ, body, or subject stops and another begins.[29]

The chivalric assemblage—problematic, masculinist, too violent, too *medieval*—nonetheless offers this line of flight: it necessarily acknowledges that a body is not a singular, essential thing but an inhuman circuit full of unrealized possibility for rethinking identity. In this way even an apparently irredeemable form of embodiment can become an important catalyst for the Foucauldian project of bringing about the "Death of Man," that monolithic figure of normalcy, the true locus of violence, oppression, and contempt for the body—the true enemy of queer. In *The Order of Things* Foucault famously argued that Man is a concept on the verge of obsolescence, about to crumble under the force of "some event of which we can at the moment do no more than sense the possibility—without knowing either what its form will be or what it promises" (Foucault 1994: 387). The inhuman circuit is perhaps that very event which promises to erase the humanist conception of man, "like a face drawn in sand at the edge of the sea."[30]

Notes

A version of this chapter with complete bibliographical apparatus appears in my book *Medieval Identity Machines* (Minneapolis: University of Minnesota Press, 2003).

  1. Caroline Walker Bynum makes this point eloquently throughout her copious work, but see especially Bynum 1992, 1995a, 1995b.

  2. The bibliography on the medieval body is too vast to reproduce in a note, but some of the work I have found useful in framing this chapter includes: Cohen and Wheeler 1997; Brown 1988; Burns 1993; Citrome 2001; Lochrie, McCracken, and Schultz 1997; Kay and Rubin 1994; Dinshaw 1999; Bullough and Brundage 1996; Lees 1994; Fradenburg and Freccero 1996a.

3. Dinshaw 1995: 76–77. Other queer work by medievalists I have found useful in framing this investigation includes: Biddick 1999; Boyd 1998; Dinshaw 1994 and 1999; Fradenburg and Freccero 1996b; Gaunt 1996; Holsinger 1996.

4. Clark and Sponsler 1997; Sponsler 1997; Kruger 1997; Lochrie 1996. For a contemporary reading of queer sensitive to its imbrication in race and ethnicity, see McRuer 1997.

5. Queer, he continues, is therefore "by definition whatever is at odds with the normal, the legitimate, the dominant." It is "not restricted to lesbians and gay men" but is "available to anyone who is or feels marginalized because of her or his sexual practices"—perhaps including "some married couples without children, for example, or (who knows?) some married couples *with* children— with, perhaps, *very naughty* children" (Halperin 1995: 62).

6. Perhaps the best adjective for Foucault's stance is "antihumanistic," but for a consideration of the body as "posthuman," see the collection of essays edited by Halberstam and Livingston (1995), as well as Hayles 1999.

7. Gilles Deleuze and Félix Guattari, *Mille plateaux, v. 2 de Capitalisme et Schizophrénie* (Deleuze and Guattari 1980: 314) trans. Brian Massumi, *A Thousand Plateaus: Capitalism and Schizophrenia* (Deleuze and Guattari 1987: 257).

8. Cf. the reading of Little Hans offered by Deleuze and Claire Parnet in a conversation that records some of the salient points of the then-forthcoming *A Thousand Plateaus:* "[Freud] takes no account of the assemblage (building-street-nextdoor-warehouse-omnibus-horse-a-horse-falls-a-horse-is-whipped!); he takes no account of the situation (the child has been forbidden to go into the street, etc.); he takes no account of Little Hans's endeavor (horse-becoming, because every other way has been blocked up). . . . The only important thing for Freud is that the horse be the father—and that's the end of it (Deleuze and Parnet 1987: 80)

9. Michael Hardt describes this Spinoza-inspired body as "a dynamic relationship whose internal structure and external limits are subject to change. What we identify as a body is merely a temporarily stable relationship" (Hardt 1993: 92). Sarah Kay and Miri Rubin similarly argue that totalized bodies are the products of "a psychic investment" or of an ideology, turning to Deleuze and Guattari for a more multiple and dispersed conception of bodiliness; see the editors' introduction to Kay and Rubin 1994.

10. "Fewer stupidities would be uttered on the topic of pain, humiliation, and anxiety in masochism if it were understood that it is the becomings-animal that leads the masochism, not the other way around. There are always apparatuses, tools, engines involved, there are always artifices and constraints in taking Nature to the fullest. That is because it is necessary to annul the organs, to shut them away so that their liberated elements can enter into the new relations from which the becoming-animal, and the circulation of affects within the machinic assemblage, will result" (1987: 260).

11. "Chivalry" is a notoriously vexed term. For a recent consideration of

its complexities, see Chickering 1988: 2–5. My use should always be glossed more specifically as Christian, aristocratic, European, martial male identity. My discussion of chivalry owes much to Barber 1974; Keen 1984; Patterson 1991: 165–79. See also Borst 1982.

12. I discuss this etymological interrelation at greater length in Cohen 1999: 104.

13. The classic (if exaggerated) reading of the technological trigger to social reality that the stirrup represents is White 1966: 1–38. White grandly claims that the Western Middle Ages as we know them would not have been possible without the catalytic power of the stirrup. Although the straightforward progress narrative White erects is no longer tenable, his holistic approach to technology resonates with what would now be called postmodern analyses of culture, especially those by writers like Deleuze, Foucault, and Bruno Latour. Indeed, Deleuze incorporates White's work into his reading of the knight-horse circuit (Deleuze and Parnet 1987: 69, 72, 74–75, 98). See also Bartlett 1993: 60–84; Duby 1977; Keen 1984: 18, 24–26.

14. The quotation is from Latour 1996: 212–13, where he is speaking of a failed subway system in France, but the point is relevant to the cultural being of objects more generally.

15. In addition to the works previously cited, see also Ascherl 1988.

16. On the increasing size of medieval equines, see Hyland 1994: 57–59. Hyland's book amounts to a short history of the early Middle Ages as told through the body of the horse.

17. "Every new development, in the greater defensive protection that armour could be designed to offer and the greater weight that a more expensive war horse had consequently to carry, made such advancement [into the "cavalier's world"] a little harder" (Keen 1984: 26–7). White estimates that in the eighth century a horse and equipment for one man cost the same as twenty oxen (ten plow-teams worth). In addition, a knight had to pay for remounts, a horse and equipment for his squire, and large amounts of grain for the animals (White 1966: 29).

18. More generally, cf. Sidney Painter on the training of squires: "The squire's body was hardened and his skill in the use of weapons developed by frequent and strenuous military exercises. While the chain mail of the twelfth century was far lighter and less cumbersome than the plate armor of later times, the mere wearing of it required considerable physical strength. To be able, as every squire must, to leap fully armed into the saddle without touching the stirrup, was a feat which must have required long and rigorous training. The effective use of the weapons of a knight—the spear, sword, and shield—was a highly intricate science which a squire was forced to master if he wished to excel at his chosen profession" (Painter 1982: 17).

19. I quote from the text edited and translated by Elspeth Kennedy in Kaeuper and Kennedy 1996.

20. *La Chanson de Roland* 1946: 11. 1326–34.

21. *Aliscans, chanson de geste,* 1992: 11. 523–24; "If Paynims took you back to Spain with them / I'd die of grief, so help me God above!"

22. Foucault writes, "What I mean by the phrase are those intentional and voluntary actions by which men not only set themselves rules of conduct, but also seek to transform themselves, to change themselves in their singular being, and to make their life into an *oeuvre* that carries certain aesthetic values and meets certain stylistic criteria" (1990: 10–11; cf. 203 on the intersubjective component of this "art").

23. Of course, not everyone finds Perceval's ignorance of chivalry so easy to countenance; one knight characterizes him as a dolt (*sot*), and conflates his stupidity with his Welshness (Chrétien 1990: 242–45).

24. The difference between chivalric and utilitarian views of the horse is expressed in Gornemant's first question to Perceval and the boy's revealing reply: "Then the gentleman asked him / how skilled he was with his horse. / 'I can make it run up hills and down, / just as I could run / my hunter, when I had it'" (Et li prudom li redemande / Qu'il set fere de cheval. / 'Jel cor bien amont et aval / Tot autresi con je coroie / Le chaceor, quant je l'avoie'" 1364–68. At this point the *prudom* realizes that Perceval's first lesson must be horsemanship (Chrétien 1990).

25. William's biography is reverently narrated in the anonymous *Histoire de Guillaume le Maréchal.* Sidney Painter composed the classic English account (Painter 1982). See also Duby 1985. A good warhorse might cost thirty to forty pounds in the twelfth century (Painter 1982: 43).

26. For the story of the cleric Herebald's "splendid horse" and the races in which he rode, see Bede 1969: 259.

27. The scene from *Aliscans* is treated at length in Cohen 1999: 170.

28. See Grosz 1995: 207–27 for a full discussion of the utility of Deleuze and Guattari to a feminist rethinking of corporeality; quotation at 227.

29. Grosz's exploration of "Animal Sex" has been instrumental to my thinking throughout this chapter; see Grosz 1995: 187–205, quotation at 198.

30. The last quotation is Foucault's famous closing line to *The Order of Things,* Foucault 1994: 387.

References

Aliscans, chanson de geste, ed. F. Guessard and A. de Montaiglon (1992). Paris: Librairie A. Franck, 1870. Trans. Michael A. Newth, *The Song of Aliscans.* New York: Garland.

Ascherl, Rosemary (1988). "The Technology of Chivalry in Reality and Romance." *The Study of Chivalry: Resources and Approaches,* ed. Howell Chickering and Thomas H. Seiler. Kalamazoo: Medieval Institute Publications, 263–311.

Barber, Richard (1974). *The Knight and Chivalry*, 2d ed. Ipswich: Boydell.

Bartlett, Robert (1993). *The Making of Europe: Conquest, Colonization and Cultural Change 950–1350.* Princeton: Princeton University Press.

Bede (1969). *Bede's Ecclesiastical History of the English People,* ed. Bertram Colgrave and R. A. B. Mynors. Oxford: Oxford University Press.

[*The Romance of*] *Sir Beves of Hamton,* ed. Eugen Kölbing. *Early English Text Society Extra Series* vols. 46, 48, 65 (1885, 1886, 1894).

Biddick, Kathleen (1999). *The Shock of Medievalism.* Durham, N.C.: Duke University Press.

Borst, Arno, ed. (1982). *Das Rittertum im Mittelalter.* Darmstadt: Wissenschaftliche Gesellschaft.

Boyd, David Lorenzo (1998). "Sodomy, Misogyny, and Displacement: Occluding Queer Desire in *Sir Gawain and the Green Knight.*" *Arthuriana* 8 (2): 77–113.

Brown, Peter (1988). *The Body and Society: Men, Women, and Sexual Renunciation in Early Christianity.* New York: Columbia University Press.

Bullough, Vern L., and James A. Brundage, eds. (1996). *Handbook of Medieval Sexuality.* New York: Garland.

Burger, Glenn (1994). "Queer Chaucer." *English Studies in Canada* 20 (2): 153–70.

Burns, E. Jane (1993). *Bodytalk: When Women Speak in Old French Literature.* Philadelphia: University of Pennsylvania Press.

Bynum, Caroline Walker (1992). *Fragmentation and Redemption: Essays on Gender and the Human Body in Medieval Religion.* New York: Zone.

——— (1995a). *The Resurrection of the Body in Western Christianity, 200–1336.* New York: Columbia University Press.

——— (1995b). "Why All the Fuss about the Body? A Medievalist's Perspective." *Critical Inquiry* 22 (1): 1–33.

La Chanson de Roland (1946). Ed. Frederick Whitehead. Oxford: Blackwell. Trans. Glyn S. Burgess, *The Song of Roland* (1990). London: Penguin.

Chickering, Howell (1988). "Introduction." *The Study of Chivalry: Resources and Approaches,* ed. Howell Chickering and Thomas H. Seiler. Kalamazoo: Medieval Institute, 1–38.

Chickering, Howell, and Thomas H. Seiler (1988). *The Study of Chivalry: Resources and Approaches.* Kalamazoo: Medieval Institute.

Chrétien de Troyes (1985). *The Knight with the Lion; or, Yvain (Le Chevalier au Lion),* ed. and trans. William W. Kibler. New York: Garland.

——— (1990). *The Story of the Grail (Li Contes del Graal or Perceval),* ed. Rupert Pickens, trans. William W. Kibler. New York: Garland.

Citrome, Jeremy (2001). "Bodies That Splatter: Surgery, Chivalry, and the Body in the *Practica* of John Arderne." *Exemplaria* 13 (1): 137–72.

Clark, Robert L. A., and Claire Sponsler (1997). "Queer Play: The Cultural Work of Crossdressing in Medieval Drama." *New Literary History* 28: 319–44.

Cohen, Jeffrey Jerome (1999). *Of Giants: Sex, Monsters, and the Middle Ages.* Minneapolis: University of Minnesota Press.

Cohen, Jeffrey Jerome, and Bonnie Wheeler, eds. (1997). *Becoming Male in the Middle Ages.* New York: Garland.

Deleuze, Gilles, and Claire Parnet (1987). *Dialogues,* trans. Hugh Tomlinson and Barbara Habberjam. New York: Columbia University Press.

Deleuze, Gilles, and Félix Guattari (1980). *Mille plateaux, v. 2 de Capitalisme et Schizophrénie.* Paris: Les Editions de Minuit. Trans. Brian Massumi, *A Thousand Plateaus: Capitalism and Schizophrenia* (1987). Minneapolis: University of Minnesota Press.

Dinshaw, Carolyn (1994). "A Kiss Is Just a Kiss: Heterosexuality and its Consolations in *Sir Gawain and the Green Knight.*" *Diacritics* 24 (2) :205–26

———— (1995). "Chaucer's Queer Touches / A Queer Touches Chaucer." *Exemplaria* 7 (1): 75–92.

———— (1999). *Getting Medieval: Sexualities and Communities, Pre- and Postmodern.* Durham, N.C.: Duke University Press.

Duby, George (1977). *The Chivalrous Society,* trans. Cynthia Postan. Berkeley: University of California Press.

———— (1985). *William Marshall, the Flower of Chivalry,* trans. Richard Howard. New York.

Foucault, Michel (1994). *The Order of Things: An Archeology of the Human Sciences.* New York: Vintage.

———— (1990). *The Use of Pleasure,* trans. Robert Hurley. New York: Vintage.

Fradenburg, Louise Olga Aranye, and Carla Freccero, eds. (1996a). *Premodern Sexualities.* New York: Routledge.

———— (1996b). "Caxton, Foucault, and the Pleasures of History." In *Premodern Sexualities,* ed. Fradenburg and Freccero. New York: Routledge, xiii–xxiv.

Frantzen, Allen J. (1998). *Before the Closet: Same-Sex Love from Beowulf to Angels in America.* Chicago: University of Chicago Press.

Gaunt, Simon (1996). "Straight Minds / 'Queer' Wishes in Old French Hagiography." In *Premodern Sexualities,* ed. Louise Olga Aranye Fradenburg and Carla Freccero. New York: Routledge, 153–73.

Grosz, Elizabeth (1995). *Space, Time, and Perversion.* New York: Routledge.

Halberstam, Judith, and Ira Livingston, eds. (1995). *Posthuman Bodies.* Bloomington: Indiana University Press,.

Halperin, David M. (1995). *Saint Foucault: Toward a Gay Hagiography.* Oxford: Oxford University Press.

Hardt, Michael (1993). Gilles *Deleuze: An Apprenticeship in Philosophy.* Minneapolis: University of Minnesota Press.

Hayles, N. Katherine (1999). *How We Became Posthuman: Virtual Bodies in Cybernetics, Literature, and Informatics.* Chicago: University of Chicago Press.

Hindman, Sandra (1994). *Sealed in Parchment: Rereadings of Knighthood in the Illuminated Manuscripts of Chrétien de Troyes.* Chicago: University of Chicago Press.

Histoire de Guillaume le Maréchal (1891–1901). 3 vols., ed. Paul Meyer. Paris: Société de l'histoire de France.

Holsinger, Bruce (1996). "Sodomy and Resurrection: The Homoerotic Subject of the Divine Comedy." In *Premodern Sexualities,* ed. Louise Olga Aranye Fradenburg and Carla Freccero. New York: Routledge, 243–74.

Hyland, Ann (1994). *The Medieval Warhorse: From Byzantium to the Crusades.* Conshohocken, Pa: Combined Books.

Kaeuper, Richard W., and Elspeth Kennedy (1996). *The Book of Chivalry of Geoffroi de Charny: Text, Context, and Translation.* Philadelphia: University of Pennsylvania Press.

Kay, Sarah, and Miri Rubin (1994). *Framing Medieval Bodies.* Manchester: Manchester University Press.

Keen, Maurice (1984). *Chivalry.* New Haven: Yale University Press.

Kruger, Steven F. (1997). "Conversion and Medieval Sexual, Religious, and Racial Categories." In *Constructing Medieval Sexuality,* ed. Karma Lochrie, Peggy McCracken, and James A. Schultz. Minneapolis: University of Minnesota Press, 158–79.

Latour, Bruno (1996). *Aramis; Or, the Love of Technology.* Trans. Catherine Porter. Cambridge: Harvard University Press.

Lees, Clare A., ed. (1994). *Medieval Masculinities: Regarding Men in the Middle Ages.* Minneapolis: University of Minnesota Press.

Lochrie, Karma, Peggy McCracken, and James A. Schultz, eds. (1997). *Constructing Medieval Sexuality.* Minneapolis: University of Minnesota Press.

McRuer, Robert (1997). *The Queer Renaissance: Contemporary American Literature and the Reinvention of Lesbian and Gay Identities.* New York: New York University Press.

Octavian (1992). In *Six Middle English Romances,* ed. Maldwyn Mills. London: J. M. Dent and Sons, 75–124.

Painter, Sidney (1982). *William Marshal: Knight-Errant, Baron, and Regent of England.* Cambridge: Medieval Academy of America.

Patterson, Lee (1991). *Chaucer and the Subject of History.* Madison: University of Wisconsin Press.

Sponsler, Claire (1997). "Outlaw Masculinities: Drag, Blackface, and Late Medieval Laboring-Class Festivities." In *Becoming Male in the Middle Ages,* ed. Jeffrey Jerome Cohen and Bonnie Wheeler. New York: Garland, 321–47.

White, Lynn, Jr. (1966). *Medieval Technology and Social Change.* New York: Oxford University Press.

10

Mourning the Autonomous Body

Debra B. Bergoffen

A Synopsis of the Drama

"Mourning the Autonomous Body" takes its title from the second act of a three-act play. The drama concerns the future of the autonomous body, a beloved idol of the modern Western world. Act I, "Motives and Murder," depicts a conspiracy inspired by Rousseau, Nietzsche, Freud, and Irigaray. It exposes the lie of the autonomous body and establishes motives for its murder. Act II, "Mourning the Autonomous Body," is under the direction of Freud and Irigaray. It enacts the mourning that follows the murder. Act III, "Celebrating Ambiguous Bodies," is inspired by Simone de Beauvoir. It introduces us to the body's new love—ambiguity—and its desires. It images the ways in which a culture grounded in the ideal of the ambiguous body would transvaluate the meaning of sexual difference.

What follows are the extended program notes to act one. These notes detail the desires of the autonomous body and establish the link between our love for the autonomous body and our patriarchal culture of violence and domination. They establish that the autonomous body's image of itself as independent and self-regulating is threatened by its experience of its desire for the other. Unable to deny its desire for the other, and unable to find itself desirable insofar as it experiences itself as desiring, the autonomous body experiences its desire for the other as a threat to its "integrity." It deals with this threat by resorting to the logic of sacrifice and/or incorporation.

Guided by Rousseau's *Discourse on Inequality* (Rousseau 1994) and *Emile* (Rousseau 1993), Act I enacts the ways in which men and women are seduced by the image of the autonomous body. It also tracks the ways in which patriarchy sexes the autonomous body as male. Rather than follow the logic of recent feminist discourse, which protests the sexing but not the value of autonomy and which argues for equal access to the autonomous body, Act I shows that men and women pursuing their love of autonomy will reproduce and intensify the war of the sexes. Equality under these conditions means that it will now be equally possible for men and women to sacrifice each other to/for the ideal of autonomy. The rule of domination will be reordered but not destroyed. There will be no transvaluation of values. Confronting us with this reality, Act I establishes motives for both men and women to murder the autonomous body.

187

The Notes: Act I: Setting the Stage

Like Nietzsche, who being born posthumously, announced the death of God before anyone understood the meaning of the disaster (Nietzsche 1974), Irigaray appears ahead of her (our) time when she identifies the issue of sexual difference as the question of our age (Irigaray 1993). She knows this. She sees that others do not find this question compelling. Realizing that we do not see the relationship between our failure to address the question of sexual difference and the destructive nihilism of our times, Irigaray accuses us of being unprepared to take up the necessary task of reinterpreting "everything concerning the relations between the subject and discourse, the subject and the world, the subject and the cosmic, the microcosmic and the macrocosmic" (Irigaray 1993: 6). We are, Irigaray says, not ready for the "revolution in thought and ethics" necessary to cure the "cancerous diseases of our age" (Irigaray 1993: 5).

Addressing us in this way, Irigaray raises at least two sets of issues. One concerns the question of sexual difference itself. In what sense does it underlie all other questions of our age? How could thinking it through be our "salvation"? The other concerns our reluctance (refusal?) to hear the question as crucial. Listening with a psychoanalytic ear, I find our resistance to the question of sexual difference telling. Raising it disturbs our most crucial values. Pursuing this thought, I hear Freud's "Mourning and Melancholia" (Freud 1959) reminding me that values are ideals and that ideals are love objects. Further, learning from Freud that as love objects, ideals are only/can only be given up after the work of mourning convinces us that loving them is no longer possible, I find that it is helpful to think of the transvaluation Irigaray advocates as the work of mourning. Pursuing this line of thought, I find myself asking: What ideals/love objects are tied up with the question of sexual difference? Which of these ideals/love objects anchors the rest? What would convince us to take up the work of mourning this object, that is, what would convince us that the object is impossible and or unworthy of our love?

I begin with the obvious. In identifying the question of sexual difference as the issue of our age, Irigaray draws us to the bodies of men and women and to the ways in which these bodies are arranged in the patriarchal order. Specifically, she calls our attention to the values embedded in the lived, sexed, and sexual body. If the question of sexual difference is the question of our age, then the question of our age must concern the value of the desiring body and the desires of the body that are valued. As Freud helps us discern the register of the question, Rousseau alerts us to the values at issue. Freud points us to the implications of resistance and directs us to the work of mourning. Rousseau gives specific content to the idea that anchors the patriarchal order of sexual difference.

Oddly enough, Rousseau's justifications of sexual subordination confirm Irigaray's insights regarding the question of sexual difference; for though Irigaray rejects Rousseau's claims regarding the natural hierarchy of the sexes, she agrees with Rousseau on this: the patriarchal moral and political order depends on silencing women's desire. Rousseau's works go further, however. They also show us that the patriarchal order of sexual difference is sustained by the ideal of the autonomous body imaged as male.

As Nietzsche taught us to see God as the ground of the values of truth, Rousseau teaches us to see autonomy as the ground of the values of patriarchy. If Rousseau is correct, then the task of the critic of patriarchy is more complex than the job of the critic of truth. God, Nietzsche said, is dead. He has already been murdered. It is therefore time to recite the requiem, take up the work of mourning, and create new values. The autonomous subject, unlike God, however, is alive, well, and well loved. It is too early to mourn patriarchy, for patriarchy has not yet experienced its love object—autonomy—as impossible, something that must be murdered, given up. To get a hearing for her question, Irigaray must motivate us to murder the autonomous body; for we will not take up the task of transvaluation unless/until we become convinced that our love affair with this ideal is doomed. We must become murderers to become mourners. As mourners we free ourselves to discover new loves.

Approaching Irigaray's question of sexual difference in this way, I find her scripting two plots. Each provides a different map for the murder and mourning necessary for the transvaluation of values called for by the injustices of patriarchy. In her first and most familiar script, Irigaray identifies patriarchy with masculine privilege—specifically the privilege to speak and have one's speech legitimated as the standard of human-being-desire. In the context of this story, autonomy per se is not the issue; for the locus of patriarchal injustice is not in the validation of the autonomous body/subject, but in the equation that identifies the autonomous subject with the male body. Here, the transvaluation/mourning of patriarchy concerns the creation of a symbolic order where the autonomous desires of women and men are spoken, recognized, and legitimated in their differences.

The second script, less fully explored by Irigaray and more radical in its implications, targets autonomy per se. Here it is not the equation autonomy = male body/desire that must be murdered and mourned, but the desire for autonomy itself that must be renounced. It is not a matter of allowing for alternative expressions of the passion for autonomy but of finding other ways of imaging desire. This second script is embedded in the essay "Wonder: A Reading of Descartes, *The Passions of the Soul* (Irigaray 1993: 72–82). In this piece, Irigaray directs us to cultivate the passion of wonder as an antidote to our passion for mastery. In this directive, however, Irigaray calls for the destruction of the ideal of autonomy, for autonomy is the passion for mastery.

Given the long list of values associated with the idea of autonomy, this last claim seems extreme. For even if it could be shown that the desires of autonomy and mastery were linked and that given this link the ideal of autonomy ought to be renounced, could it not also be said that insofar as autonomy carries the meanings of integrity, independence, sovereignty, and freedom, the autonomous subject is worthy of our love? Perhaps, but I am not convinced; for I think the link between the ideal of autonomy and the desires of mastery are essential rather than accidental, and I believe that as long as the values of integrity, independence, sovereignty, and freedom are understood as expressions of an autonomous subject, the law of domination will prevail and patriarchy will endure.

In linking the power of patriarchy to the passion for mastery and its validation of/in the autonomous body/subject, I am identifying modern and contemporary patriarchy with a social system characterized by the subordination of women to men and am treating this systemized legitimation of domination as the effect of a fundamental commitment to the value of autonomy. I do not claim that patriarchy has always been grounded in the value of autonomy or that the image of the autonomous body has always structured the desires of patriarchal men and women. My claim is more limited. It is that at this point in our occidental (on its way to becoming global?) history patriarchy legitimates itself by aligning itself with the values and images of autonomy and that as long as autonomy retains its value patriarchy (at least in its modern guise) will remain secure. (Pateman 1988, 1989)

Rousseau's *Discourse on Inequality* (Rousseau 1994) and *Emile* (Rousseau 1993) detail the relationship between the ideal of autonomy, the image of the autonomous body, and the autonomous subject's passion for mastery. These works record the ways in which the ideal of autonomy and the image of the autonomous body establish our desire for the other as alienating and necessitates the subordinations of the patriarchal order. Within the context of Rousseau's works the rule of the autonomous subject appears benign. The husband loves his wife and children. He cares for them as he takes care of them. It is merely a matter of "Father knows best." The benign appearance of the rule of autonomy is belied in the woman's anorexic body. Here we are confronted with the disaster of the will to autonomy. I offer this tortured body as a concrete motive for the murder of the autonomous subject.

Rousseau, Autonomy, and the Question of Sexual Difference

Rousseau's *Discourse on Inequality* provides an account of the transformation of humanity from its existence as a natural species to its existence as a social and moral species. Rousseau's *Emile* provides an extended account of the transformation of a boy child into a husband, father, and citizen and an abbreviated account of the transformation of a girl child into a wife and mother. We would expect these accounts of species and individual development to mirror each other. They do not. Instead they reveal the fissures in Rousseau's thought. These fissures expose the fault lines of patriarchy's account of sexual difference.

According to the *Discourse* autonomy is the human natural condition. It is the birthright of both men and women. In the state of nature men and women are equally autonomous even if they are not quite each other's equals. Natural women, like natural men, are self-sufficient, independent, and self-reliant. Though Rousseau describes women's bodies as relatively weaker than men's, he does not use this relative weakness to argue that women are essentially weak. He never depicts natural women's birthing and nursing bodies as helpless. Natural mothers and their children do not need paternal protection.

Given Rousseau's refusal to use differences in bodily strength as an argument for sexual inequality in the state of nature, we might expect him to take Mary Wollstonecraft's (Wollstonecraft 1992) position and argue that the sexual inequalities established by society are unnatural and therefore unjust. Were Rousseau a straightforward binary thinker, this line of thinking might have been his. He does not, however, establish the state of nature as the truth of our being. It is the truth of our prehistorical being. Nature is not to culture as true is to false. Culture is not simply an alienation from nature. It is our second nature—the truth of our being as rational, moral persons. The "fact" that, as natural, we were each other's equals insofar as we were equally autonomous and independent has no standing when considering the moral positions of men and women after their second moral birth as members of the family, society, and the body politic. Natural autonomy, the self-sufficiency of indifference, is incompatible with the requirements of social life. According to Rousseau, however, the requirements of social and moral life place different demands on the woman's birthing and nursing body and the man's instrumental/working body. Working bodies can reconcile their autonomous nature with their social being through the process of sublimation. For these bodies are also familial and political bodies. They can, as fathers, husbands, and citizens, assert their moral and political autonomy. Though they can no longer be indifferent to others, they may still claim the right to be self-determining. As fathers and husbands their desires are recognized as the desire of the family. As citizens their will is expressed in the general will. Literal autonomy, the self-sufficiency of an independent being, is sublimated. It becomes social autonomy, the authority to be the author of the family's and/or state's desire/will. So long as men are established as the head of the family or recognized as a citizen of the state their desire for autonomy diverted from its natural course, will find moral, social paths to travel.

Women, on Rousseau's account are denied travel permits. In their rebirth as moral beings, birthing and nursing bodies lose their autonomy. Marked as dependent, women are confined to the private domain. As daughters, wives, and mothers they are required to acknowledge the authority of men. This requirement is essential for men's sublimations of their desire for autonomy. Deemed unfit for citizenship, women play no role in formulating the general will. Forgetting that in the *Discourse* he established the natural autonomy of women as well as men, Rousseau asks women to abandon their natural autonomous bodies/ desires. This request is crucial for the moral well-being of humanity; for if women do not effect this repression men's sublimation strategies will fail and the social and political fabric of patriarchy will unravel. Rousseau is unaware of the repetition compulsion, the return of the repressed and the death drive. Coming to Rousseau after Freud, however, we begin to understand why Irigaray says that the question of sexual difference engages the issues of nihilism and destruction.

In *Emile* the relationship between the ideal of the autonomous body and the question of sexual difference is straightforward. Unlike other treatises of that period (and ours) where the ambiguity of the term "man" seduces us to read the subject of the text as unsexed, *Emile* is unambiguous. There is no single form of humanity. As differently bodied, men and women perform different natural, social, and political functions and are guided by different moral codes. As corrupted by society, both men and women are alienated from their nature and natural differences; but, according to Rousseau, however corrupt society may be, its alienating fantasies follow nature in this—men and women are different. They are seduced/produced by different imagineries.

Perhaps we were not meant to read the *Discourse* and *Emile* together. Perhaps we were not meant to attribute any importance to the discrepancies between the ways in which these texts depict the nature of men and women. Irigaray's question, however, alerts us to the significance of these discrepancies. I pause to consider their meaning. In *Emile* Rousseau argues that the sexual differences of patriarchy reflect the natural order of the sexes. Here, culture is said to imitate nature. In *The Discourse*, however, Rousseau shows us that there is no smooth transition between nature and culture. In fact, *The Discourse*, having insisted that in the state of nature men and women live autonomously and independently, fails to explain why men ought to legislate for women in the moral, political, and social worlds. It is a matter, Rousseau tells us, of being born again. Perhaps we are meant to accept, without further explanation, that births are not smooth transitions but radical breaks, but that will not help us understand the difference between the birth marks of men and women. For we are not told why men in their second birth as moral beings are required to substitute one image of autonomy for another, but not required to renounce their nature as autonomous beings; while women in their second birth as moral beings are required to deny their natural autonomy by displacing the image of autonomy with an image of femininity.

According to Rousseau, it is as members of families rather than as members of the species that we become moral beings. Prior to the advent of the family, we were, Rousseau says, autonomous beings. Our desire for the other was short lived and indiscriminate. It was sufficient, however, for our satisfactions and for the procreation and preservation of the species. Attending to the family as the site of our second birth, Rousseau discovers the power of love. It is through love that our natural, promiscuous passions are tethered to one particular person. Sounding very much like Freud, Rousseau aligns love with the notion of the imaginary. Both Emile and Sophy love images of the ideal man and woman before they love each other. They fall in love with each other because they find in each other a concrete imitation of the imaginary object. They fall in love with each other because they have been educated to love images of femininity and masculinity. They are prepared to idealize each other because they already idealize the image each has been educated to embody.

Love demands inequality. It requires me to single you out from and elevate you above all others. It is because you and only you meet the requirements of the ideal that I love only you. Love does not, however, require the inequalities of patriarchy—that is, that (though not how) the inequalities demanded by love became the inequalities of patriarchy, i.e. that women to be loved had to reflect the image of femininity (dependency and fragility) and that men to be loved had to assume the image of the master—can (perhaps) be understood if we return to Rousseau and his account of the ideal of autonomy. Rousseau's descriptions of love may be read as an account of the way in which the promise of love lures men and women toward their second birth and as an account of the way the promise of love though different for men and women appeals to an image of autonomy as mastery.

Following Rousseau's discussions, we realize that we are thrown off track if we confuse the promise of love with the promise of sex; for according to Rousseau the desire for sex is fleeting. It is the desire for autonomy that is fundamental. Love must lure us to marriage by promising more than sex. It must promise to fulfill our desire for autonomy. To be properly understood, love's promise must be heard as both erotic and political. As political, love promises the lovers power. It lures each party to the family by promising that the image of the autonomous body as independent can be safely exchanged for an image of autonomy as mastery. Luring men and women to marriage with the same promise, patriarchal love does not fulfill its promise to men and women in the same way. Designated as the head of the couple, men's affirmations of mastery are recognized as morally right and politically just. Designated as seductive, women's claims to mastery are called immoral. In insisting that it is natural, necessary, and moral for men to rule the women they love and that it is both unnatural and immoral for women to use the power of love to establish their power over men (Rousseau 1994: 49), Rousseau shows us that patriarchy recognizes men's right to sublimate their desire for autonomy and recognizes that the success of men's sublimation requires that women's sublimations be condemned. He also shows us that the desire for autonomy, understood as the desire for self-mastery, must, within the social context of human life, refigure itself as the desire for mastery of/over the other. Disagreeing with Hobbes's description of the state of nature as the condition of perpetual war, Rousseau shows us that social life would be impossible if the rebirth of autonomy as the desire for mastery were not stabilized by the order of sexual difference that grounds the patriarchal family.

Yet even *Emile,* which never overtly recognizes the legitimacy of women's desire for autonomy, covertly acknowledges its rights. What is especially interesting in Rousseau's account of Emile's and Sophy's courtship and marriage are the instructions he allows the tutor to give Sophy. On the one hand these instructions feed Emile's sublimations. Sophy must never openly challenge his position as head of the house. On the other hand they acknowledge that Sophy, the perfect instantiation of the ideal feminine, experiences her sexual body as powerful and also, given this experience, desires autonomy. The tutor does not tell Sophy that her desires are immoral; nor does he insist that she repress them. Rather he teaches her how to use them effectively—the first rule being: never *appear* autonomous, independent or in control. In this ambiguity surrounding the woman's right to rule, we find Rousseau attending to the fissure in his thought; for though he calls women's power immoral he also seems to recognize that, as originally autonomous, women cannot abandon their desire for autonomy. They too must mourn their loss and be offered substitute love objects.

For us, the idea of a natural man and woman is decidedly problematic. We know that the ideal of autonomy is powerful currency in today's marketplace of ideas. We know that calling it natural serves to solidify its power. Knowing that exposing its unnaturalness is essential to divesting it of its idealized position, we are (perhaps) surprised to find Rousseau, the advocate of "natural" autonomy, showing us the ways in which autonomy is constructed as natural; for *Emile* may be read as a set of instructions for creating a natural childhood.

Emile's autonomy is from the very beginning, contrived. It is the effect of the tutor's control. Emile lives in the nature of an English garden. His spontaneous actions are preprogramed. His experiences of independence are sheltered. Given only one book to read, *Robinson Crusoe,* he is educated to value autonomy. Further, this education requires that he be taken from his mother and removed from the world of women. The one experience that the tutor cannot control, the rush of sexual desire, exposes the lie of the education for autonomy. (Might we go so far as to say that all of the prepubic education is designed to protect Emile/the ideal of autonomy against the implications of this irrefutable experience of our need/desire for the other?)

Emile experiences his passion as an alienation. It threatens his identity as an autonomous being. The tutor teaches Emile how to resolve the conflict. He introduces Emile first to love and then to Sophy, such that the logic of sexual desire is taken up by the logic of autonomy and incorporated in marriage. As husband, Emile acknowledges his desire for the other without acknowledging the other per se; for as his wife Sophy is a part of him. As man and wife Emile and Sophy become a new moral person where Emile is recognized as the head that rules the body. As ruler of the desired (non)other Emile may forget his need of Sophy and once again call himself autonomous.

Reading the *Discourse* and *Emile* under the influence of Freud, we may say this: Autonomy, imaged as the self-sufficient body, functions as the lost, impossible object that sets our desire's course. As the wife substitutes for the mother, the controlling body comes to stand for the autonomous body. Turning on the slight of hand that allows the one who controls the other to appear to be self-sufficient, and appealing to the phenomena of sexual difference, patriarchy aligns bodily strength with the idea of the right to control. The male body may now function as a legitimate substitute for the lost autonomous body. Men sublimate their desire for autonomy by controlling the bodies of women.

Women's bodies, insofar as they are figured as weak, cannot function as suitable substitutes for the lost autonomous body. Women's loss, at least according to the official ideologies of patriarchy, is without compensation. When women discover that they can control others, they are told that access to this control will be their ruin. Barred from sublimation their desire must either be repressed or express itself as melancholia. Denying their desire, they become feminine. Living it, they may, like the melancholic, turn their desire for the impossible object upon themselves and attempt to destroy the body that cannot serve as a surrogate for the lost object. They may speak the language of the anorexic body.

The anorexic body may be read in many ways: An image of feminine narcissism, an obsession with contemporary standards of beauty, an attempt to become bodiless, an expression of masochism (Thompson 1994). Within the context of this discussion, the anorexic body may be read as a clear and concrete motive for the murder of the autonomous body. It is tempting to say that this goes too far, that the anorexic body, in its self-destructive attempt at autonomy teaches us that legitimate routes to autonomy must be opened for women, not that the value of autonomy per se be rejected. As I see it, however, reading the anorexic body in this way ignores the logic of the ideal of autonomy. Autonomous bodies cannot acknowledge their desire for each other. Mastery or incorporation are their only possibilities. Neither possibility evades the logic of sacrifice and/or domination. Allowing women to mourn the ideal of autonomy like men would not change this and this, I think, is what must be changed.

Between Rousseau's love stories and the anorexic body we confront the different routes by which men and women, guided by the patriarchal ideal of autonomy, attempt to claim their bodies as their own. Both routes are disastrous. The disaster of the anorexic body is flagrant. The disaster of the love story is invisible (most of the time, there are the bodies of battered women). We may read these disasters as signs of the wrongness of the routes taken by patriarchy in imaging the ideal of autonomy or as signs of the problematic status of the ideal itself. Reading the anorexic body and listening to Emile's body, I find the trouble more in the ideal than in the ways in which it has been imaged and sexed.

With these notes to Act I: Motives and Murder, the curtain rises. I leave the dialogue and action to your imagination. I leave the notes for Act II: Mourning the Autonomous Body and Act III: Celebrating Ambiguous Bodies for after intermission.

References

Beauvoir, Simone de (1974). *The Second Sex,* trans. H. M. Parshley. New York: Vintage.

Bordo, Susan (1993). *Unbearable Weight: Feminism, Western Culture and the Body.* Berkeley: University of California Press.

Freud, Sigmund (1959). "Mourning and Melancholia," trans. Joan Riviere. *Freud: Collected Papers,* vol. 4. New York: Basic Books.

Irigaray, Luce (1993). *An Ethics of Sexual Difference,* trans. Carolyn Burke and Gillian C. Gill. Ithaca: Cornell University Press.

Nietzsche, Friedrich (1974). *The Gay Science,* trans. Walter Kaufmann. New York: Vintage Books.

Pateman, Carol (1989). *The Disorder of Women.* Stanford: Stanford University Press.

——— (1988). *The Sexual Contract.* Stanford: Stanford University Press.

Rousseau, Jean-Jacques (1994). *Discourse on Inequality,* trans. Franklin Philip. Oxford: Oxford University Press.

——— (1993). *Emile,* trans. Barbara Foxley. London: Everyman Press.

Thompson, Becky W. (1994). *A Hunger So Wide and Deep: A Multiracial View of Women's Eating Problems.* Minneapolis: University of Minnesota Press.

Wollstonecraft, Mary (1992). Vindication of the Rights of Woman. New York: Knopf.

CONTRIBUTORS

Debra B. Bergoffen is professor of Philosophy, a member of the Cultural Studies faculty, and Director of Women's Studies at George Mason University. Her writings examine the epistemological, ethical, political, and feminist issues raised by the work of Nietzsche, Lacan, Irigaray, and Beauvoir. She is the author of *The Philosophy of Simone de Beauvoir: Gendered Phenomenologies, Erotic Generosities.* Her most recent articles include: "Message à trois: Freud, Beauvoir and the Marquis de Sade" (Continental Philosophy Review Fall 2001); and "Oedipal Dramas: Why Nietzsche Still?" in *Reflections on Drama, Culture, Politics,* ed. Alan D. Schrift (Berkeley: University of California Press, 2000).

Sara Castro-Klarén is professor of Latin American Culture and Literature at the Johns Hopkins University. She has published extensively on the work of José María Arguedas, Julio Cortázar, Mario Vargas Llosa, Garcilaso de la Vega, Inca and Guamán Poma and Diamela Eltit. Her books include *Escritura, transgresión y sujeto en la literatura latinoamericana* (1989) and *Women's Writing in Latin America* (1991). Questions in postcolonial theory and subaltern studies have occupied her research. Her most recent work on the intersection of the trope of cannibalism and colonialism has appeared in *Revista de crítica latinoamericana* and *Nepantla.* She is finishing a book on the imaginary of cannibalism and coloniality.

Jeffrey Jerome Cohen is associate professor of English and Human Sciences at The George Washington University. His monographs include *Of Giants: Sex, Monsters, and the Middle Ages* and *Medieval Identity Machines,* both from the University of Minnesota Press. He has also edited three collections of essays: *Monster Theory: Reading Culture* (University of Minnesota Press, 1994), *Becoming Male in the Middle Ages* (Garland, 1997) and *The Postcolonial Middle Ages* (Palgrave, 2000). His current research focuses on the intersections of body, trauma, and race in the multiethnic England of the twelfth century.

William A. Cohen is associate professor of English at the University of Maryland and the author of *Sex Scandal: The Private Parts of Victorian Fiction.* The present essay is drawn from his current work on human interiors and the senses in Victorian literature and culture.

Laura Doyle is associate professor of English at University of Massachusetts-Amherst. She works in the areas of modernism, the novel, existential phenomenology, and sexuality and race studies. Recent publications include essays in modernism, modernity, and American literature and an edited collection, *Bodies of Resistance: New Phenomenologies of Politics, Agency, and Culture* (Northwestern, 2001).

Rosemarie Garland-Thomson is associate professor of Women's Studies at Emory University in Atlanta, Georgia. Her work focuses on feminist theory and disability studies in the humanities. She is the author of *Extraordinary Bodies: Figuring Physical Disability in American Literature and Culture,* editor of *Freakery: Cultural Spectacles of the Extraordinary Body,* and co-editor of *Enabling the Humanities: A Sourcebook for Disability Studies in Language and Literature.* She is currently writing a book on staring and another on the cultural logic of euthanasia.

Elizabeth Grosz is professor of Women's and Gender Studies at Rutgers University. Her research interests include feminist and contemporary French Philosophy. She is the editor of *Becomings: Explorations in Time, Memory and Futures* (Cornell, 1999); and the author of *Architecture from the Outside: Essays on Virtual and Real Space* (MIT Press, 2001).

Linda S. Kauffman is professor of English and Distinguished Scholar-Teacher, University of Maryland, College Park. She is the author of numerous books and articles on contemporary fiction, film, and performance art, including *Bad Girls and Sick Boys: Fantasies in Contemporary Art and Culture* (University of California Press, 1998), *Discourses of Desire: Gender, Genre, and Epistolary Fictions* (Cornell, 1986) and *Special Delivery: Epistolary Modes in Modern Fiction* (Chicago, 1992). She is also the editor of *American Feminist Thought at Century's End* (Blackwell, 1993).

Robert McRuer is an assistant professor in the Department of English and the Program in Human Sciences at The George Washington University. He is the author of *The Queer Renaissance: Contemporary American Literature and the Reinvention of Lesbian and Gay Identities* and other articles on queer theory, disability studies, cultural studies, and composition theory. He is guest editor, with Abby Wilkerson, of a special issue of *GLQ: A Journal of Lesbian and Gay Studies* on the intersections of disability studies and queer theory.

Gail Weiss is associate professor of Philosophy and director of the Human Sciences graduate program at The George Washington University. She is the author of *Body Images: Embodiment as Intercorporeality* (Routledge 1999) and the co-editor of *Perspectives on Embodiment: The Intersections of Nature and Culture* (Routledge 1999) and *Feminist Interpretations of Maurice Merleau-Ponty* (Penn State Press 2003). Her research and published work focuses on intersections among continental philosophy, feminist theory, and literature.

INDEX